The
EVERYTHING
Wine Book
2nd Edition

Dear Reader:

There was a time when we didn't know the difference between Sangria and Sangiovese (except that one had fruit in it). But we had the opportunity with our radio show to interview lots of winemakers and we learned two things above all:

There are no stupid questions. (Goodness knows, if anyone could ask them, it would have been us.)

Winemakers are the most generous and un-snobby people you'll ever meet.

Through our new acquaintances we had the opportunity to learn about wines from their makers. Not only did they bring their wines for us to try (often, on the air) . . . they let us taste from their barrels and bite into grapes in their vineyards (not necessarily recommended). It started us on a journey of discovery that has given us daily pleasure.

We hope that our book will inspire you to try new wines and take chances on the unfamiliar. We guarantee you won't regret it.

Cheers!

Barbara Nowak   *Beverly Wichman*

The EVERYTHING® Series

Editorial

Publishing Director	Gary M. Krebs
Associate Managing Editor	Laura M. Daly
Associate Copy Chief	Brett Palana-Shanahan
Acquisitions Editor	Kate Burgo
Development Editor	Karen Johnson Jacot
Production Editor	Casey Ebert

Production

Director of Manufacturing	Susan Beale
Associate Director of Production	Michelle Roy Kelly
Cover Design	Paul Beatrice
	Matt LeBlanc
Design and Layout	Colleen Cunningham
	Holly Curtis
	Erin Dawson
	Sorae Lee
Series Cover Artist	Barry Littmann

Visit the entire Everything® Series at *www.everything.com*

THE
EVERYTHING®
WINE
BOOK

2nd Edition

Completely Updated!

By the Saucy Sisters
Barbara Nowak and Beverly Wichman

Adams Media
Avon, Massachusetts

To Mom and Dad

———————

An Everything® Series Book.
Everything® and everything.com® are registered trademarks of F+W Publications, Inc.

Published by Adams Media, an F+W Publications Company
57 Littlefield Street, Avon, MA 02322 U.S.A.
www.adamsmedia.com
ISBN 13: 978-1-59337-357-3
ISBN 10: 1-59337-357-0
Printed in the United States of America.

J I H G F E D C B

Library of Congress Cataloging-in-Publication Data
Nowak, Barbara.
The everything wine book. — 2nd ed. / Barbara Nowak and Beverly Wichman.
p.   cm.
An everything series book
Rev. ed. of: The everything wine book / Danny May and Andy Sharpe. c1997.
ISBN 1-59337-357-0
1. Wine and wine making. I. Wichman, Beverly. II. May, Danny.
Everything wine book. III. Title. IV. Series: Everything series.
TP548.M4585 2005
641.2'2—dc22
2005011016

This book is available at quantity discounts for bulk purchases.
For information, please call 1-800-289-0963.

Contents

Foreword

The Saucy Sisters were touring California Wine Country a number of years ago and I had the great fortune to meet them. I was immediately captivated by their curiosity about wine and food and their quest for understanding everything related to wine and food. Their enthusiasm has now been captured in their book.

The *Everything*® *Wine Book* is the product of the Saucy Sisters' passion and knowledge conveyed in a meaningful way that any reader will find interesting. I grew up in a wine family and in the wine business and have read innumerable books to expand my learning. I found *The Everything*® *Wine Book* provided a historic perspective on wine worldwide. A broad range of facts on how wine is made, and how it tastes, how to buy it are just a few of the morsels that are covered in a concise, authoritative and authentic manner. The Saucy Sisters have also dealt with and helped to dispel many myths often associated with wine. I will share this book with everyone I know as a fun and informative read. Anyone who picks up this book will thoroughly enjoy it!

The Top Ten Wine Myths

1. **Aged wine is better than young wine.** (Not all wines need aging. Generally speaking, red wines—particularly those high in tannins—require more aging than whites.)

2. **Red wine should never be chilled.** (Some light reds, like Beaujolais, benefit from chilling.)

3. **"Reserve" wines are top of the line.** ("Reserve" on American wine labels has no legal meaning. Winemakers can use the term at their whim.)

4. **Wines with sulfites will give you a headache.** (Sulfites are the cause of headaches in only about 1 percent of the population—mostly asthmatics.)

5. **All German wines are sweet.** (German wines come in all degrees of sweetness—from dry to very, very sweet. "Trocken" on a German wine label means "dry.")

6. **Screwtops are a sign of cheap wine.** (Au contraire! Increasingly, top winemakers are using screw tops to avoid cork contamination of their wines.)

7. **Wines should always breathe.** (In general, breathing is only necessary for wines that need further aging.)

8. **All wines have the same amount of alcohol.** (The level of alcohol depends on the amount of sugar that has been converted during fermentation.)

9. **The more a wine costs, the better it is.** (Price is related to many factors: the cost of the vineyard land, the type of grapes used, whether it's aged in oak barrels, and—most of all—the reputation of the winery or winemaker.)

10. **Zinfandel is a pink wine.** (Zinfandel is a red grape, but it can be made into a red wine or a blush wine.)

Introduction

"Would you care for a bottle of wine to go with your dinner?" These words have struck terror in the hearts of four-star generals and million-dollar-a-game athletes. What if you choose . . . the WRONG one! Who knows how wine got to be so intimidating? In most of the wine-drinking world, wine is just a part of daily life. No big deal. It's something to be savored and appreciated—but not something to lose sleep over.

Maybe you haven't lost any sleep, but chances are, you've been overwhelmed by the sheer volume of wine choices out there. You walk into a wine shop or discount warehouse and don't know where to start. Even when you've decided between red and white, that still leaves half. Okay, you focus on reds from California. Now what: Cabernet Sauvignon, Merlot, Pinot Noir, Zinfandel? Then you have to narrow it down further to region (Napa? Sonoma? Santa Barbara?) and producer. Napa alone has over 300 wineries. Yikes! It just makes you want to throw up your hands and let someone else choose for you.

Wine shouldn't be nerve-racking. It should be fun. And the interesting thing about wine is that the more you learn and taste, the more you *want* to learn and taste. Even the exalted Master of Wine professionals who can tell a Zinfandel from a Shiraz at 100 paces started just like you: one wine at a time. And every one of them will tell you that you can never know everything there is to know about wine. It's a subject that, by its very nature, changes every day—new vintages, start-up wineries, young winemakers, DNA revelations about old grape varieties. And that, of course, is part of the challenge and part of the enjoyment.

Wine is essentially social. It's part of family gatherings, friendly dinners, holidays, celebrations, impromptu visits, and romantic interludes. When you choose a wine to accompany a social event, you want others to enjoy your selection. Sure, there's some pressure there. And when you gain confidence in your wine knowledge and in your own palate, the pressure diminishes. Instead of feeling anxious about pleasing your friends, you look forward to sharing something you value.

You'll find out how to taste—really taste—wines with all your senses . . . and learn how to express in words what you're tasting. Having a vocabulary for wine helps you get what you want.

There's nothing like the euphoric feeling when you find a bargain. But you have to recognize the relative quality before you know whether it's a true bargain. *The Everything® Wine Book,* 2nd Edition, will give you some handy tips when you go out shopping. Whether you're looking to build a wine collection or just picking up a bottle for dinner with a friend, you'll have the facts you need to make a purchase that's right for the occasion.

Nunc est bibendum.

Acknowledgments

A special thank-you goes to Cheryl Charming, who's always at the ready to invent new drinks for us to try, including some sparkling wine recipes in our book; to David Gay, who always surprises us and challenges us with his knowledge of wine and unpredictable wine recommendations—like some you'll see in the following chapters; to Vicki Turner, our friend and the best wine broker in the South, who has introduced us to the finest winemakers in the world—some of whom are mentioned in these pages; and to our family and loved ones who have shared their love and support.

CHAPTER 1

A Brief History of Wine

The discovery of wine was probably an accident. It didn't have to be "invented," because wine can happen all by itself. It's safe to assume that, way back, people learned to store their fruits of summer for the bleak winters ahead. More than likely, they put their grapes into a hollow in a rock, where nature took over, and fermentation turned the grapes into a bubbling liquid. Wine!

2nd Edition

Wine in the Ancient World

We may not know how humans were first introduced to wine, but we do know that people have been imbibing since at least 4000 B.C. Maybe as far back as 6000 B.C. And maybe even further back than that. Mesopotamia (Persia), near present-day Iran, and Egypt—the end-points of the Fertile Crescent—seem to be the birthplace of ancient winemaking. And recent discoveries point to winemaking in China during the same period.

A Persian fable has it that an ancient king kept his beloved grapes in an earthen jar labeled "poison." A discontented member of his harem drank juice from the jar in a suicide attempt, but instead of dying, she found her spirits quite rejuvenated. She shared the drink with her king, who took her into his favor and decreed that, henceforth, grapes would be allowed to ferment. Men have been buying their women drinks ever since.

Ancient Persia was truly wine country. Not only did the Persians give toasts to their gods with wine, they also paid salaries in wine. Men earned ten to twenty quarts a month, and women earned ten. The grape varieties they used to make wine are believed to be the precursors of those we use today.

The ancient Egyptians cultivated grapes and made wine in a surprisingly modern fashion. They developed the first arbors and pruning methods. And the grapes were stomped and fermented in large wooden vats. The wine was mostly sweet white wine, probably made from the grape we now know as the Muscat of Alexandria. As a matter of respect to the gods, the Egyptians used wine in their funeral rites. Depending on the status held by the deceased, his body and belongings were anointed with wine prior to being entombed.

Message in a Bottle

Most of the cultivated Muscat of Alexandria ends up as table grapes or raisins. But you can find modern wines using the grape in Spain's Moscatel de Málaga, which is heavy, sweet, and golden brown, or in Portugal's Moscatel de Setúbal, which is a sweet fortified wine.

Situated between Egypt and Mesopotamia along the Fertile Crescent were the Phoenicians, who sailed the Mediterranean from what is now the coast of Lebanon. Thus the grapevine—and wine—found its way to Greece, Sicily, and north-central Italy.

The earliest written account of wine that we have is in the Old Testament of the Bible. After the Great Flood, Noah planted a vineyard and made wine. With the first wine came the first occasion of drunkenness—and a lesson about moderation.

During ancient times, everyone drank wine and beer—children included. That's not as decadent as it might sound. Frankly, drinking the water was hazardous to one's health, and wine was a good substitute thirst-quencher. If you sipped one of those old-style wines today, you'd probably notice that it was lower in alcohol than modern day wines and tasted more like vinegar with a hint of cider. But it was certainly better than the water that was available. While wine was a staple of daily life, it was consumed mostly by the rich and powerful. Beer was the drink of the common folk.

Greeks Democratize Wine

Greeks embraced wine drinking more enthusiastically than any culture before them. Wine became a drink not just for the elite—but for everyone. It is said that of all the vessels Greeks used daily, more than half related to the consumption of wine. Wine was considered to be a gift from Dionysus, the patron god and symbol of wine, and was used in religious rituals. Wine was used in commerce. And Greek doctors, including Hippocrates, prescribed it for their patients.

Greeks considered it barbaric to drink wine straight, so they diluted it in varying proportions with water. And they learned to add herbs and spices to mask spoilage. Another addition to this delicious taste profile was the flavor of pine resin. Greeks typically stored their wine in porous clay jugs, which had to be sealed to preserve the wine. They caulked the jugs with the resin of pine trees, which imparted its unique essence.

Retsina is a traditional wine of Greece with a long history and the distinctive taste of pine resin. The taste that permeated the wine in ancient times became so accepted that long after resin-caulked containers were discontinued, chunks of resin were added to the wine during fermentation to reproduce the flavor. Most people who have tried Retsina—Greeks included—say it's an acquired taste.

Wine was important to the economies of Greek cities. It was traded within Greece and exported throughout the Mediterranean world. As Greece began to colonize the western Mediterranean, the Greeks took their grapevines and winemaking technology with them.

Romans Advance Winemaking

The Roman Empire covered, at its greatest outward expansion, most of the Mediterranean lands and a good part of Europe. The Romans found grapes already under cultivation in many of their conquered lands, the wine culture having been widely distributed by their Greek and Phoenician predecessors. The Romans, too, loved wine and fostered its development throughout the empire.

By about 1000 B.C., Romans were classifying grape varieties, charting ripening characteristics, identifying diseases, and increasing yields through irrigation and fertilization. They developed wooden barrels to store the wines in place of the skins and jars previously used. And, as glass blowing became more common, the Romans may have been the first ones to put wine into glass containers.

Romans knew that contact with the outside air was bad for their wine. In order to protect it from oxidation and evaporation, they added olive oil to the pitchers. The oil floated on top of the wine, keeping the air out and maintaining the freshness of the wine.

By the first century A.D., Rome was awash with wine. Each person in the city of Rome drank on average half a liter each day. Winemaking techniques had spread from Italy to Spain, Germany, England, and France, and those regions developed their own vineyards. A boom was created. Corner bars popped up all over cities like Pompeii. The supply (or oversupply) of wine drove down the prices—so much so that Emperor Domitian ordered the great vineyards of France be uprooted to eliminate the competition of French wines with the local Italian wines. Fortunately that order wasn't fully executed, and it was rescinded two centuries later. When the Roman Empire fell for good in 476, the great wine regions of Europe were under vines.

Vino Veritas

Archaeologists discovered the remains of vineyards in the ruins of Pompeii. Those vineyards have been replanted—replicating those of A.D. 79 when Mount Vesuvius erupted and buried the city. Using ancient frescoes, root imprints, Roman authors, and DNA, scientists identified the grape varieties. Campania winemaker Mastroberardino produced wine from the grapes and named it Villa dei Misteri (Villa of Mystery).

Wine in Europe

Wine and its extraordinary properties have always been associated with spirituality and religion. While most of the religions practiced in the eastern Mediterranean incorporated wine in their rituals, it was the spread of Christianity in the fourth century that ensured the survival of viticulture and winemaking after the collapse of the Roman Empire. Because wine was such an integral part in the celebration of the Eucharist, the monasteries and cathedrals that sprang up across Europe took up winemaking and amassed substantial vineyard holdings. The monks—who had the education, the financial resources of the Catholic Church, and the requisite time for cultivating land and trying new techniques—became some of the most important winemakers of the Middle Ages.

Monastic wineries established extensive vineyards across Europe— and especially in Burgundy, Bordeaux, Champagne, the Loire Valley, and the Rhone Valley. During this time France emerged as the pre-eminent winemaking region in the world.

Wine and War Don't Mix

In 1152 Henry II of England married France's Eleanor of Aquitaine, whose dowry included the vineyard areas of Bordeaux and neighboring Gascony. The light-red wine produced there gained favor in England and came to be called claret. By 1350, the port city of Bordeaux was shipping 1 million cases of claret a year. But the sporadic fighting between the kings of England and France—known as the Hundred Years' War (1337–1453)—put an end to England's access to her much-loved wine. Any ship transporting the wine faced piracy, and protecting the ships became prohibitively expensive. England had to look beyond western France for wine imports.

A trading friendship with Portugal began that led, ultimately, to the creation of Port wine. The journey by sea from Portugal to England was hard on wine. The shippers in Oporto, the port city, began adding a couple buckets of brandy to the wine to stabilize it so it would arrive in good condition. Then, they started adding the brandy earlier and earlier until they were adding it during fermentation. This wine became known as, quite appropriately, *Porto*—or Port.

Inventions Spur Change

Even though the Romans may have used blown-glass containers to serve wine, pottery and stoneware jugs were the norm. That is, until the seventeenth century and the advent of commercial glass making. The first glass bottles were onion-shaped but eventually evolved into cylindrical bottles that could be stacked on their sides.

Needless to say, there would be no sideways stacking without some effective bottle stopper. Enter the cork.

Originally corks were tapered so they could fit a bottle with any size neck and so they could be manually removed. But with the production of mold-made bottles and horizontal stacking, a standard cylindrical cork was developed that could be driven into the bottle for maximum wine containment. Now a special tool was required to remove the cork. Corkscrews of all kinds were introduced—and continue to be introduced to this day.

Reaching Out to the New World

With the discovery and colonization of new lands, emigrating Europeans took their vines and their winemaking knowledge elsewhere. Exploration and settlement brought wine to the Americas and South Africa in the 1500s and 1600s and to Australia in the 1700s. The wine history of Europe thus became intertwined—for better and for worse—with that of the New World.

Wine in the Americas

The wine-guzzling conquistadors who arrived in South and Central America from Spain in the 1500s were responsible—directly or indirectly—for introducing winemaking to those lands. Hernando Cortés, perhaps the most successful of the conquistadors and later governor of Mexico, defeated the Aztecs in 1521. After much celebration, he and his soldiers were out of wine. One of his first orders of business was to direct all new Spanish settlers to plant vines on the land they'd been granted. Winemaking flourished. In fact, it flourished to such an extent that the settlers needed to import less and less wine from Spain.

Vino Veritas

Mexico was home to the oldest commercial winery in the Americas. The first wine was produced there in 1596. The winery was known as "Santa Maria de las Parras"—or Holy Mary of the Vines. It's still operating today as Casa Madero in the Parras Valley.

As you can imagine, the king of Spain, who wanted a captive market for Spanish goods, wasn't too happy about this. He levied heavy taxes and ordered vineyards destroyed in all of Spain's new colonies. The edict was enforced most aggressively in Mexico, and the growth of the burgeoning wine industry there came to an abrupt halt.

The church was the sole exception to the king's edict. Just like in Europe, vineyards survived under the care of the church. Missions—particularly, Jesuit missions—were established early in Chile, Argentina, Peru, and Mexico. Later, a series of missions along the Pacific Coast would bring winemaking to California.

Colonial Experiments in North America

Early settlers brought with them a mighty thirst for wine. Imagine their delight when they found a landscape practically smothered by grapevines. Upon closer inspection, however, they found vines unlike any they were familiar with back in Europe. Being the pioneers they were, they forged ahead and fermented anyway. The first wine from native American grapes was made in Jamestown in 1609 and it was . . . well, not like what the colonists were used to. And not really what they wanted either.

The colonists' next step was to import vine cuttings of *Vitis vinifera* from Europe so they could grow the more familiar varieties—Cabernet Sauvignon, Merlot, Chardonnay. All up and down the Atlantic coast settlers planted vines from every great European wine region. Even Thomas Jefferson, the wine geek of his era, planted vines at Monticello. No one succeeded. Each vineyard would die off after only two or three years. It was thought that the extremes of weather were the reason for failure. Or that indigenous diseases were at fault. A hundred years later, another possible cause came to light.

Even though the vinifera vines failed, the side effect of these experiments was the emergence in the 1800s of new American varieties. No one knows for sure, but it's generally assumed that they were produced by chance through pollen exchange between the vinifera and earlier American varieties. These hybrids became the foundation for the wine industry in the eastern United States. Winemaking centers emerged in Ohio, Missouri, on the shores of Lake Erie, and in the Finger Lakes region of upstate New York. The American wine industry was on its way.

California Dreamin'

Beginning around 1770, Franciscan monks established missions— and planted vineyards—up the coast of what would become California. Father Junípero Serra led the way when he planted the first vineyard at Mission San Diego. He traveled north and established eight more missions. His work got him the name of "father of California wine."

The Gold Rush of 1849 brought frenzied growth both in terms of population and vineyards. By this time Sonoma had 22,000 acres under vine, and Napa had 18,000. The Santa Clara Valley and Livermore Valley were widely planted and had numerous wineries at this same time. Many pioneer vintners settled south and east of the San Francisco Bay where most of the bottling plants were located. Railroads arrived, and now California wines were available in eastern markets and shipped around the world. By the end of the century, all of the state's winemaking regions were producing wine. California had become the premier wine-growing region in the country.

An International Wine Crisis

In 1863 an unidentified vine disease was being talked about in France's Rhone Valley. By 1865 the disease had spread to Provence. By the late 1860s vine growers all over France were watching their vineyards die before their very eyes. And over the next twenty years it decimated nearly all the vineyards of Europe.

The scourge was called phylloxera, and it all started with a louse indigenous to the eastern United States. This insect is barely visible to the naked eye, but its powers are devastating. It sucks the nutrients from the roots of grapevines and slowly starves the life out of the vines. Native American grapevines have a thick and tough root bark and suffer no damage from this sucking parasite. But vinifera vines had no such evolutionary protection.

The Ripe Stuff

How did phylloxera get to Europe?

It was popular in nineteenth-century Europe to import living plants. Between 1858 and 1862 large numbers of rooted American vines were sent to Bordeaux, England, Ireland, Alsace, Germany, and Portugal. Phylloxera probably hitched a ride.

The parasite spread and affected vines in California, Australia, New Zealand, and South Africa. For a while, eradicating phylloxera seemed hopeless. Eventually a solution presented itself: graft vinifera vines to pest-resistant American rootstocks. It worked, but it was a long and laborious undertaking to graft and replant each and every vine in Europe.

Prohibition Wipes Out an Industry

The winemaking business had its ups and downs—sometimes due to insects and other times to economics. But in 1920 it crashed and burned because of politics. The Eighteenth Amendment to the U.S. Constitution made Prohibition the law of the land. The Prohibition movement in America wasn't a sudden twentieth-century phenomenon. It was a long time in the making. It started county by county, state by state, and grew.

In 1816 Indiana forbade Sunday sale of alcohol. In the 1840s "dry" towns and counties emerged in seven states. In 1851 Maine outlawed the manufacture and sale of alcohol. By 1855, New Hampshire, Vermont, Delaware, Michigan, Indiana, Iowa, Minnesota, Nebraska, Connecticut, Rhode Island, Massachusetts, and New York had followed suit. At the outbreak of World War I, thirty-three states had gone dry.

The Eighteenth Amendment was ratified on January 29, 1919, and one year later Prohibition began, making virtually all alcoholic beverages illegal. Even after ratification by the states, the amendment still needed an act of Congress to make it enforceable. That came in the form of the Volstead Act, spearheaded by the Minnesota congressman of the same name. Many supporters of the Eighteenth Amendment had assumed that the "intoxicating liquors" to be banned were the high-alcohol distilled spirits, with 40 percent alcohol—surely, not beer, with its 3 to 7 percent alcohol, or wine, with its less than 15 percent alcohol. But Volstead defined intoxicating liquors as any beverage containing more than one-half of 1 percent alcohol.

There's been some debate that the quality of wine declined in the post-phylloxera era. No one will ever know for sure. But if you want to try a wine from vinifera vines grown on their own roots, try a Chilean wine. Chile is the only wine-producing country in the world that escaped phylloxera.

Savvy Sipping

Lasting Effects

The almost immediate result of these acts was the decimation of the American wine industry. Vineyards were uprooted. Equipment was abandoned. Growers and producers—if they didn't go completely under—had to find creative ways to stay in business. Cooking wine could still be produced, as long as it was salted and undrinkable. Sacramental and religious wines were still allowed—and somehow found their way to secular markets. Medicinal alcohol was legal, too, because it wasn't for "beverage purposes." Doctors began prescribing more and more of it. And home producers were permitted to make up to 200 gallons of wine a year.

But the overall effect of Prohibition was to annihilate a once-thriving industry. The art of winemaking, which had been practiced for centuries, became illegal. People who had invested their lives and savings in research and equipment had their investments wiped out. Thousands of workers involved in making, bottling, distributing, serving, and selling wine were out of jobs. In 1919 the United States produced 55 million gallons of wine. In 1925 it was 3.5 million gallons. Winemakers weren't compensated in any way. Mostly they just went out of business.

By 1933, when the Twenty-first Amendment repealed Prohibition, the damage had been done. The country had lost its winemakers and had lost an entire generation of wine drinkers. And there were other effects of this

"Noble Experiment" that last to this day in the form of direct-shipping and distribution laws. By 1936 fifteen states had laws that created state monopolies on wine sales and prevented free-market competition. Other states, while allowing hotels and restaurants to serve wine, banned bars and "liquor by the drink." And still other states left serving and selling options to local jurisdictions. The aftermath of Prohibition is a hodgepodge of laws that vary from state to state and community to community.

Vino Veritas

Some ingenious California grape growers introduced a product they named Vine-Glo. While they weren't permitted to make wine, the growers could still make grape juice. They sold their juice with instructional material telling consumers what *not* to do—lest their juice turn to wine in sixty days.

The Wine Boom in the United States

As the wine industry rebuilt itself after the repeal of Prohibition, it found a market much changed in its thirteen-year hiatus. The quality of wine was very poor, in part because California grape growers were raising grapes that shipped well, rather than grapes that made fine wine. Wineries mostly sold their wines to wholesalers who bottled them under their own brands and then, in turn, sold them under generic names like Chablis and Burgundy. In 1940 Americans were drinking one gallon of wine a year per person compared to the French, who were consuming forty gallons. Nevertheless, the American wine industry slowly recovered.

Savvy Sipping

To get a taste of one of these "grapey" wines, you need look no further than Manischewitz. It produces the sweet style of kosher wine from the native American Concord grape. It's the same grape used to make grape juice and jelly.

A major development that helped this process was the introduction of French hybrids. French hybrids crossed American and European vines to resist phylloxera. These resultant new varieties were hardy enough to withstand a northeastern winter, yet yielded good-quality wine without the "grapey" taste of many native varieties.

JFK and Julia Child Join Forces

The American wine boom really began with the affluence of the late 1950s. Wine was attractive to educated suburbanites, especially those wealthy enough to travel abroad. Wine, which to most of the wine-drinking world is a simple beverage, had become a status symbol in the United States.

A few role models helped. When John F. Kennedy was sworn in he brought with him, among other things, a new sense of internationalism—and his wife, Jackie, who loved all things French. French restaurants—and French wines—became very trendy. And from a kitchen in a Boston television studio, Julia Child taught a generation of Americans how to prepare French cuisine, how to match it with French wine—and how sipping and cooking can go together.

New products appeared in wine stores to meet the growing demand. Portuguese Rosé in the form of Mateus and Lancer's hit the shelves. They were sweet and fruity and slightly fizzy. And the fact that they were imported from Europe gave them cachet. From West Germany came Liebfraumilch, a flowery, fruity, and slightly sweet blend of Riesling and other lesser grape varieties.

Vino Veritas

This was not the first time American wines won international acclaim. In 1880 Charles Wetmore, California's first Commissioner of Agriculture, brought cuttings from France to California. In 1889 he sent the first wine from these vines to the Gran Prix in Paris where it won top honors. And after Prohibition in 1939 Wente Bros. sent a wine to the same world wine tasting and won the Gran Prix.

Meanwhile, California's reputation for world-class fine wines rapidly grew. In the early 1970s resourceful winemakers, many educated in their craft at the University of California at Davis, developed a whole new genre of California wine—high-alcohol, fruity wine that took full advantage of the long California growing season. In a blind tasting that pitted several California wines against top French wines in 1976, the American wines—Stags' Leap Cabernet and Château Montelena Chardonnay—won. The decision, by a panel of all French judges, shocked the world.

Varietals Take Over

American winemakers began labeling their wines according to the grape variety they were made from. This was in distinct contrast to the often confusing custom of European winemakers of naming their wines after the place where they were produced. Now wine-drinking ladies no longer ordered a glass of "white wine" with dinner. It was more likely, "I'll have a glass of Chardonnay, please."

Americans became attached to their new varietals: Cabernet Sauvignon, Merlot, Sauvignon Blanc. One California variety, however, wasn't having as much success in the 1970s. It was Zinfandel. Unfortunately, many growers had acre upon acre of Zinfandel vines whose grapes matured effortlessly in the California sunshine. The growers might have replanted their vineyards with other varieties had it not been for Bob Trinchero, owner of Sutter Home Winery, who was the first to make a fruity, pink, slightly sweet Rosé from this red wine grape. It was an instant and enormous success in the American market. Its popularity helped to drive yearly wine consumption in the United States up to two gallons per person.

New Wine Regions

The boom in wine production happened in areas far removed from California. Historical wine regions like New York and Ohio experienced intense growth after a long period of relative dormancy. In addition to benefiting from French hybrids, these areas could now also grow traditional vinifera vines because of the new understanding of plant pathology.

Areas that had modest wine production in the past picked up speed. Wines from Texas, Virginia, Pennsylvania, New Mexico—to name a few—are commonplace. The Northwest underwent significant planting, and Oregon and Washington developed outstanding reputations for their wines.

Today, every state in the Union has a winery.

The Last Twenty Years

As wine-drinking Americans, we've upgraded our taste in wines. The proliferation of wine classes, tastings, dinners, and publications has helped us do that. While White Zinfandel is still a staple for millions, there's an enthusiasm for venturing beyond those pink borders. The White Zin craze morphed into a Chardonnay trend and Merlot fad. And now there are "newer" fashions: Pinot Grigio and Shiraz. There will always be new wines in vogue. It used to be that the popular wines of choice were the ones that people could pronounce. Now, at least, brave wine drinkers dare to say "Gewürztraminer."

Message in a Bottle

Gewürztraminer is pronounced "guh-VURTS-trah-mee-ner." If you like White Zinfandel, chances are you'll enjoy a glass of Gewürztraminer—particularly if it's a German Gewürztraminer. It's a fragrant white wine with a hint of sweetness. Drier versions are produced in Alsace, California, and Oregon.

California has taken up growing more Old World grapes. So-called "Cal-Ital" varieties like Barbera and Sangiovese are popular. As are Syrah and Grenache—the traditional grapes of the Rhone Valley of France.

International collaboration as well as international competition have picked up. Famous names in wine—Mondavi, Lafite Rothschild, Lapostolle—have invested heavily in land and facilities in places like South America to produce high-quality wines. On the other hand, Australian wineries have been able to give American producers a run for their money with well-made inexpensive wines. They've been so successful that some U.S. wineries are labeling their bottles of Syrah with the Aussie name, Shiraz.

Technology is ever advancing. But who would have thought just a few years ago that people would be seriously discussing screw tops in the same breath as fine wines? The fact is that tainted corks have spoiled too much wine. And winemakers—even though they are artists—still have to make enough money to produce another bottle of wine tomorrow. So the seventeenth-century invention may be replaced by the same kind of closure you find on a bottle of Bud.

Consolidation in the wine industry—larger wineries buying up smaller ones—has become a fact of life. It enables one producer to market many brands and gain shelf space in retail stores. For consumers, the positive effect of consolidation is lower prices and ease of purchase. But it has also limited choice as supermarkets and large retailers stock only the well-known and highly promoted brands from large companies. Only time will tell how all the buying and selling of wineries will flush out. But with the growing number of educated wine drinkers like you, there should continue to be a market for quality wines.

CHAPTER 2

Categories of Wine: More Than Red, White, and Pink

After seeing Lucy sprawled out in a vat of red goo in old TV reruns, it's hard to take the crushing of grapes seriously. But, like all winemaking processes, it's serious business. Every winemaking process has a direct effect on what we drink: whether the wine is red or white or pink; whether it's sweet or dry; whether it has bubbles, oak, or tannins; and even how much alcohol it contains. They're all created on the fascinating journey from grape to glass.

2nd Edition

How Wine Is Made

When you think about it, winemaking is pretty basic. It's almost as if the grapes themselves want to be turned into wine. Wine grapes will grow almost anyplace that has a warm to temperate climate. Ripe grapes contain lots of sugar. And the skins of the grapes are the perfect surface for natural yeasts to thrive. All the conditions you need to make wine.

First you pick a bunch of ripe grapes and crush them. Crushing releases the sugar inside the grapes and causes the yeast to come in contact with the sugar. The yeast "eats" the sugar and turns it into alcohol and carbon dioxide. The process is called *fermentation*, and it transforms plain old grape juice into sublime wine.

When nature is in balance, all goes according to plan. The reality, of course, is that nature can be annoyingly unpredictable, and a winemaker can run into a plethora of problems in the quest to produce an outstanding bottle of wine. Fortunately, technology has come to the aid of winemakers in an activity that is a careful balance of art and science.

There are many technological options available to the modern winemaker. But—whether the end product is red, white, or pink, or whether it's cheap or expensive—there are several principles common to all winemaking.

Harvesting and Preparing the Grapes

The quality of a wine depends, first and foremost, on the grapes, which have to be picked at just the right moment of ripeness. As grapes ripen, the sugar content increases. At the same time, their acidity declines. The trick is to harvest them when the sugar and acid levels are in balance. This is always a subjective judgment by the winemaker and is based on what style of wine he is producing.

It's crucial that the grapes are picked and transported to the winery without prematurely splitting the skins. While handpicking is best, mechanical harvesting machines can handle grape bunches with care. This equipment tenderly squeezes the juice from the grapes so that the bitter seeds aren't crushed. The resulting substance is called *must*—a combination of juice, skins, and seeds. Depending on what kind of wine is being produced, the skins and seeds are either discarded or left in for a period of time.

Fermenting the Juice

Winemakers can "manage" fermentation to enhance the resulting wine. Fermentation usually takes place in large stainless steel tanks, but winemakers can choose to substitute oak barrels to add flavor and complexity. Because high temperatures kill yeast and end fermentation, winemakers control the temperature through refrigeration and circulation. Instead of relying solely on naturally occurring yeasts, they can add cultured yeasts to the juice that are better suited to the kind of wine they're producing. For wines that have fermented with their skins, winemakers decide the appropriate time to separate the skins from the liquid.

Message in a Bottle

If a wine is fully fermented to produce a dry wine, about 40 percent of the grapes' sugar is converted to carbon dioxide and about 60 percent becomes alcohol. If all the sugar is not converted, you get a low-alcohol wine that will have some degree of sweetness. The leftover sugar, called *residual sugar*, determines how sweet a wine will be.

When grapes don't fully ripen and lack enough natural grape sugar to produce reasonable alcohol levels, the winemaker can add sugar to the juice. This practice, called *chaptalization*, is illegal in some winemaking areas—Italy and California, to name two—but perfectly allowable in France and other U.S. states.

After fermentation, coarse sediment particles called *lees* settle at the bottom of the fermentation vessel. This sludgelike material is made up of dead yeast cells and small grape particles. The wine is usually separated from the lees when fermentation has run its course. But a winemaker can choose to extend the lees contact for further aging to produce a wine with more complexity. This is more often done with white wines than with reds.

Wines, by nature, are cloudy because of the dead yeast and tiny particulate matter. Once fermentation is complete, most wines are clarified by *fining*, a process that removes those microscopic elements. When fining agents—such as charcoal, bentonite clay, casein (milk protein), or egg whites—are added to the wine, they grab onto the solid particles and drag them, over a period of days, to the bottom of the tank. The wine can then be separated from the sediment by *racking*, the siphoning off of the clear juice. Some winemakers will further clarify the wine right before bottling by filtering it through layers of paper filters or synthetic fiber mesh.

Savvy Sipping

Some winemakers think that fining and filtering remove too much flavor and body from the wine, and forego those processes. The resultant wines (sometimes, but not always, labeled "unfined" and "unfiltered") may have a small amount of sediment in the bottle, but the winemakers believe a fuller flavor will more than offset any inconvenience to the consumer.

Sometimes, between fermentation and aging, a winemaker will add special bacteria to encourage an extra fermentation called *malolactic fermentation*—ML or MLF, for short. This process makes the wine less acidic. It converts malic acid in the wine, which has a sharp taste, to lactic acid, which gives the wine a creamy or buttery flavor. In terms of what you sense in your mouth, imagine an apple at one end of the spectrum and milk at the other. Most reds and some whites undergo MLF.

Aging the Wine

After fermentation, some wines are ready for immediate bottling. Rosés, many whites, and light reds are bottled soon after fermentation and should be drunk while still young. Others will be aged—either in stainless steel or oak—for several months or up to several years. Fine red wines, in particular, need to age to reach their full potential. This is accomplished in oak barrels, which allows the wines to soften and absorb some of the wood's flavors and tannins.

Many wines, both red and white, are blends. Before bottling, a winemaker may combine several different grape varieties—like adding some Merlot to some Cabernet Sauvignon—or different barrels (or *lots*) of the same wine in order to make the best-tasting bottle of wine.

Grape skins rise to the top of the fermenting must, forming a "cap" over the juice. This cap needs to be broken up and mixed back in to extract the desirable qualities from the skins. The cap is pumped or manually punched back with a paddle. A "punched-cap" wine, it's said, reflects the winemaker—a big, strong winemaker will force more extract from the skins, resulting in a big, highly tannic wine.

Vino Veritas

Bottling the Wine

When a wine is ready for release, it's bottled in a highly mechanized process that keeps the wine from contact with the air, germs, and impurities. Sparkling clean bottles are filled, corked, capped, and labeled with little human intervention. For the finest wines it is often advantageous for the winery to keep the bottles in storage for two or more years. This makes for better wine when it finally reaches the market and, in many cases, substantially increases the value of the wine.

Red Wine

All grapes, regardless of color, have the same greenish pulp and colorless juice. So where does a red wine get its color? The skins. Red wine grapes are crushed leaving the juice, skins, seeds, and, sometimes, stems together in the fermenting vat, during which time the skins impart their color and tannins to the juice.

When fermentation is complete—one to three weeks later—the new wine is drawn from the vat. This first run of juice, called *free-run juice*, comes forth voluntarily. Afterward, the mixture is pressed, yielding *press wine*, which is darker and more tannic. The winemaker may, at this point, choose to blend the two in order to adjust the tannin level. Now the wine is clarified and transferred to either oak barrels for aging or stainless steel vats for holding in an oxygen-free environment.

Savvy Sipping

Oak barrels are expensive and usually reserved for premium wines. But wineries sometimes use less-expensive techniques for their cheaper wines, like adding oak chips to the wine in the tanks. The results, however, aren't usually as good. If you see an inexpensive wine labeled "oaked" with no mention of "barrel," you can be pretty sure no barrel was used.

Aging in Barrels and Bottles

Prolonged barrel aging before bottling is desirable for most types of red wine to allow all the flavor components time to harmonize. The oak barrel imparts flavor to the wine, sometimes reminiscent of vanilla or wood (surprise!) and other times described as spicy. The barrel also allows a very slight and controlled exposure to oxygen. Winemakers usually try to avoid exposing their wines to the air. But this low-level oxidation is actually beneficial to the structure and character of the wine.

Some wines improve with further aging in the bottle—particularly fine reds that begin life high in tannins. They include California Cabernet Sauvignon and Zinfandel, French Bordeaux and Italian Barolo—and they can continue to improve after many years and, sometimes, even decades. Their harsh tannins soften. Their aromas become more complex. And their textures become silky.

White Wine

Because the juice of all grapes is colorless, white wine can be made from any kind of grape. In practice, though, most whites come from "white" grapes—which are actually greenish, greenish yellow, golden yellow, or pinkish yellow.

In contrast to making red wine, the juice for white wine is fermented without the skins and seeds. The result: no tannins and little color. White wines can take on a pale straw color or greenish to deep gold tones depending on the grape variety and aging treatment.

Vino Veritas

White wines have a propensity to produce crystals known as "wine diamonds." They're harmless—but a nuisance. They form from tartaric acid and potassium (both naturally occurring in grapes) that bind together when wine gets too cold. Many winemakers force crystals to form under extremely cold conditions during fermentation so they can remove them. The process is called *cold stabilization*.

In making red wines, malolactic fermentation is a given. With white wines it's an option. A winemaker can choose to perform it or not. When you peruse wine shelves, you'll be able to find clean, crisp whites that have not undergone any MLF, full-bodied whites that have undergone full MLF, and whites somewhere in the middle.

Winemakers have similar decisions to make regarding aging white wines in oak barrels. Chardonnay, for example, can benefit from oak. Others such as Riesling and Sauvignon Blanc rarely do.

Most white wines are meant to be drunk young, but there are exceptions. Some age-worthy whites are white Burgundies, white Bordeaux, and German and Alsace Rieslings.

Rosé Wine

Rosé is French for "pink." And that's how you identify a Rosé wine: by its color. The preferred method for producing Rosés is to crush red wine grapes but allow the skins to sit with the juice for only a short time before separating the juice—anywhere from a few hours to several days. Just long enough to kiss the juice with color. It's the winemaker who determines how long the kiss will last. When the color is to the producer's liking, the winemaking process continues as it would for white wine. An alternative technique involves adding a small amount of finished red wine to a white wine. However, the result is more like a tinted white and has a different taste than a true Rosé.

Message in a Bottle

Even though a Rosé has acidity and tannins acquired from the grape skins, its fruit flavor disappears quickly—which is why you should always buy the most recent vintage available. And, like a white wine, a Rosé should be served well chilled.

Rosés have always been drunk in southern France. Originally they were made from leftover grapes that didn't make it into the local red wine. But the winemaking philosophy has changed, and Rosés are now being made on purpose and have acquired respect. They're made in a dry style.

Some of the best Rosés come from France—from Tavel (which makes *only* Rosé wines) in the Rhone region and Anjou in the Loire Valley. Back in the 1960s, Rosés were quite popular in the United States but fell out of fashion. Enter *blush wine* in the '80s. Same concept, different term. It was a marketing success. White Zinfandel—the first blush wine introduced—became all the rage and spawned many other pinks-from-reds: white Grenache, Merlot Blanc, Cabernet Blanc. Most of them are low in alcohol and sweet—which led to the perception that all Rosés are sweet. In fact, many are dry and off-dry.

Rosé wines can be found by other names. Rosado is a Rosé from Spain. Rosato is a Rosé from Italy. Vin Gris ("gray wine"), from France, is a very pale Rosé made from very lightly pressed red grapes.

Sparkling Wine

What a difference a few bubbles make! Sparkling wine starts out as still wine and then undergoes a second fermentation. More carbon dioxide is formed—but, this time, it's captured and not allowed to escape. Voilà! A party ready to happen.

There are all sorts of sparkling wines: Cava (from Spain); Prosecco and Asti (from Italy); Sekt (from Germany); blanc de noir (from the Pinot Noir grape); blanc de blanc (from the Chardonnay grape)—and, the most famous, Champagne. Not all sparkling wines are Champagne. In order to legitimately be called Champagne, a sparkling wine must meet the following criteria. It must:

- be produced in the Champagne district of France.
- be produced from the Chardonnay, Pinot Noir, and/or Pinot Meunier grapes grown there.
- get its bubbles via the *méthode champenoise* (Champagne method).

The Champagne method is an expensive and labor-intensive means of naturally carbonating a wine. First, wine is made from local grapes. This is no easy feat. The vineyards of Champagne lie so far north that ripeness is an issue in most years. After clarification and a measure of aging, the wine is put into thick Champagne bottles, along with enough yeast and sugar to initiate a second fermentation. It is this second fermentation in the tightly sealed bottle that puts the bubbles in the bubbly. The carbon dioxide can't get out, so it's dissolved in the wine.

The wine is aged—sometimes for years—along with the dead yeast that accumulates as sediment. The trick is to get rid of the sediment without losing all the bubbles. By gradually tilting the bottle a little bit each day until it is inverted, the dead yeast is coaxed into the neck of the bottle where it can quickly be removed. At that time, the bottle is topped off and adjusted for sweetness and then immediately corked so that the wine doesn't lose its effervescence. The Champagne method, because it's so time-consuming and labor-intensive, is expensive—one reason for the high price tag of Champagne. Sparkling wines that are carbonated in other, cheaper ways can be sold for much less.

Fortified Wine

Fortified means that extra alcohol has been added to a wine. In the beginning it was done to preserve the wine for shipping, but fortified wines have become specialties to be enjoyed on their own terms.

If you were making regular table wine, you'd crush the grapes and let fermentation take its course. You'd end up with a dry wine with about

12 percent alcohol. For a fortified wine you would add a brandy (usually made from the same grape as the wine) or a neutral spirit. If you add the brandy after fermentation, the fortified wine is dry, with no residual sugar. If it is added before fermentation is complete—before all the natural fruit sugar is consumed—the alcohol stops the yeast from converting the sugars, and you have a sweet fortified wine.

Vino Veritas

The alcohol level of a table wine in the United States, as mandated by government regulations, is 7 to 14 percent. Fortified wines generally have between 17 and 21 percent alcohol. As a result, they're more stable than table wines and less apt to spoil once they've been opened.

There are four primary types of fortified wines: Port, Sherry, Madeira, and Marsala. The popular drinking wines are Port and Sherry. Madeira and Marsala are better known as cooking wines, but there are good bottles of each for drinking.

Port is sweet and is most often served after a meal. True Port comes from the Douro Valley in Portugal.

Sherry, from the vineyards of southern Spain, can range from dry to sweet. Pale, dry Sherry is served chilled as an apéritif. Darker, sweet Sherry is usually enjoyed as an after-dinner drink.

Madeira is named after its birthplace, a Portuguese island off the coast of Africa. Unlike other fortified wines, Madeira is heated in its production. It can be sweet or dry.

Marsala, named for the town on the western tip of Sicily, comes both dry and sweet. Of all the fortified wines, Marsala is the least distinctive as a beverage and is mostly used for cooking.

Dessert Wine

Dessert wines are called "dessert" because, well, they're sweet. They're served either with dessert or as dessert. Timing is everything when it comes to making a dessert wine. The time you pick the grapes, that is.

The grapes are harvested very late in the growing season when they're ripe, ripe, ripe. Because of the high concentration of sugar, not all of it converts to alcohol during fermentation. The result is that the wine is extremely sweet. At the same time, the overabundance of sugar means the wine can ferment to a high level of alcohol. The high sugar content also helps preserve the wine so it can improve in the bottle for years.

Exactly how long the grapes are left on the vine before picking is determined by what wines are being produced. Grapes that are harvested late in the season produce *late harvest* wines. The grapes can be left on the vine even longer until they shrivel up and their flavors become concentrated. German wines labeled Auslese, Beerenauslese, and Trockenbeerenauslese come from these grapes.

Other wines—notably Sauternes, Barsac, Tokay, and many California late harvest wines—are produced from grapes that have been allowed to develop a mold (*Botrytis cinerea*). Endearingly called *noble rot*, this mold concentrates the grapes' flavors and adds some of its own.

Grapes, especially those from northern vineyards, can be left on the vine until they freeze. They're picked and pressed before they can thaw, separating out the frozen water and leaving concentrated juice. These are made into *ice wines*.

Kosher Wine

Wine has played an important part in Jewish tradition and rituals for thousands of years. Most important religious ceremonies begin with the *Kiddush*, the prayer over the wine. During Passover, celebrants drink four cups of wine to symbolize the four dimensions of freedom. In ancient times, before the Roman conquest drove the Jewish inhabitants out of what is now Israel, vineyards and winemaking were common. Because tradition mandated the drinking of wine, Jewish winemakers took their skills with them into exile. When Jewish immigrants settled in the Northeast United States a century ago, the only grapes available to them were the native American Concord grapes. The wines made from these grapes were very high in acid and had a musty character, often referred to as "foxy." In order to make them palatable, the wines had to be heavily sweetened.

This heavy and cloyingly sweet style became synonymous with kosher wine. But it's not a religious dictate. Kosher wines can be—and are—made from any variety of grapes. Since the mid-1980s kosher winemaking has changed. Kosher wines are increasingly made from popular grape varietals like Chardonnay, Merlot, and Cabernet Sauvignon.

The Ripe Stuff

What does *kosher* mean?

It's Hebrew for good, fitting, or proper. According to Jewish dietary code, foods can be naturally kosher (like fruits and vegetables); not kosher but with the potential to be made so by special processing; or not kosher—without the possibility of ever becoming kosher (like pork and shellfish).

What Makes Wine Kosher?

Kosher wines are produced under the strict supervision of a rabbi. To qualify as kosher, certain regulations have to be followed. Because the Holy Land has such a sanctified status in Judaism, some practices are mandated for wineries in Israel but not for those outside of Israel. Qualifying for kosher status extends from the vineyard to the table:

- The vines have to be at least four years old before the grapes can be made into wine. (In Israel, this applies both to grapes grown in one's own vineyard and to purchased grapes.)
- For wineries in Israel, the vineyard must be left fallow every seventh year, and the growing of other fruits or vegetables in the vineyard is prohibited.
- Only Sabbath observant workers are allowed to take part in making the wine. Even after the wine has gone into barrels and been given a rabbinical seal, a *shomer*—or watchman—has to guard it. And none of the work can be done on a holy day.
- All the equipment, tools, materials, and storage facilities may be used only for making kosher products.

- No animal products may be used to produce kosher wine. Instead of using gelatin or egg whites in the fining process, nonanimal fining agents (such as bentonite clay) or kosher fish gelatin are used.
- No leavens are permitted. While yeasts are part of winemaking, they must be certified kosher.
- In Israel, 1 percent of the finished wine has to be discarded. This practice commemorates the time before the Roman conquest when tithing was mandatory.

A wine's label tells you if a wine is kosher. You'll see an *O* with a *U* inside of it with a *P* near it—a sign that the world's largest kosher certification organization has approved it. A wine label that reads "Made from grapes that are not *orlah*" indicates that the winery observed the age rule—that the vines were at least four years old.

Vino Veritas

Two Types of Kosher Wine

For observant Jewish people, kosher wine is holy in nature. And to retain its "kosherness," it must be opened and poured by equally observant Jewish individuals. In answer to the social and economic limitations this poses—to restaurants, for example—there is *mevushal* wine. It undergoes an additional process to retain its religious purity no matter who opens and pours it. In a sense it's super-kosher.

Mevushal means "boiled." In reality, the wine isn't boiled; it's subjected to flash pasteurization. Wines are pasteurized by heating them to about 185°F for one minute—or flash pasteurized by heating them to 203°F for a few seconds—followed by rapid cooling.

Pasteurization changes a wine's characteristics to some degree. Some winemakers say it actually enhances a wine's flavor. For non-kosher wines, pasteurization is done to kill bacteria (which includes bacteria necessary for aging) and is primarily used for ordinary, less expensive wines that are meant for early consumption.

Savvy Sipping

Who Makes Kosher Wines?

In the United States, the largest producer and importer of kosher wine is the Herzog family, whose labels include Baron Herzog, Herzog Wine Cellars, and Weinstock Cellars. In Europe, a number of well-known wineries have set aside a portion of their production for kosher wines. And in Israel, a new generation of winemakers is producing outstanding wines. Here are just a few of the high-quality kosher wine producers:

- Hagafen Cellars *California*
- Gan Eden Winery *California*
- Château Sarget de Gruaud Larose *France*
- Barkan *Israel*
- Gamla *Israel*
- Bartenura *Italy*
- Ramon Cardova *Spain*
- Hafner Koscher Wein *Austria*
- Backsberg *South Africa*
- Teal Lake *Australia*
- Alfasi *Chile*

Organic Wine

It was only a matter of time before the organic movement reached the vineyards. Most winemakers are farmers. The wines they produce will be only as good as the grapes they grow. So they have a natural interest in growing the best-tasting fruit and maintaining the health of the land for years to come.

Conventional vs. Organic Farming

All grape growers face the same natural obstacles: weather, pests, disease, weeds. Conventional techniques adopted over the last fifty years to meet nature's challenges have come from man's own inventions—insecticides, chemical fertilizers, fumigants, and herbicides.

Organic farming forsakes chemicals in favor of more "natural" techniques. From a practical viewpoint this means that organic farmers will:

- Fertilize using composted animal manure or algae.
- Combat weeds by mowing them periodically and allowing them to rot back into the ground, providing organic fertilizer.
- Get rid of insects by growing other plants in the vineyard to attract "beneficial" bugs to act as predators.

Organic farming is as much philosophy as practice. The objective is balance in nature and the long-term health of the soil, the plants and, ultimately, the wine drinker. Grapes grown in this fashion can be government certified as organic grapes. The wine can then be advertised as wine from "organically grown grapes."

The irony is that many producers are using organic techniques because they make good sense—but not seeking certification because of the rigidity of government oversight.

Conventional vs. Organic Winemaking

The term *organic*—or, more precisely, the government certification of a wine as "organic"—doesn't stop at the harvest. Organic winemakers have to use only approved organic methods in cellar operations as well. The subject of "organic" has been muddied over the practice of adding sulfur dioxide (sulfites), which is the main ingredient wineries use to extend the shelf life of wine.

The health effects of sulfites are negligible except for a small percentage of people who have a sensitivity to them. It's difficult to make a wine that will keep for any length of time without adding at least some sulfites to those that are naturally produced by the yeasts during fermentation. But to be able to call a wine "organic," the winemaker has to abide by strict, government-mandated sulfite rules.

How to Know You're Getting "Organic"

Organic claims on store shelves are just plain confusing. When you want an organic alternative to conventional wine, who and what should you believe? The answer is on the label—if you understand what the terms mean. There are four categories that organic wines can claim:

- **100% Organic.** The wine must be from 100 percent organically produced ingredients. There can be no added sulfites. It can have naturally occurring sulfites from fermentation, but they have to measure less than 100 parts per million.
- **Organic.** The wine must be from 95 percent organic ingredients. The nonorganic 5 percent has to be either an agricultural ingredient that's not organically available or another substance like added yeast. There can be no added sulfites, but naturally occurring sulfites can measure up to 100 parts per million.
- **Made with Organic Ingredients/Organic Grapes/Organically Grown Grapes.** The wine must be from 70 percent organic ingredients. Sulfites have to measure below 100 parts per million.
- **Some Organic Ingredients.** The wine has less than 70 percent organic ingredients. The label can't have any information about a certifying agency or any other reference to organic content.

Simply put, "organic" wines are made from certified organic grapes and contain no additives such as sulfites. Wineries that use organic grapes but add sulfites or other additives can only be labeled "made with organically grown grapes."

To give you a leg up on your next organic wine-buying expedition, here are some wineries that produce certified organic wines:

- **Frey Vineyards** *California*
- **Badger Mountain Vineyard** *Washington*
- **Bonterra Vineyards** *California*
- **Cooper Mountain Vineyards** *Oregon*
- **Organic Wine Works** *California*

Vegetarian and Vegan Wine

Vegetarians and vegans adhere to a diet of vegetables, fruits, grains, and nuts. While vegetarians limit their intake of animal product—sometimes making exceptions for milk and cheese—vegans eliminate animal products altogether.

Winemakers—both organic and nonorganic—often use animal-based products in the fining process to clarify the wine. The fining agents act as magnets to attract the unwanted material, then fall to the bottom of the tank. The clear wine is siphoned off, but trace amounts of the fining agent may linger in the finished wine.

Wines suitable for vegans use earth-based fining agents such as bentonite clay, diatomaceous earth, carbon, and kaolin (similar to bentonite). But the fining agents aren't listed on the label, and you have to do some investigating. It's not that vegan wines are scarce. There are lots of them. They're just not advertised as vegan.

Savvy Sipping

Often, kosher wines may be the answer for vegans—but not always. Kosher gelatin, sometimes used as the fining agent, can be made with fish bones and the skins of beef or pork. Because the product is not real flesh and has undergone significant changes to make it kosher, it's considered not to be meat.

A word to the wise vegan: A suitable wine in one vintage may not be suitable in the next. Winemakers can change their fining agents from one year to the next. You might have to make a call to the producer or exporter to find out. A simpler solution to finding a vegan-friendly wine is to look for "unfined" wines. And that's what it will say on the label.

Filtering is another process to remove impurities. A wine can be both fined and filtered, it can undergo one process without the other, or it can undergo neither. "Unfined" on the label means that no clarifying agent has been used.

CHAPTER 3

Types of Wine: What's in a Name?

Wine is only as good as the grapes that go into it. It's the grapes that determine the wine's varietal character. Sure, a winemaker can tinker with the juice and add new dimensions to the wine, but the grape is still the taste determiner. Whatever is right or wrong with a wine grape will show itself in the final product. Producing the highest-quality wine is only possible when you start with the highest-quality fruit.

The Grapes

Thousands of years ago wine was made from the grapes available to the ancient winemakers. It happens that the grape species *Vitis vinifera* was native to Europe and central and east Asia, where the first known winemaking took place. Most of the world's wines are still made from these grapes.

Ten thousand varieties of *Vitis vinifera* exist, but only about 230 varieties ever make it into a bottle. In the normal course of enjoying wine, you might run into a mere 50 varieties.

Vino Veritas

Recent findings by researchers at the University of Pennsylvania suggest that Chinese villagers were fermenting alcoholic beverages as long ago as 7,000 B.C. The chemical evidence came from examining shards of pottery. The team found tartaric acid, an organic acid present in wine.

Personality Traits of Grapes

Color is the most obvious visual trait that distinguishes one grape from another. Grapes are categorized either as white wine grapes or red wine grapes based on the color of their skins when ripe. (Never mind that, in reality, white grapes can be green and red grapes can be black.) Except for a handful of red grape varieties that have red pulp, all grapes have the same white-colored pulp and clear juice.

Grapes come in all sizes—some large, some small. Their skins can be thick or thin. Certain grapes have naturally higher acid levels, and some have an aromatic component that you can easily smell in the wine. Viognier, for example, has decidedly floral aromas. Sauvignon Blanc has an herbaceous quality.

Some vines produce grapes in dense clusters. That too can affect the wine. In warm, moist climates mildew can grow between the grapes. Left unchecked, it will make the wine taste moldy.

Noble Grapes

Good breeding and good taste will get you far. For six grape varieties, it got them nobility status. They were once thought to produce the best wines in the world and defined the artistry of wine. The so-called "noble grapes"—Cabernet Sauvignon, Merlot, Pinot Noir, Chardonnay, Sauvignon Blanc, and Riesling—are the basis for the legendary wines of France and, in the case of Riesling, Germany.

Hmm. No mention of Sangiovese or Nebbiolo of Italy. Or Tempranillo of Spain. Or Zinfandel of California. And that's probably the reason that the term has outlived its usefulness: Grape growing and production of fine wines have expanded to regions far removed from France.

Why aren't grapevines grown from seeds?

The Ripe
Stuff

Grapes start out in the spring as blossoms that are fertilized by the pollen from another vine. The "other" vine may be a different variety altogether. The new grape, then, has seeds with the genetic material from both parents—just like humans. There's no telling the result when those grape seeds are planted. Cuttings are more predictable.

Not So Noble

When the early American settlers made wine, they made it with grapes from vines they found growing in their neighborhoods. They weren't *Vitis vinifera* grapes. They were different species altogether. The wines had tastes that were unfamiliar (and sometimes not particularly agreeable), but some of them survive to this day.

- ◆ *Vitis labrusca*—found primarily in Canada and the northeastern United States. The best-known varieties are Concord and Catawba.

- *Vitis aestivalis*—found mainly in Missouri, Arkansas, and Tennessee. Cynthiana (also known as Norton) is the most recognizable variety.
- *Vitis rotundifolia*—native to the area around the Gulf of Mexico. The best-known variety is Skuppernong, used to make sweet wines popular in the South.

Growing the Grapes

Grapevines are pretty adaptable. But if they had their way, they'd live in temperate climates with warm, dry summers and mild winters. (Who wouldn't?) If you were going to plant grapevines, you'd have several important considerations: normal weather conditions, type of soil, drainage, sun exposure, natural pests, and—not least—the average length of the ripening season.

Choosing an inappropriate location for a grape variety will have disastrous—and expensive—results. Every grape variety has its own timetable for ripening. If a grape variety with a long ripening period is planted in an area with short summers, the grapes won't ripen sufficiently and will produce a tart wine. If a variety that ripens early is planted in a very warm climate, the grapes may get overripe and cause the wine to taste like mushy fruit.

Planting Vines

Modern grapevines begin as cuttings from other plants rather than from seeds. The cuttings are usually grafted to rootstocks that have been specially cultivated for their sturdiness.

Every grape variety has its favorite type of soil. Chardonnay and Pinot Noir like limestone. Cabernet prefers gravelly soil. Riesling is at its best in slatey soil. The common denominator for healthy plants is good drainage.

If a vine was left to its own devices (as vines were in ancient times), it would grow wildly, sprouting roots everywhere the branches touched the ground. It could easily cover an acre of land all by itself. But that's not the way to get the best fruit. The vine spends most of its energy putting down lots of shallow roots and spreading itself, so it has little left over to nurture the grapes. Today, vines are supported off the ground by trellises and are carefully pruned back.

A grape's skin, seeds, and stem all contain tannin, the bitter-tasting substance that's an important component of red wines. While the stems are usually removed during winemaking, the skins and seeds are left in the grape juice as it ferments. Varieties that have thick skins and small grapes will have a greater skin-to-juice ratio and will make more tannic wines.

Vino Veritas

Better Grapes Through Strength Training

Have you noticed how people who suffer through aggressive workout sessions and reduce their caloric intake have good bodies to show for it? The same goes for grapes. If you make their lives comfortable, making water and nutrients easily accessible, they become lazy and produce poor grapes.

This may seem counterintuitive, but if you plant the vines close together and make food and water hard to find, they have to send their roots deep into the ground for resources to survive. They end up producing strong and fit vines and great grapes. For whatever reason, stressed vines spend more of their energies on the fruit, producing lower yields and better quality.

Not all plants of the same variety are alike. Cabernets, for example, can vary in flavor, aroma, ripening traits, and disease resistance. A winemaker decides which plant best suits his or her purposes and buys a cutting from that plant to propagate. The resulting plant, genetically identical to its "mother," is known as a clone.

Message in a Bottle

Harvesting the Grapes

The harvest in warm climates may start in mid-August and, in cooler areas, may extend to late September. The determining factor is the ripeness of the grapes, and that's the decision of the winemaker. Ripeness is established largely by color and sugar level. In the United States the sugar content is measured according to the Brix scale, named after a nineteenth-century German inventor. Using a hydrometer, the winemaker can get a Brix reading for the grapes, which, for most table wines, will be between 19° and 25° Brix. The measurement translates directly into what level of alcohol will be produced from the grapes during fermentation.

Message in a Bottle

Each degree Brix equals 1 gram of sugar for every 100 grams of grape juice. About 55 percent of the sugar is converted to alcohol. So, you can predict the alcohol level by multiplying the Brix reading by .55. A 20° reading will make a wine with 11 percent alcohol.

Grapes are harvested either by hand or with mechanical harvesters. Handpicking is labor-intensive and costly but better for the grapes. The pickers reject unripe or diseased grapes right in the vineyard. They collect the rest in small buckets and carefully transfer them to larger bins, keeping the risk of damage to the grapes low. Mechanical harvesters shake the grapes from the vines and store them until they're unloaded at the winery. The risk of damage to the grapes increases, but the harvest can be accomplished with little labor.

To put grape growing into a wine drinker's perspective, look at what you get from an acre of vines. Keep in mind that lots of variables are at work—like the number of vines planted, grape yield, varieties producing larger or smaller clusters, and varieties yielding more or less juice. On average, one acre will produce:

- 5 tons of grapes
- 13.5 barrels of wine
- 3,985 bottles of wine
- 15,940 glasses of wine

Hybrids

Hybrids are the offspring of two or more different species (like vinifera and labrusca), although the term has also come to mean a cross between two varieties of the same species (vinifera and vinifera). Hybrids can occur naturally through cross-pollination. Cabernet Sauvignon developed that way—as a cross of Cabernet Franc and Sauvignon Blanc. Or, a hybrid can be created under controlled conditions, usually with a specific purpose in mind. Müller-Thurgau is such a grape. Professor Müller from Thurgau, Switzerland, wanted to produce a prolific grape that would ripen early but would taste like Riesling. He successfully crossed Riesling and Sylvaner. Today, Müller-Thurgau is the most cultivated grape in Germany.

Phylloxera Becomes a Driving Force

The real impetus for hybrids was the phylloxera epidemic of the late 1800s. This small yellow louse feeds on the roots of grapevines and eventually starves the vines. By the time France had lost 75 percent of its grapevines, everyone in the wine world was looking for a solution.

Growers had discovered that the roots of native American grapevines were immune to the effects of the louse because the roots were so thick. The answer to the phylloxera problem came in the form of grafting European vines onto American rootstocks. The vines flourished and produced good wines with all the desired vinifera characteristics.

American and French Hybrids

Some hybrids sprang up naturally in the eastern United States. Their ranks include the Catawba, Delaware, Isabella, and Alexander. Then there are the man-made hybrids, including the Niagara and Diamond.

Americans weren't the only ones in the hybrid business. French researchers were busy too. In order to eliminate some of the "foxy" taste they detected in wines from *Vitis labrusca* vines, they used other American vine species and American hybrids as parents. Some of the more popular French hybrid grapes, named after their creators, are:

- Baco Noir and Baco Blanc
- Seyval Blanc
- Maréchal Foch
- Vidal Blanc
- Ravat Blanc

Ironically, French planting regulations have discouraged hybrid vine varieties. But you'll run across them in the wine regions of the eastern United States, Canada, Australia, and Brazil.

Naming Wines: Region vs. Grape

In France, Italy, Spain, and most of what is known as the Old World, wines are named for the place where they're produced. It can be a huge area (France), a broad region (Bordeaux), smaller areas like villages, or even a specific slope within a vineyard. Chianti, Pouilly-Fuissé, and Rioja are all places. The name tells you nothing about the grapes in the bottle.

Savvy Sipping

Regional wine names may tell the uninitiated nothing about the bottle's contents, but wine drinkers familiar with the regions know exactly what grapes they're drinking. They have learned that the primary grape in Chianti is Sangiovese. In Pouilly-Fuissé, it's Chardonnay. And in Rioja, it's Tempranillo.

How Regional Names Evolved

Europeans have a long history of winemaking. Through centuries of experimentation, they learned which grapes grew best where. And certain regions became known for using those particular grapes in their wines. European winemakers were all about blending their wines. Not just one grape . . . but two, three, or many more. Châteauneuf-du-Pape wines can have up to thirteen different grapes.

When the European governments got involved in overseeing winemaking to ensure quality and protect against unethical producers, they divided their respective countries into specific growing areas—called appellations—and set down laws to regulate winemaking. While each country is different, the French system, established in 1935, is the one most copied. For a wine to qualify for appellation status, it has to meet rigid requirements. The rules govern such things as:

- What grape varieties can be grown and put into the bottle
- Growing methods like pruning and fertilizing
- Maximum production per acre
- Minimum alcohol content
- Winemaking practices

Europeans came to associate an appellation or region with a particular type of wine. They didn't need a label to tell them what grapes were inside the bottle. For people unfamiliar with the regional differences, choosing a European wine makes them want to tear their hair out.

Naming their wines after geographical locations has a philosophical element, too. Old World winemakers say their wines reflect the earth—that the characteristic taste comes from all the growing conditions of soil, sun, rain, altitude, and drainage. The winemakers have such a reverence for what they term *terroir* (French for "soil") that their winemaking practices tend toward minimalist. Let the New World winemakers tinker! The Old World style of winemaking is to let the grapes and the terroir speak for themselves.

Varietal Wines

In the New World—meaning everywhere outside of Europe—wine names are all about the grapes. Winemakers became enamored with producing wines using one grape variety as opposed to the European practice of blending the grapes. The wines were named after the grape variety they used. Chardonnay, Chenin Blanc, Merlot, Pinot Noir, Cabernet Sauvignon: They're all named after the grapes and are classified as varietal wines.

The New World has appellations too, but the rules are much more lax and don't come into play as often with wine names as they do in Europe.

Vino Veritas

In the United States the regional growing areas are known as American Viticultural Areas (AVA). The only requirement for a wine to use an AVA on the label is that 85 percent of the contents have to come from grapes grown in that area. New AVAs are designated all the time.

Old World and New World Meet

Realities of the wine marketplace have brought the Old and New Worlds closer together. The United States is a big market for European wines. If Americans can't tell what's inside the bottle, they're not going to be buying it. As a result, European wines destined for export are increasingly adding grape variety names to their labels. When American wine drinkers find out that red Burgundies are made from Pinot Noir grapes and white Burgundies are made from Chardonnay, their comfort levels go up.

New World wine names have made some accommodation to the marketplace as well. As general wine knowledge has increased and as wine enthusiasts have recognized the contribution of growing regions to a wine's quality, wine names came to incorporate the locations of the vineyards. Geographical names like Napa Valley, Russian River Valley, and Stags' Leap became synonymous with quality and prestige.

Made-Up Names

As the Old and New Worlds have copied each other for marketing purposes, they've also borrowed from each other in the styles of wine they produce. European winemakers sometimes deviate from the finesse they're known for in favor of the bigger, more fruit-forward wines that have been so popular in America. In the United States many winemakers began to adopt the European practice of blending wines, realizing that the final product can benefit from more than one ingredient.

Proprietary Wines

For a wine to carry a varietal name, the bottle has to contain at least 75 percent of that variety. The regulation is intended to protect against diluting wines with inferior varietals, but it put creative limits on some producers. If a wine is half Cabernet and half Merlot, it's easy enough to call it a Cab-Merlot blend. But potential names get a little unwieldy when you start combining several different varieties.

Aha! Make up a name. Ford did it: Mustang. Mattel did it: Barbie. Why not winemakers? It turns out that using brand names for wine can be effective marketing tools. Some European producers had already figured that out years ago. Remember Blue Nun, Lancers, and Mateus? More and more winemakers around the world are using trademarked names for the whole spectrum of wines from low-end to very high-end. The names themselves range from thought-provoking to blatantly funny: Goats do Roam, Cat's Pee on a Gooseberry Bush, Fat Bastard, Marilyn Merlot.

Meritage Wines

In the 1980s a group of California winemakers who were really Francophiles at heart began producing Bordeaux-style blends from the traditional grapes of Bordeaux. They decided to formalize their group and establish standards for the category of wine. And the Meritage Association was born.

Message in a Bottle

Meritage rhymes with *heritage*. In fact, the name is a combination of *merit* and *heritage*. The term was created through a contest held by the members of the unnamed association. The winner got two bottles of each member's Meritage wines for ten years.

Meritage is a registered trademark of the association. If a winery producing a Bordeaux-style wine wants to use the term on its labels, it must meet certain criteria, including:

- The wine has to be a blend of two or more Bordeaux grape varieties.
- No single variety can make up more than 90 percent of the blend.
- The wine should be the winery's most expensive offering.

Unlike most proprietary names, Meritage is shared by a group of wineries. A similar sharing of a name comes from Alsace: Gentil. Any producer in the region can use the term if at least 50 percent of the wine comes from the region's Riesling, Gewürztraminer, Muscat, or Tokay Pinot Gris varieties.

Savvy Sipping

Generic names like Burgundy, Chablis, Port, and Sherry on American jug wines can be misleading. The contents don't come from those famous and distant wine regions and don't taste like they do either. The wines are mass-market blends of who-knows-what grapes. As wine drinkers have become more savvy shoppers, you'll find fewer generic names on wine store shelves.

How to Read a Label

Wine labels and the regulations governing them vary from country to country. The specific information on the label has to conform to the rules where the wine is eventually sold—not where it's produced. If a wine is sold in the same country where it's produced, it will have one label. If the wine is also destined for export, it may well have another version of the label—and both labels have to be approved by government agencies in the countries where the wine will be sold.

In the United States, most wine bottles have a front label to get your attention on the shelf and a back label geared to get you to buy. Very little of what's on the label actually tells you how the wine will taste. All the flowery language on the back label came from a marketer's imagination—not from unbiased tasting notes. While the back label is unregulated, the front label is highly regulated and overseen by the Alcohol and Tobacco Tax and Trade Bureau (TTB) within the Department of the Treasury. As a creative ploy to skirt the regulations, some wineries reverse the front and back labels. Many back labels are actually approved as the front label—so the front label is more whimsical in nature.

TTB Label Requirements

The name of the wine is the first essential on the label. Sounds easy enough. For U.S. wines you'll likely see a winery name or a brand name. If there's no mention of a varietal, it's probably a blend. If the varietal is part of the name, you know that 75 percent of what's in the bottle is that varietal. In Europe the name and the region are one and the same.

Message in a Bottle

The label will give you the class of wine. Terms like *table wine, sparkling wine, fruit wine,* and *apéritif wine* all have specific definitions in the regulations. Table wine, for example, means that the alcohol content is between 7 percent and 14 percent by volume.

The appellation or growing region is necessarily on the label of Old World wines because it's the default name. When it appears on New World wines, it's usually because the growing area is held in high esteem. If the appellation mentioned is an official AVA like Napa Valley, 85 percent of the wine has to have come from there. However, if a vineyard is mentioned, 95 percent of the grapes used must be from that vineyard.

The alcohol content is required on wines containing more than 14 percent alcohol. Wines over that amount are considered "fortified"—and taxed at a rate four times higher than regular table wines. Even if a wine—say a big Zinfandel—has achieved a high alcohol level the natural way (without adding extra alcohol), it's still taxed at the higher rate. Wines under 14 percent alcohol can state the actual amount or get by with just giving its class designation. A 1 percent variation is permitted for fortified wines, and a 1.5 percent variation is allowed for table wines.

The bottler and producer are mandated on the label. And here's where confusion enters.

- "Bottled by" means someone else produced it.
- "Produced and bottled by" means the bottler produced at least 75 percent of the wine.
- "Made and bottled by" says the bottler either produced 10 percent of the wine or changed its class status—say, turning it from a still wine into a sparkling wine.
- "Cellared," "vinted," or "prepared" means the winery exposed the wine to some sort of cellar treatment.
- "Blended and bottled by" means the winery combined wines of the same type.
- "Estate bottled" or "Grown, produced, and bottled by" means the winery controlled all aspects of production. It grew the grapes on its property before making and bottling the wine. And, further, the vineyard and winery have to be in the same viticultural area stated on the label.

The name of the producer differs according to country. New World wines come from wineries. French wines are produced by a château in Bordeaux or a domaine in Burgundy. Wines from Germany, Italy, and Spain come from estates. The real importance of the producer is that getting to know one producer and its track record over time will probably tell you more about a wine than anything else on the label.

Some countries have rating systems for their wines. In those cases, the labels may include the quality rankings of the wine. The accepted standard bottle size is 750 ml. You'll find the volume of the bottle's contents either on the label or molded into the glass.

Besides the government health warning about birth defects, ability to operate machinery, and health problems, the label also carries a sulfite advisory. The law says that wines with sulfite levels above ten parts per million must carry the phrase "contains sulfites" on the label.

The vintage year may be listed on the label. If a wine in the United States carries a vintage date on the label, 95 percent of the wine in the bottle has to be from that year. A wine that is blended from multiple years will either have no date on its label or have a "nonvintage" (NV) designation.

Is Vintage Important?

Somehow, the term *vintage* has come to imply quality. Very simply, a wine's vintage is the year the grapes were harvested. Everyone knows that crops are affected by weather conditions and that conditions vary from year to year. Grapevine crop quality—meaning healthy, ripe grapes with good sugar-acidity balance—can be compromised in two crucial growing stages.

At the beginning of the growing season, there's risk that frost will damage the flowers and reduce the potential size of the crop. But the weather at harvest and the couple weeks leading up to the harvest is the real key. Rain is the biggest threat. Too much rain will make the grapes bloat—diluting the wine—and encourage fungal diseases. What does a grower do with a weather forecast of rain? Harvest early to be safe or take a risk, hoping for full ripeness?

Variations in the harvested fruit will occur from year to year—to a greater or lesser extent—due to weather conditions. In some wine regions—like France, Germany, and Oregon—the variations will be more extreme and less predictable than in the sunny regions of California, southern Italy, Australia, and South Africa.

The vintage year isn't necessarily the year the wine went into the bottle. In wine regions in the northern hemisphere, even the freshest white wines are rarely bottled in the same calendar year that the grapes are picked. Reds—especially long-lived reds—are bottled two or three years or more after the harvest.

Message in a Bottle

Differences Within Regions

Even within wine regions, the weather isn't consistent. A vineyard on the valley floor will experience different weather conditions than one on a hillside or mountainside. Or a mold encouraged by moisture could destroy one vineyard and leave nearby vineyards unscathed.

The grape variety makes a difference, too. Cabernet is tough-skinned and able to withstand rain and rot that can wipe out the more sensitive Pinot Noir. So what turns out to be a really good year for one grape may not be so good for another. The same goes for the producers. In any year, some winemakers will produce better wines from the same grapes than other winemakers.

All this boils down to the fact that thinking about vintages as either good or bad is a bit simplistic. There are few universally dazzling vintages and few completely dismal years. Yet, there are times when vintage is a valuable consideration: when you're a devoted fan of a certain kind of wine from a certain region or when you're about to spend lots of money. In that case, have a vintage chart at the ready.

CHAPTER 4

A Primer on Red Grape Varieties

All wine grapes have signature characteristics that they impart to the wines: body, flavor, texture—and, in the case of red wine grapes, color and tannins. You can predict how a wine is likely to taste by the grapes that are crushed to make it. You'll find a grape's true varietal character in a wine regardless of winemaking practices. You may not always see the grape name on the label, but each variety has contributed something special to the mix.

2nd Edition

Cabernet Sauvignon

For a wine that's consistently captivated audiences around the world, you'd expect Cabernet Sauvignon (Cab, for short) to have a long history. Not so. It's less than 600 years old, which, in wine terms, is a relative youngster. Recent genetic studies at UC Davis revealed that, far from being an ancient variety, Cabernet Sauvignon is really the offspring of Cabernet Franc and Sauvignon Blanc.

One Tough Customer

The Cabernet grapes are small, black, and very tough-skinned. The thick skins make Cab grapes pretty resistant to disease and capable of withstanding hard autumn rains, which is a good thing because the grapes don't ripen until long into the growing season. The skins are also what give the wine its highly tannic nature. Cab grapes are adaptable and can grow in almost any climate that's not too cool. They grow in most major wine-producing regions of the world. Even in Spain and Italy where local grapes have dominated the landscape for centuries, Cabernet is being planted and used in nontraditional blends.

Message in a Bottle

Some Napa Cabernets have reached "cult" status. They're made in extremely small quantities and are sold almost exclusively by mailing list. When you find one for resale on the open market, you can pay thousands. Some of these elite wineries are Harlan Estate, Screaming Eagle, Grace Family Vineyard, Dalla Valle Vineyards, Bryant Family Vineyard, Araujo Estate Wines, and Colgin Cellars.

The planting of Cabernet Sauvignon got a real jump-start in the 1800s when it was used to replant the vineyards of Europe that had been ravaged by phylloxera. It became the primary grape of the famous Bordeaux blends from Médoc and Graves. But its popularity has spread around the world—particularly to California, where high-quality (and sometimes super-high priced) Cabs reign.

The Wines

Because of their high tannins, Cabernets start out life on the harsh side. But aging—first in oak barrels and later in bottles—softens and smoothes them. Serious Cabs can age for fifteen years or more. Think of Rod Stewart as a Cab. In his youth, he was an in-your-face rocker. In his maturity, he's crooning mellow ballads. Same voice, same showman. But age has added subtlety.

Savvy Sipping

Rubired is one of the major grapes grown in California. You may not recognize the name—because, frankly, it's not held in the highest esteem. It's one of the few grapes that produce red juice instead of white. For that reason, it's added to other wines to boost the color. It's also used to "stretch" jug wines—including some low, low-priced Cabs.

Typical tasting comments on young Cabernets usually praise the black currant, bell pepper, chocolate, and spice flavors. Older vintages are often described as having a taste of tobacco.

While 100 percent Cabernet wines are made (many in California), the trend seems to be toward blending. Bordeaux has always blended its Cabernet wine with Merlot, Cabernet Franc, Petit Verdot, or Malbec. Merlot and Cabernet Franc, in particular, add a soft fruit finish.

In Australia, Shiraz is added to the Cabernet, giving the wine a spicy pepper flavor. In Italy winemakers have introduced Cabernet to their Sangiovese-based wines, producing a new breed of wine referred to as "Super Tuscans." In Spain Cabernet is blended with their native Tempranillo.

Vino Veritas

The first recorded reference to planting Cabernet Sauvignon came from Château Mouton in the eighteenth century. Only, the grape was called by a different name: Vidure. It was derived from *vigne dure,* French for "hardy vine." The name is still used today in parts of Bordeaux.

A Sampling of Cabernet Blends
Try these Cab blends on for size:

- Nicolás Catena Zapata (Mendoza, Argentina) Cabernet/Malbec—$100
- Parador (Napa Valley) Cabernet/Sangiovese/Tempranillo—$36
- Van Ruiten Vineyards (Lodi, California) Cabernet/Shiraz—$12

Merlot

The '90s thrust Merlot into the spotlight, as it became the easy-drinking red varietal of choice, a less tannic alternative to Cabernet. Even in wine-making circles, Merlot didn't always have star status. It was relegated to the role of blending grape. But its mass-market appeal led to mass plantings around the world. In California alone, Merlot acreage went from 2,000 acres in 1985 to 50,000 in 2003.

Second Fiddle, No More

Merlot's small, dark blue grapes are relatively thin-skinned, making them earlier ripening and less tannic than Cabernet Sauvignon. The Merlot grape can be traced back to first-century France, but it wasn't named as a distinct variety until the 1800s.

While Cabernet gained recognition in Bordeaux's Médoc district, Merlot became prominent in the cooler Bordeaux districts of Pomerol and Saint-Emilion. Merlot is the third most planted red grape in France. Besides France, Merlot is important in California, Washington, New York's Long Island district, northeastern Italy, and Chile.

Savvy Sipping

When Merlot is good, it's really good. The famous Château Pétrus in Pomerol makes possibly the world's most expensive Merlot. Its 1990 bottling earned a perfect score of 100 from *Wine Spectator* magazine and sells for $2,500 or more—if you can find it.

Merlot has a reputation for low acidity and softness. It makes beautiful wines all by itself or blended with others—sort of the Miss Congeniality of the wine world. With its soaring popularity, however, came overproduction in some areas and a tarnished image for many undistinguished wines that were shaped more by market forces than the winemaker's art.

Merlot doesn't get particularly complex, and, on its own, doesn't benefit much from bottle aging. It's a "drink now" wine. Typical descriptions of Merlot flavors are plum, black cherry, currant, violet, and rose.

Merlot with Distinction

To get a taste of what different Merlots have to offer, here are some suggestions:

- Pahlmeyer (Napa Valley) Merlot—$80
- Andrew Will Klipsun Vineyard (Columbia Valley) Merlot—$53
- Bell Wine Cellars Aleta's Vineyard (Napa Valley) Merlot—$28

Pinot Noir

Pinot Noir has been frustrating winemakers since the ancient Romans. It's recognized worldwide as a premier grape, but it presents obstacles to winemaking every step of the way—from its propagation to bottle aging.

Pinot Noir first earned its reputation for making magnificent wines in the Burgundy region of France—and, more specifically, the two-mile-wide stretch called the Côte d'Or. Pinot Noir is also grown in the Champagne region, where it's one of the three grape varieties allowed to be used in its sparkling wine.

A Handful of Trouble

How difficult can Pinot Noir be? Let's count some of the ways. It's finicky about where it's planted and requires a long, cool growing season. The vine is genetically unstable, making the fruit from parent and offspring vines inconsistent. It's susceptible to bugs, spring frost, and disease. It lacks sufficient leaf cover to protect the grapes from birds. And even if the fruit survives the birds, the thin-skinned grapes can shrivel and dry out.

Message in a Bottle

Pinots have a huge family tree. At last count, there were more than 1,000 of them. The Pinot vine mutates easily and produces new offspring—both red and white. A few of the more familiar ones are Pinot Blanc, Pinot Gris, and Pinot Meunier.

Pinot Noir produces the best wines when it's grown in limestone soil and in relatively cool climates. Outside of France it's grown in such areas as Germany, Austria, Italy, Eastern Europe, South America, South Africa, Australia, Canada, and the United States. Its emergence in America began in the 1930s in California and it has gained prominence farther north in Oregon.

You might wonder, with all its difficulties, why anyone would go to all the trouble of producing a wine from Pinot Noir. One sip will give you the answer. Pinot Noir is like a demanding diva. She may be a complete pain in the neck prior to her performance, but it's all worth it as soon as she sings her first note.

Pinot Noir has been described as liquid silk. The texture is soft and velvety. Because the grape is less pigmented than other red wine grapes, the wine is lighter in color too. It's full-bodied but not heavy. It's high in alcohol—yet neither acidic nor tannic. Typical Pinot Noir flavors are raspberries, cherries, and smoke.

Picking the Perfect Pinot
See what Pinots are all about with one of these examples:

- Saintsbury Brown Ranch (Carneros, California) Pinot Noir—$70
- Patz & Hall Hyde Vineyard (Carneros, California) Pinot Noir—$45
- Ponzi (Willamette Valley, Oregon) Pinot Noir—$30
- Louis Jadot (Beaune, France) Chorey-Les-Beaune—$19

Syrah/Shiraz

It's called Shiraz in Australia, but everywhere else in the world the grape is known as Syrah. It has grown in France's Rhone Valley since at least Roman times. The grape arrived in Australia in the 1800s and became one of the most widely planted varieties in the country. Not too long after that, Syrah arrived in the United States, but only in the last ten years or so has the grape become very fashionable.

Syrah has all sorts of legends attached to it. One legend has it that Syrah was brought by the Crusaders from Shiraz, Persia, to the Rhone. Another says the ancient Romans brought it from Syracuse in Sicily. But DNA testing has shown that Syrah is really a native of the Rhone Valley.

Vino Veritas

In the 1980s a group of California winemakers who were particularly fond of the French wines of the Rhone pooled their experience and resources and started the movement toward the planting of Syrah and other Rhone varietals. They called themselves "The Rhone Rangers."

Survivor

The Syrah grape is black, thick-skinned, and can survive almost anywhere. That's why you'll find Syrah in places as diverse as France, Australia, California, Washington, and Oregon. Even within those areas, Syrah thrives both in cool climates and in warm and sunny conditions.

In the northern Rhone, Syrah is used in the wines from Cornas, Côte Rôtie, Hermitage, and Crozes-Hermitage. The Syrah is rarely blended there. When young, the wines are deeply colored and tannic with a distinct spiciness. As they age, they ease into flavors of blackberries, plums, and smoke. In the southern Rhone, Syrah is blended with other varietals to produce such well-known wines as Châteauneuf-du-Pape. In Australia Shiraz is made in two distinct styles: the big, rich tannic style; and the lighter, fruitier, drink-me-now style.

Qué Syrah Shiraz
Whatever will be, will be with these fine examples of the grape:

- Two Hands Barossa Valley (Australia) ARES Shiraz—$100
- d'Arenberg McLaren Vale (Australia) "The Dead Arm" Shiraz—$60
- Clos Mimi Bunny Slope Vineyard (Paso Robles, California) Syrah—$50
- Marquis Phillips McLaren Vale (Australia) Shiraz 9—$37

Sangiovese

Sangiovese is one of Italy's oldest red varieties and is said to have been cultivated by the Etruscans, the early inhabitants of the Italian peninsula. But it wasn't until about 1600 that Sangiovese finally got its name. It comes from the Latin *sanguis Jovis*—"blood of Jupiter." Sangiovese grows all over its native Italy, but its real home base is in Tuscany. It's only recently that the grape's popularity has risen dramatically in the United States.

All in the Family

Sangiovese is the main component of Chianti. Sangiovese has a lot of subvarieties. Both Vino Nobile de Montepulciano and the potent and long-lived Brunello di Montalcino are made from them. For the most part, wines made with Sangiovese have pronounced tannins and acidity—but not great depth of color. In the 1960s Italian winemakers began producing 100 percent Sangiovese wines and also blending the grape with Cabernet Sauvignon—wines that became known as "Super Tuscans."

Sampling Sangiovese
Here are four distinct examples of Sangiovese wines:

- Altesino (Italy) "Montosoli" Brunello di Montalcino—$90
- Ruffino (Italy) Riserva Ducale Oro Chianti Classico Riserva DOCG—$42
- Allegrini (Italy) Palazzo della Torre IGT—$22
- Masciarelli (Italy) Montepulciano d'Abruzzo—$20

Tempranillo

Tempranillo has been called Spain's answer to Cabernet Sauvignon. It's the country's most important red grape variety and is the main grape in Rioja wines. It was once rarely used outside of Spain except for blending. Today it's making itself known in California, Australia, and South America.

The Name Game

Tempranillo (from the Spanish word *temprano*) means "early"—so named because it ripens earlier than most red varieties. Tempranillo has a bewildering array of aliases. Inside Spain it goes by Cencibel, Ojo de Liebre ("eye of the hare"), Tinta de Pais, Tinto Fino, Tinta de Toro, and Tinto de Madred. In Portugal it's known as Tinta Roriz. It's also been grown in California for grape juice and jug wines and called Valdepeñas.

Savvy Sipping

When young, Tempranillo is a mellower, easier-drinking wine than a Cabernet. Yet, like Cabernet, it has the alcohol and tannins to age well. In Spain's Rioja region, Tempranillo is blended with Grenache and Carignan to produce brighter, more acidic wines.

Tempranillo Wines to Try
Here are a few Tempranillo wines to check out:

- Bodegas (Spain) Muga Rioja Torre Muga—$65
- Marques de Riscal (Spain) Rioja Gran Reserva—$26
- Truchard (Napa Valley) Tempranillo—$26
- Marques de Caceres (Spain) Rioja Reserva—$25

Zinfandel

Zinfandel: the All-American grape! Well, sort of. Although Zinfandel was brought to California from elsewhere in the 1800s, the BATF (Bureau of

Alcohol, Tobacco and Firearms, which administers wine labeling regulations) classified Zinfandel as a native grape. After its introduction to America, it became a huge success. It was easy to grow, produced big crops, and could be made into an amazing number of different styles.

However, Prohibition, the Depression, and World War II put an end to all that. Zinfandel vineyards might have disappeared if it hadn't been for an unexpected marketing phenomenon in the '70s: White Zinfandel. And a new interest in Zinfandel (both colors) was sparked.

Vino Veritas

Many Zinfandels are labeled "old vines." As vines age, they produce fewer grapes and—as the theory goes—more flavorful and intense grapes. This is obviously good for the wine. But the term *old vines* isn't regulated. So it can mean different things to different producers.

Zin's True Identity Is Revealed

Southern Italy produces a dry red wine from the Primitivo grape that was thought to be related to Zinfandel. Cousins? Brothers? Nope. The same grape. DNA investigation revealed them to be identical. Later, their ancestor was discovered: a wild vine that grows on the Adriatic Coast in Croatia in the former Yugoslavia.

Zinfandel is a chameleon. It can be vinified in many styles from a light, claret-style wine to a high-alcohol monster. The more robust styles have berry and spicy, black pepper flavors.

Zinfandel vs. Primitivo
Compare for yourself with these blockbusters:

- Storybook Mountain Vineyards (Napa Valley) Estate Reserve Zinfandel—$45
- Montevina Terra d'Oro Deaver Vineyard (Napa Valley) Zinfandel—$30
- Coturri Vineyards Chauvet Vineyard Estate (Sonoma Valley) Old Vine East Block Zinfandel—$28
- Hendry (Napa Valley) "Block 24" Primitivo—$28

Other Red Grape Varieties

Each variety of vinifera has its own characteristics and something unique to bring to a wine. More often than not, wines are blended so that the final product—the sum of all the parts—is greater than any single wine by itself. Perhaps a wine's contribution is acid, maybe texture, maybe tannins. Here are some other red grape varieties that put their distinctive mark on wines.

Barbera

Barbera is an Italian grape that contributes deep garnet colors, medium to full body, and light tannin levels. In warmer growing areas, it develops high sugar levels and, consequently, high alcohol levels. Barbera makes Italy's Barbera d'Asti, Barbera d'Alba, and Barbera del Monferrato.

Message in a Bottle

Barbera d'Alba and Barbera d'Asti are neighbors to Barolo and Barbaresco in Italy's Piedmont region, but they're miles apart in taste. The Barberas are more like the people's wine because they're easy-drinking and go so well with "peasant" food. Their light tannins mean that these wines aren't meant for long aging. In contrast, Barolo and Barbaresco are big and brawny.

Carignan

Originally from northern Spain, this high-yielding vine grows extensively in France and around the Mediterranean. It's popular as a blending grape because it brings red fruit characteristics, deep purple color, strong tannin structure, and high levels of alcohol. Carignan is also known as Carignane, Carignano, Carinena, Mazuelo, and Monestel.

Carmenère

A historic variety once heavily planted in Bordeaux, Carmenère was one of the six varieties allowed for use in making red Bordeaux wines. Because of low yields and ripening problems, it was almost completely abandoned in Bordeaux. But it has found a new home in Chile. It was imported there in 1850 but mislabeled as Merlot. In 1991 its true identity was discovered. Carmenère produces deeply colored, full-bodied wines.

Gamay

Gamay is the French variety solely responsible for the distinctive wines of Beaujolais—which are light-to-medium bodied, high in acid, low in tannins, and meant to be drunk young. Beaujolais Nouveau is a special category of "new" Gamay wine (seven-to-nine weeks old) that's released on the third Thursday of each November.

Vino Veritas

Beaujolais Nouveau is the first wine made from each year's harvest. Originally, it was made for the winery workers, but its popularity quickly spread to local bistros and beyond. Today, festivals around the world celebrate the wine's release the third Thursday in November.

Grenache

Grenache is a sweet grape that can produce wines with 15 or 16 percent alcohol because of its high sugar level. It's one of the official blending partners in Châteauneuf-du-Pape. In Spain it's known as Garnacha, where it's blended with Tempranillo to produce the red Rioja wines.

Malbec

A French grape permitted as one of the blending grapes in the famous wines of Bordeaux, Malbec is soft, yet robust, intense, and full-bodied. Malbec has found a new home in Argentina, where it is extensively produced as a rich and earthy varietal.

Nebbiolo

A thick-skinned grape grown mainly in Italy's Piedmont region, Nebbiolo is used as a varietal and for blending with other Italian wines. It is most famous for making two of Italy's great reds: Barolo and Barbaresco. It generally needs long aging in wood to soften.

Pinotage

A uniquely South African grape created in the 1920s by crossing Pinot Noir and Cinsault, Pinotage has a distinct spicy and peppery flavor. Although winemakers elsewhere have been experimenting with Pinotage, it remains primarily a product of South Africa.

CHAPTER 5

A Primer on White Grape Varieties

Grapes are the dominant factor in determining a wine's taste. Different varieties have different aromas, flavors, and colors—the grape's varietal character. Even though varietal character is fairly predictable within limits, it's not precise. Every grape variety has multiple clones that will have an effect on taste. Grapes picked at various times throughout the harvest can influence taste. And so can a winemaker's techniques. With all that taken into account, take a look at what you can expect from some prominent varieties.

2nd Edition

Chardonnay

DNA profiling has concluded that Chardonnay is a cross between a member of the Pinot family and an ancient, and almost extinct, variety called Gouais Blanc. Gouais Blanc originated in Croatia and was probably brought to France by the Romans. The first recorded reference to Chardonnay goes back to 1330. Some historical theories have Chardonnay coming from Lebanon, but there are no written references to that until long after 1330.

The Chameleon

As they say in the wine business, Chardonnay is low in varietal character. That means that the grapes have fairly neutral flavors that are less identifiable than in other grape varieties. A lot of what determines the taste of a Chardonnay is what the winemaker does to the grapes. Using oak to ferment and/or age the wine produces a richness and the familiar oak flavors of toast and vanilla. Leaving the wine on the lees adds complexity. Conducting malolactic fermentation reduces the overall acidity and produces a softer, creamier wine. All these are flavors not derived from the grapes themselves.

Message in a Bottle

Corton-Charlemagne vineyards in Burgundy, home to one of the most venerated Chardonnay wines of all time, was once planted in all red grapes. Or, at least that's the legend. It seem Mrs. Charlemagne got tired of seeing her husband's red-stained beard and convinced him to rip out the vines and start over with white wine grapes.

Location, Location, Location

Chardonnay is hardy and versatile and can grow successfully in all but the most extreme wine regions around the world. It can make great—though somewhat different—wines almost anywhere it's reasonably comfortable. Cool-climate Chardonnays tend toward a dry crispness and clean fruit flavors. Warmer-climate Chardonnays lean toward richer honey and butterscotch flavors.

In Burgundy, where it's been considered *the* noble white wine grape, Chardonnay goes into all the region's great white wines, such as Montrachet, Meursault, Pouilly-Fuissé, and Chablis. It's one of the three grapes—along with Pinot Noir and Pinot Meunier—allowed in Champagne and the only grape in blanc de blanc.

ABC

"Anything but Chardonnay." You've probably heard the mantra. Chardonnay is ubiquitous. Some would say boring. Others might say over-oaked. Chardonnay is particularly compatible with oak and usually receives some oak treatment—with the exceptions of Chardonnay wines from northern Italy, Chablis, and France's Mâconnais district. Recently, a bunch of unoaked Chardonnays have entered the arena and are gaining momentum.

Chardonnay didn't become the most popular white wine in the world for no reason. You can expect a tremendous variety of flavors, medium to high acidity, medium to full body, and minimal fruit to tropical fruit. And you can count on a wine that's dry.

Examples of big, oaky, and creamy Chardonnays:

- Lewis Cellars (Napa Valley) Reserve Chardonnay—$52
- Martinelli Vineyards Martinelli Road Vineyard (Russian River Valley, California) Chardonnay—$40
- Château Potelle Winery (Napa Valley) "VGS" Chardonnay—$35

Some unoaked Chardonnays:

- Kalin Cellars (Sonoma Coast) "Cuvée Le Charles" Chardonnay—$45
- Jermann (Friuli, Italy) Chardonnay—$29
- Scarpantoni Estate Wines (McLaren Vale, Australia) Unwooded Chardonnay—$16

Chenin Blanc

The traditional home of Chenin Blanc is the Loire Valley of France, where it's been cultivated among picturesque châteaus since the Middle Ages. Chenin Blanc is a sturdy grape with high natural acidity and the versatility to produce crisp, dry table wines, sparkling wines, and sweet dessert wines. From France you'll find dry Chenin Blancs from Saumur and Savennières, off-dry wines from Vouvray and Anjou, dessert wines from Coteaux du Layon, and sparkling wines labeled Crémant de Loire.

Message in a Bottle

If you've ever tasted a Vouvray, you know that it can be dry or it can be sweet, but there's nothing stated on the label that tells you in advance what to expect. As a general rule, as Vouvray moves up in price, the sweeter it gets.

Outside of France Chenin Blanc is often used as a blending grape, with only a small percentage of it going into varietal bottlings. However, South Africa produces the full range of Chenin Blanc wines, referring to the grape as Steen. It's even used in their fortified wines and spirits.

The Model of Cooperation

Chenin Blanc is a cooperative sort of grape. It ripens in the middle of the season so that no extraordinary harvesting measures have to be taken. With its compact clusters it's easy to pick. The grapes have tough skins that minimize damage as they make their way to the crusher. And their natural acidity helps the aging process. A number of California producers make the classic dry style of Chenin Blanc that typifies the Loire. Some excellent and reliable producers to look for:

- Chalone Vineyard (Monterey County) Chenin Blanc—$23
- Chappellet (Napa Valley) Dry Chenin Blanc—$13
- Ventana Vineyards (Monterey County) Dry Chenin Blanc—$12
- Weinstock Cellars Clarksburg (Santa Maria) "Contour" Chenin Blanc—$12

Gewürztraminer

Most people either love Gewürztraminer . . . or hate it. It's got intense aromas and strong flavors and is fairly difficult to enjoy with food. Sommeliers typically suggest pairing Gewürztraminer with highly seasoned food and spicy Asian and Mexican dishes. But it's probably best sipped all by itself.

Vino Veritas

In 1996 after thirty years of development, Cornell University introduced a new grape variety, called *Traminette,* that's a cross of Gewürztraminer and a hardier variety. Traminette has the same floral aroma and spicy flavor but can withstand the harsh winters and unpredictable temperature swings of cold-weather climates like that of New York State. Traminette is being successfully produced in the Finger Lakes region with both dry and sweet examples.

The grape is thought to be a mutated form of the Traminer grape. And because of its taste, it got *gewürz* (meaning "spicy") attached to it by Alsatians in the nineteenth century. The name caught on, but it wasn't until 1973 that the term *Gewürztraminer* was officially adopted.

Sweet 'n' Spicy

The first thing you'll notice is that Gewürztraminer smells like flowers. And when you taste it, you'll see that it can be sweet and spicy at the same time. Not all Gewürztraminers are sweet. It depends on who's making them.

Alsace has had arguably the most success with Gewürztraminer. Producers there make it dry, dry, dry—unless they're using the grapes for dessert wines, in which case the wines are exceptionally sweet, sweet, sweet.

In Germany Gewürztraminers are usually off-dry to medium sweet. They have less alcohol and more acidity than their Alsatian counterparts. The high acidity camouflages the perception of all that sweetness.

Here are some fine examples of Gewürztraminer:

- Trimbach (Alsace, France) Gewürztraminer—$17
- Tiedl (Austria) Gewürztraminer Spätlese—$14
- Mon Ami Winery (Ohio) Gewürztraminer—$9

Because Gewürztraminer grows best in cool climates, it has found good homes in Austria, eastern Europe, New Zealand, Canada, and the United States—especially Oregon, Washington, and New York. A few U.S. producers offer a dry version of the wine, but most produce Gewürztraminer with a perceptible sweetness.

Muscat

Muscat is the world's oldest known grape variety and has grown around the Mediterranean for centuries. Early records show Muscat was shipped from the port of Frontignan in southwest France during the time of Charlemagne. Actually, Muscat is a family of grapes with more than 200 varieties. The grapes range from white to almost black. And the wines vary from fine and light—even sparkling—to deep, dark, and sweet. Muscat is the only variety that produces aromas and flavors in wine just like the grape itself. Among the most familiar of the Muscat varieties are:

- **Muscat Blanc à Petits Grains**—considered the best of the Muscats. It's responsible for the sweet, fortified Muscat de Beaumes-de-Venise; for Italy's sparkling Asti; and for Clairette de Die. The grape is also known as Muscat Blanc, Muscat Canelli, Moscat d'Alsace, and Moscatel Rosé, among others.
- **Muscat of Alexandria**—thought to date back to the ancient Egyptians. It's most widely grown in Spain and is one of the three varieties permitted in making Sherry. The grape also goes by Moscatel de Málaga, Moscatel, Moscatel Romano, Moscatel Gordo, and Gordo Blanc, among others.

- **Muscat Ottonel**—a lighter flavored grape. Also called Muskotaly, it's used for dry, perfumy wines in Alsace and dessert wines in Austria.
- **Muscat Hamburg**—used primarily as table grapes. But eastern European winemakers produce thin red wines from it. It's also called Black Muscat and Moscato di Amburgo.

Pinot Gris

The French call it Pinot Gris. The Italians call it Pinot Grigio. Americans produce both and drink a lot of it. The Pinot Gris grape exhibits a range of colors from grayish blue to brownish pink. It's in the same family as Pinot Noir and Pinot Blanc but has a character all its own. Pinot Gris (meaning "gray") has been known to produce wines that range from white to light-tinged pink.

Pinot Gris is thought by many to reach its pinnacle in Alsace, where it's called Tokay Pinot Gris or Tokay d'Alsace. The grapes are harvested from thirty-year-old vines and turned into a full-bodied, fruity, and creamy wine with a rich gold color.

Pinot Grigio has been called the "new Chardonnay" because of its soaring popularity among both casual drinkers and serious wine enthusiasts. Santa Margherita was the first winery to make its mark as an import to the United States in 1979. In the last five years, small growers all over Italy's northeast have been planting Pinot Grigio to take advantage of the demand.

Message in a Bottle

That's a far cry from what most people know as Italy's Pinot Grigio—often a light (some might say thin), pale, and herbal wine for easy quaffing. Some of the best Pinot Grigios come from the Friuli region of Italy, where leading producers show full, rounded versions.

The current hot spot for Pinot Gris is Oregon. It was introduced there in 1966 and has become the state's premier white grape. Oregon producers prefer the name Pinot Gris to Pinot Grigio, although there's no single style of wine made. Some winemakers use oak. Others use only stainless steel. Most produce a completely dry wine. Some leave a little residual sugar.

Savvy Sipping

Don't confuse "Tokay d'Alsace" with the world-famous sweet wine from Hungary, "Tokay Aszú." The Hungarian government was concerned that you and other consumers might. So, during the negotiations for Hungary's accession to the EU, it got France to agree to add the grape variety to the bottles. So now the label will say "Tokay—Pinot Gris d'Alsace."

Riesling

Before Chardonnay came to be the belle of the ball, it was Riesling. In the nineteenth century, Riesling was considered the best white grape variety because it produced wine of such "elegance." The physical and spiritual home of Riesling is Germany, where it's been grown for at least 500 years and possibly as long as 2,000 years. It thrives in the coldest vine-growing climates and has found excellent homes in Alsace, Austria, Canada, and in the northern United States, in areas of New York, Washington, Oregon, and Michigan.

Does Not Play Well with Others

Riesling is rarely blended with other grapes. It doesn't need to be. It produces wines that run the gamut from bone dry and crisp to ultrasweet and complex. Riesling is one of the few whites that have a long aging capacity. Some will last for twenty years or more. Unlike Chardonnay, which relies on winemaker interventions for its style, Riesling relies on nature for its diversity. The winemaker really has only two decisions to make: when to pick the grapes and how long to ferment the juice.

Riesling grapes take a long time to ripen and are picked at various times throughout the harvest. The stage of ripeness of the grapes roughly corresponds to the sweetness and alcohol levels of the wines. The earliest harvested grapes produce the lightest, driest wines, which are categorized as *Kabinett*. The next category up the sweetness chain is known as *Spätlese* (late picked), followed by *Auslese* (hand-picked bunches).

"Dry" Riesling

Riesling is the favored grape for the sweet and acclaimed late harvest wines and ice wines. However, for table wines the preference in recent years has been for dry wines. Producers have been deliberately making Rieslings in a dry style. Rieslings are typically crisp and low in alcohol. To lower the sugar levels, winemakers extend fermentation, which also raises the alcohol content. For the resulting German wines, the labels will say *trocken* (dry) or *halbtrocken* (off-dry).

In Alsace, the French wine region across the Rhine from Germany, Rieslings are usually fermented bone dry. Compared to a German Kabinett Riesling with between 7.5 percent and 8.5 percent alcohol, an Alsatian Riesling will have at least 12 percent alcohol.

Riesling is sometimes labeled as Johannisberg Riesling, Rhine Riesling, or White Riesling.

These Rieslings are worth trying:

- Dr. Konstantin Frank (Finger Lakes) Johannisberg Riesling—$14
- Handley Cellars Anderson Valley (California) Late Harvest Riesling—$12
- St. Urbans-Hof (Germany) Riesling—$10

Sauvignon Blanc

Sauvignon Blanc is widely cultivated in France and California. The Loire Valley produces wines that are 100 percent Sauvignon Blanc—most notably from Sancerre and Pouilly-Fumé. You'll find them crisp and tart. In Bordeaux Sauvignon Blanc is usually blended with Sémillon that's been aged in oak. While not the primary grape, Sauvignon Blanc plays an important part in the sweet and revered dessert wines of Sauternes.

Sauvignon Blanc came to North America in 1878 when winemaker (and California's first agricultural commissioner) Charles Wetmore acquired cuttings from the famed Château d'Yquem vineyards in Sauternes and planted them at his Cresta Blanca Winery in Livermore, California. He propagated some of the vines in his 300 acres of nursery vineyards and sold others to California winemakers, including Carl Wente. The vines thrived, and Sauvignon Blanc became an early California favorite. A postscript to the story is that Wente Bros. (as the winery was then known) produced California's first Sauvignon Blanc–labeled varietal wine in 1933 and in 1981 purchased Cresta Blanca—making the original Wetmore vineyards part of the current Wente Vineyards property.

Sauvignon Blanc is also produced successfully in Italy, Australia, South America, and—met with much recent acclaim—in New Zealand.

The Ripe Stuff

How did Charles Wetmore acquire the Sauvignon Blanc cuttings?

Prior to his trip to France, Wetmore was given a letter of introduction to the Marquis de Lur Saluces, owner of Château d'Yquem, by his friend and fellow winemaker, Louis Mel. Mel happened to be married to the marquis' niece. Oh, to have well-placed friends!

Sauvignon Blanc's Alias

Back in the 1960s when Robert Mondavi introduced a dry style of Sauvignon Blanc, he wanted to distinguish it from the sweet version he was already producing. He called the new wine Fumé Blanc—after

Pouilly-Fumé. Rather than trademark the name for his exclusive use, he permitted other winemakers to use it. Many American wineries label their Sauvignon Blanc wines Fumé Blanc. The variations in labeling cause a lot of confusion, but Sauvignon Blanc and Fumé Blanc are the same.

Whatever the particular style, you can recognize a Sauvignon Blanc by its distinctive aromas and flavor—often described as grassy or herbaceous.

Some Sauvignon samplings from diverse locations:

- Pascal Jolivet (Loire Valley, France) Pouilly-Fumé—$40
- Warwick Estate (South Africa) Sauvignon Blanc—$16
- Spy Valley (New Zealand) Sauvignon Blanc—$13
- Casa Lapostolle (Chile) Classic Sauvignon Blanc—$11
- Wente Vineyards (Livermore Valley, California) Sauvignon Blanc—$9

Viognier

Viognier is no easy grape to grow. Until the vines are about fifteen, they don't give their best fruit. The plants are susceptible to all kinds of diseases and pests. Their yields are sparse. And the grapes ripen irregularly.

Maybe that's why the grape was headed toward extinction. In 1965 only a few acres of Viognier remained under cultivation in Condrieu, in the grape's Rhone Valley homeland. Since then, Viognier has been making a comeback—first in Condrieu and then in the south of France in Languedoc-Roussillon and Provence. Later, the plantings spread to California and Australia. To give you an idea of the escalation: In 1993 California crushed 231 tons of Viognier grapes. Ten years later that increased to 9,800 tons.

A Gift of Flowers and Perfume

Viognier is aromatic with vibrant floral qualities, sometimes even perfumy. The classic Old World style of Viognier is crisp, dry, and intense. As winemakers around the world craft their own Viogniers, more style variations appear. While cooler regions of California produce a style closer to the French classic, wines from warmer areas are richer and fuller.

Vino Veritas

It's rare for France to permit using a white wine grape in a high-quality red wine. But in an unusual twist in the vineyards of the Côte Rôtie, Viognier vines are planted among Syrah vines. The white and red grapes are harvested and vinified together to produce the highly regarded Côte Rôtie red wines.

A few Viognier selections to try:

- Alban Vineyards (California) Viognier—$30
- Château de Campuget (France) Viognier—$11
- Yalumba (Australia) Viognier—$10
- Windmill Estates (California) Viognier—$13

Up-and-Comers

Grape varieties go in and out of fashion. Or they'll be popular in one part of the world and then somehow catch on elsewhere. As Americans have tired of ordering the same old familiar varietals, they've looked for excitement in "new" grapes.

Grüner Veltliner

Austria has jumped onto the American scene with its dry, crisp Grüner Veltliner. It's the most extensively grown grape variety in Austria, accounting for 37 percent of all vine plantings. The wine has different expressions depending on how the grapes are grown and how they're treated by the winemaker.

Grüner Veltliner used to be treated as a high-production commercial grape. The high-yield grapes produced light and refreshing sippers that were popular in Austria's *heurigen* (wine taverns). In the 1980s Austria's wine industry made a conscious step toward higher quality. With lower yields and higher ripeness, the resulting wines are more complex and fuller-flavored. The wines have a peppery quality and naturally high acidity. The best bottles of Grüner Veltliner have potential for some aging. These examples will give you a taste of Austria:

- Pfaffl, Grüner Veltliner Hundsleiten Sandtal—$20
- Leopold Sommer Grüner Veltliner—$14
- Weingut Bründlmayer Grüner Veltliner Berg Vogelsang—$12

Fiano

Italy's Campania wine region, the area around Naples and Mount Vesuvius, is the current rage. And Fiano is the trendy grape. Hardly "new," Fiano's history—and popularity—date back to ancient Rome. While the origin of the word is the subject of conjecture, *Fiano* may have come from "apiano" because the ripe grapes attracted bees (*apis* in Latin).

The towns of Avellino and Lapio and their surrounding areas are the primary growing centers. Hence, the wines are called Fiano di Avellino and Fiano di Lapio. They can be fairly light and dry with a creamy texture or (when the grapes are harvested late and fully fermented) full-bodied and ripe. Take a taste of one of these Fiano wines:

- Villa Raiano, Fiano di Avellino "Ripa Alta"—$26
- I Favati, Fiano di Avellino Pietramara—$16
- Feudi San Gregorio, Fiano di Avellino—$15

Albariño

Albariño presents certain roadblocks to its producers. Even though it's high-quality (perhaps a relative of Riesling), it's low-yielding. And its skins are so thick that only a small amount of juice can be squeezed out. Albariño's scarcity made it one of Spain's most expensive wine grapes.

In the mid-1980s only five commercial wineries existed in the Rias Baixas region of northwest Spain where Albariño is produced—so very little Albariño was made. Since then, the number of wineries has multiplied to 100—with a positive (if not overwhelming) effect on production. Albariño is produced across the border in Portugal, where it's called Alvarinho.

Test the waters with these quality producers:

- Morgadío (Spain) Albariño—$19
- Valminor (Spain) Albariño—$16
- Varanda do Conde (Portugal) Vino Verde Alvarinho—$11

The wine has a creamy texture with complex flavors of apricots, peaches, and citrus. Albariño is rarely barrel fermented—so the flavors are clean and vibrant. In spite of its high acidity, Albariño doesn't age well and should be consumed within the first two years.

CHAPTER 6

Wine Regions of the "Old World"

In winespeak, Europe and the rest of the Mediterranean basin are called the "Old World"—because it was there that the grapevines were first so widely established. The Old World is more than a geographical area. It's a tradition. Old World winemakers have always favored terroir ("the soil") over technique. It's the sense that the earth, the sun, and the climate should have (and do have) more influence on the nature of the wine than the winemaker.

France

As Julius Caesar concluded 2,000 years ago, France is a pretty good place to grow wine grapes. Through trial and error, and after centuries of careful cultivation and meticulous record-keeping, the French learned how to make excellent wine. Many people (particularly the French) would say they defined good wine. Even the grapes that have been transplanted halfway around the world retain their French names: Cabernet Sauvignon, Cabernet Franc, Sauvignon Blanc, Pinot Noir.

It's generally accepted that France produces many "best of" types:

- ◆ Champagnes are the best sparkling wines.
- ◆ Alsace produces the ultimate Gewürztraminer.
- ◆ The Pauillac and Margaux districts of Bordeaux produce the finest Cabernet Sauvignon–based wines.
- ◆ Merlot best displays its qualities in the Bordeaux regions of Saint-Emilion and Pomerol.
- ◆ The grand cru vineyards of the Côte de Beaune produce the finest Chardonnays.
- ◆ Some of the most refined Sauvignon Blanc–based wines come from Sancerre.
- ◆ Chenin Blanc is in its glory along the Loire River.
- ◆ Sauternes is widely acclaimed as the world's finest dessert wine.
- ◆ The prototype of Pinot Noir comes from the vineyards of Côte de Nuits in Burgundy.

And there's plenty to brag about from France's other regions as well. Because some of the regions are not so high-profile, they offer real bargains for wine lovers.

Savvy Sipping

While France has always been in the forefront of winemaking, it's not without its troubles. They've done a better job of producing wine than marketing wine—with the result that Australia and South American countries have knocked it out of its prominent position in world wine exports.

Reading French Wine Labels

In order to understand the degrees of specificity of French wine labeling, think of an archery target. The outer circle is all of France. The next-largest circle is a region of France, such as Bordeaux. The next circle in is a district—Médoc, for example. Within that circle is the commune—say, Pauillac. Finally, the bull's-eye: the individual producer—a château or domaine. The better—and usually more expensive—the wine, the more specific is the indicated source of the wine.

It's a telling fact that there is no word for "winemaker" in French, Spanish, Italian, or German. In France the word used is *vigneron*—meaning "grower."

Vino Veritas

The French are très concerned about the quality of their wines. So they created a system for regulating the quality and ranking the wines. The rankings appear on the labels.

- Appellation d'Origine Contrôlée (**AOC or AC**)—the most widely applied standard used on French wine labels. It indicates that the wine meets the rigorous legal standards for the area indicated. The more specific the area of origin, the higher the standards.
- Vins Délimité de Qualité Supérieure (**VDQS**)—a second set of standards for wines in areas not covered by AOC law. Although a notch down in quality, VDQS is still a reliable government guarantee of quality.
- Vin de pays—a third, and slightly more relaxed set of rules that regulate "country" wines. The phrase is always followed by a place name—be it larger (region) or smaller (community).
- Vin de table **or** vin ordinaire—"table" wines whose place names are "France." This is the lowest category of wine in the French system.

Within France, each region has its own system of organization and classification. And each region is known for producing specific wines.

Bordeaux

Bordeaux, an industrial city in southwestern France, is the center of the world's most famous wine region. Several types of wine are produced there:

- **Dry white wines**—blends of Sauvignon Blanc and Sémillon
- **Sweet dessert wines**—blends of Sauvignon Blanc, Sémillon, and Muscadelle afflicted with *Botrytis cinerea* (noble rot)
- **Medium-bodied red wines**—blends of Cabernet Sauvignon, Merlot, Cabernet Franc, Malbec, and Petit Verdot (Some subregions produce wine made primarily from Cabernet, while Merlot is the dominant grape in other areas.)

The most important subregions of Bordeaux are Sauternes (famous for its dessert wines), Pomerol (known for Merlot-dominant reds), Saint-Emilion (more Merlot-based reds), Entre-Deux-Mers (light whites), Graves (home of both fine dry whites and Cabernet-based reds), and Médoc (Cabernet-based reds). Médoc is probably the most famous of the Bordeaux subregions and has communes within its borders that also qualify for village appellation status: Saint-Estephe, Saint-Julien, Margaux, Pauillac, Listrac, and Moulis.

Premier Cru Wines

Back in 1855 Napoleon III went to the wine brokers of Bordeaux and asked them to rate the red wines of Médoc. This they did by looking at the price history of the wines—the operating theory being that the most expensive wines would be the best. The brokers came up with the sixty-one "best" wine estates in Médoc and then ranked them one through five—with one being the highest rank. This classification is called *premier cru* (meaning "first growth").

The four châteaus that were first awarded this classification are Lafite Rothschild, Latour, Margaux, and Haut-Brion. In 1973 Château Mouton-Rothschild was upgraded to premier cru status. You'll see "Premier Grand Cru Classé" on their labels.

With a total of only sixty-one châteaus listed in the original classification, thousands of other producers in Médoc were left out. In 1932 another classification, *cru bourgeois*, was created to include the best of them.

Burgundy

In Bordeaux, the wine estates are called châteaus. In Burgundy, they're called domaines. That's just your first clue that the two regions are figuratively (and geographically) miles apart. While Bordeaux is dominated by large producers, Burgundy has thousands of small growers who often own only very small pieces of vineyard land. And one vineyard can be divided up into dozens of owners.

However, one thing about Burgundy is pretty predictable. Red wines are made from the Pinot Noir grape. White wines are made from Chardonnay. And Beaujolais, in the southern part of the region, makes light and fruity reds from the Gamay grape.

Traveling from north to south through the heart of France, you pass through the subregions of Burgundy in sequence:

- **Chablis**—known for its dry white wines
- **Côte de Nuits**—home of the most noteworthy reds
- **Côte de Beaune**—producer of both reds and whites, but known especially for great whites
- **Côte Chalonnaise**—regarded as a lesser region but still home to good reds and whites
- **Mâcon**—known for whites that offer excellent values
- **Beaujolais**—home to Gamay production

Premier cru is top dog in Bordeaux . . . but *grand cru* ("great growth") is the cat's meow in Burgundy. The designation is reserved for specific vineyards that, based on their location and long-term track record, produce the best wines. The labels will bear only the name of the vineyard—not the name of any village.

Role of Négociants

Négociant is French for "merchant" or "dealer." Traditionally, *négociants* bought wines, blended and bottled them, and shipped them. They could take wines from small producers and market them on a more commercially viable scale. More recently, their roles have expanded to buying grapes and making wine. They represent wines of all quality levels—including grand cru.

Large *négociant* houses blend wines to produce their own house styles. Some of these well-known houses include Louis Jadot, Joseph Drouhin, Georges Duboeuf, and Louis Latour.

Côte de Nuits and Côte de Beaune, together, are known as the Côte d'Or—the "slope of gold." The area has a lot of grand cru and premier cru vineyards that produce some of Burgundy's most famous and most expensive wines, including Corton-Charlemagne, Montrachet, Romanée-Conti, Chambertin, Bonnes Mares, and Clos de Vougeot.

Rhone

Continuing south from Burgundy, you enter the Rhone Valley—home to earthy, gutsy wines, both red and white. The northern and southern regions are distinctly different in terms of their wines. Northern reds are Syrah-based and worthy of aging. You'll run into names like Côte Rôtie, Hermitage, Crozes-Hermitage, Cornas, and St. Joseph. The whites are made from Viognier (like Condrieu) or a blend of Marsanne and Roussane (like Hermitage).

Most Rhone wines come from the south—in the form of Côtes du Rhone. The primary grape variety is Grenache. Southern Rhone is also famous for its Châteauneuf-du-Pape, which can be made with as many as thirteen grape varieties—both red and white (although Grenache, Mourvèdre, and Syrah predominate).

Vino Veritas

Châteauneuf-du-Pape means "new home of the pope." It dates back to the fourteenth century when the papal court was relocated to nearby Avignon and a summer palace was built in a village just north of the city (now known as Châteauneuf-du-Pape).

Southwest of Châteauneuf-du-Pape is Tavel, where they produce France's best-known and most distinguished Rosés. They're dry and full-bodied and have an international reputation.

Loire

The Loire Valley stretches across northwest France, following the Loire River. The area has a reputation for its non-Chardonnay white wines. The most important ones are:

- **Muscadet**—a light, dry wine that (unlike most other French wines) is named after the grape variety
- **Vouvray**—made from the Chenin Blanc grape into wines that can range from bone dry to off-dry to sparkling
- **Pouilly-Fumé**—straight Sauvignon Blanc made in a rich style
- **Sancerre**—unblended Sauvignon Blanc in a lighter, drier, more lively style than the Pouilly-Fumé

It's easy to confuse the names Pouilly-Fumé and Pouilly-Fuissé, but they're two different wines from two entirely different areas in France. Pouilly-Fuissé is a Chardonnay from the Mâcon region of Burgundy and is a much more full-bodied wine.

Alsace

Historically, Alsace (the area across the Rhine River from Germany) has belonged to whoever won the most recent war between France and Germany. Since World War I, it's been a part of France. Because of its background, Alsace has much in common with Germany. Both Alsace and Germany grow the same grapes—although the wines of Alsace are generally drier than those of Germany. And, contrary to the rest of France, Alsace labels its wines with the varietal name. Regulations in Alsace require that a wine carrying a varietal name contain 100 percent of that grape. The most important varietals are:

- Riesling
- Gewürztraminer
- Pinot Gris
- Muscat
- Sylvaner

A small amount of Pinot Noir (the only grape permitted for red wine) is grown in Alsace and is often used for Rosé wines.

Italy

Italy produces—and drinks—more wine than any other country. Yes, little Italy. An area like Bordeaux may have well over 12,000 producers, but Italy has 1.2 million growers. And on the consumption side, Italians drink twenty-six gallons per person each year—compared to just three gallons for Americans.

Savvy Sipping

Italy makes more than 2,000 kinds of wine within its borders. Everywhere you go in Italy, you see grapevines growing. And the grapes are overwhelmingly Italian: Nebbiolo, Sangiovese, Barbera, Dolcetto.

Don't expect to find the grape names on the labels . . . except sometimes. For the most part, Italians name their wines after places—just like the French do. Take Chianti Classico as an example. It's made primarily from the Sangiovese grape, but the wine is named after the Chianti Classico winemaking district. Then there's Barbera. It's the name of a grape. In the town of Asti, they name their wine Barbera d'Asti. In Alba, they call it Barbera d'Alba. All right, simple enough. But not all Barbera wines use the grape name on the label.

In 1963 Italy developed a system—modeled after the French one—to control the quality of their wines and classify them. The regulations govern yields, grapes that can be used for specific wines, viticultural practices, and alcohol levels. From top to bottom, the categories are as follows:

- Denominazione di Origine Controllata e Garantita (**DOCG**)—Meaning "Controlled and Guaranteed Denomination of Origin," it's the highest category of wine and indicates that the quality is not only "controlled"—it's "guaranteed" by the government.
- Denominazione di Origine Controllata (**DOC**)—The wines must meet certain standards and come from specific geographic areas.
- Vino da tavola—Italy's "table wine" category, it indicates a simple, everyday wine.

It's important to remember that DOC/DOCG status is a guarantee of where and how the wine is produced. It's not a guarantee of how it will taste. Some of the "best" and priciest wines from Italy don't have DOC status.

In the 1970s a group of winemakers in Tuscany ran afoul of the DOC regulations by using disallowed grape varieties—like Cabernet Sauvignon and Merlot—in addition to the native Sangiovese or by producing 100 percent Sangiovese wines. The wines turned out to be terrific and much sought-after, but (because they were against the law) they were labeled "vino da tavola." They skyrocketed in price anyway. They're known as "Super Tuscans."

Since then, a new official quality category has been created whose rules are less strict than those of the DOC. It's called *IGT* (Indicazione Geografica Tipica). Some of the esteemed Super Tuscans were thus upgraded to IGT status.

Italy's Wine Regions

Italy has twenty wine regions that are geographically identical to its political regions. The regions in the north are the most recognized, but southern Italy—viticultural areas such as Campania, Umbria, Basilicata, and the islands of Sicily and Sardinia—are making huge inroads in producing wines of quality and marketability. Unique indigenous varieties—like Fiano di Avellino from Campania and Vermentino from Sardinia—have really taken off.

In the north, the regions of Piedmont, Tuscany, and Veneto are the most familiar. Piedmont (meaning "foot of the mountain") in the northwest lies at the base of the Alps. Nebbiolo reigns, producing the famous Barolo and Barbaresco—two robust reds. They're very similar to each other, but Barolo is fuller-bodied and needs more aging. (Barolo is sometimes referred to as the "king" of Italian wines.) Other popular reds include Barbera, Dolcetto, and Bonardo. Among the whites are the Muscat-based Asti Spumante and Moscato d'Asti and the dry white Gavi from the Cortese grape.

Tuscany, with its enchanted landscapes and historic castles, is responsible for the world-famous Chianti—whose production goes back centuries. Much more recent is Brunello di Montalcino, made in an area south of Chianti from a Sangiovese clone. It's big, tannic, and powerful and has one of the longest aging requirements (four years) in Italy.

Message in a Bottle

Rosso di Montalcino is made from the same Brunello grape in the same area of Montalcino. The difference is that it only has to age for one year before its release. It's lighter, less intense . . . and cheaper.

Another Tuscan favorite is Vino Nobile di Montepulciano from 60 percent to 80 percent Sangiovese. Tuscany's most important white grape is Trebbiano.

Veneto in the northeast is the third largest region in terms of production and serves up some of the more familiar Italian exports: Soave, the sparkling Prosecco, and Valpolicella. While Valpolicella is rather light and fruity, another version—Amarone della Valpolicella—is rich, high in alcohol (14 to 16 percent), and long-lived. Known simply as Amarone, the wine is made from grapes that have been dried on mats for several months before fermentation, concentrating the sugars and flavors.

And what about the ubiquitous Pinot Grigio, the number one imported table wine in the United States? Probably the best ones come from the two northeastern-most regions of Alto Adige (which borders Austria) and Fruili (bordering Slovenia).

Germany

Talk about intimidating! Who can read a German wine label? If they want you to drink their wines, you'd think they would make buying one easier. Actually, they're trying.

In the German quality rating system, the highest quality wines are labeled QmP (Qualitätswein mit Prädikat), meaning "quality wine with distinction." QmP wines (the ones primarily exported) are categorized by the ripeness of the grapes when they're harvested. Because Germany's vineyards are so far north, it's difficult to get the grapes to ripen. Hence, grape sugars are highly prized. The riper the grape, the higher the sugar content—and, in Germany's opinion, the higher the quality of the wine. From the least ripe (lowest) to the ripest (highest) are:

♦ Kabinett
♦ Spätlese
♦ Auslese
♦ Beerenauslese
♦ Trockenbeerenauslese
♦ Eiswein

At the two lower levels, the grapes can be fermented to produce a completely dry wine. So, a rule-of-thumb for choosing a dry German wine is to look for Kabinett on the label. At the highest ripeness levels, the grapes have so much sugar at harvest that the wines can't help but be sweet.

Some wine drinkers equate German wines with sweetness. In today's environment of "dry is better," German producers are trying to make it easier for consumers to identify their dry wines. Words to look for if you're trying to find a dry style:

- **Trocken.** It means dry; *halbtrocken* is "half dry."
- **Classic.** It indicates a dry, uncomplicated varietal. The term will appear next to the grape name.
- **Selection.** In addition to being dry, these are premium varietals that have to come from an individual vineyard named on the label. The term will appear after the vineyard site.

When all is said and done, it's really Germany's sweet wines that take the prizes. The late harvest wines from grapes picked long into the fall, the botricized grapes whose sweetness comes from noble rot, and the ice wines whose grapes were left to freeze on the vines: They're internationally acclaimed.

The Ripe Stuff

Why do German wines come in different color bottles?

The color of the tall, slender bottles tells you what region the wine comes from. Brown bottles come from the Rhine region. Green bottles come from the Mosel area or from Alsace. The shape is used elsewhere around the world for wines made from grape varieties associated with Germany—like Riesling and Gewürztraminer.

Germany's Wine Regions

With the exception of a couple of regions in the east, most of Germany's wine regions are concentrated in the south and southwestern part of the country. They are among the most northerly wine regions in the world. Germany's most famous winemaking areas are the Mosel-Saar-Ruwer region (along the Mosel River and its two tributaries) and the three contiguous regions along the Rhine River—Rheingau, Rheinhessen, and Pfalz.

With Germany's climate, 85 percent of the country's wines are white—because red grapes don't ripen well under cool conditions. The wines they produce are relatively low in alcohol. Riesling is Germany's signature grape. But other varieties are more widely planted. Müller-Thurgau, a cross between Riesling and Sylvaner, ripens earlier than Riesling and takes the anxiety out of harvesting. However, the grapes don't reach the same heights of great wine as Riesling.

German Wine Labels

German labels can contain both a varietal and a geographic location. In the German language, adding *er* at the end of a noun makes it possessive. On wine labels, *er* is added to the name of the town or village where the wine was made. The name of the town in the possessive form is followed by the name of the specific vineyard. So, a label that reads "Niersteiner Oelberg Riesling Spätlese" tells you that the name of the town is Nierstein, the vineyard (in the town of Nierstein) is Oelberg, the varietal is Riesling, and the ripeness level is Spätlese.

Spain

There was a time not too long ago that Spain was known for producing inexpensive and unremarkable reds. Well, times have changed—due, in part, to regulations (similar to those in France) that were adopted to improve the quality of the wines. On top of that, Spanish winemakers adopted modern production methods and expanded into new regions. All had a positive effect on Spain's wines. Spain's rating system from highest quality to lowest is as follows:

- ♦ Denominación de Origen Calificaca (**DOCa**)—meaning "qualified designation of origin"
- ♦ Denominación de Origen (**DO**)—meaning "designation of origin"
- ♦ Vino de la tierra—a table wine category the equivalent of France's vins de pays

Rioja

Rioja, Spain's oldest and most famous wine region, became the first DO when the system was set up in 1926. And when the system was refined in 1991, Rioja became the first region to be promoted to DOCa status. Tempranillo is king in Rioja. Other grapes—Garnacha, Graciano, and Mazuelo—are used for blending, but Tempranillo takes center stage.

The wines range from delicate to big and alcoholic. The traditional method of production included significant aging in oak barrels. Reds that are aged for two years are labeled *crianza*. After three years of aging, they become *riserva*. And five years or more makes them *gran reserva*. Because the oak dominated the fruit flavors in an era when international wine drinkers preferred fruit, winemakers have begun replacing some of the barrel aging with bottle aging.

Vino Veritas

After the phylloxera epidemic in the late nineteenth century, France imported wines from Spain to make up the local shortfall. The wines were not exactly up to French standards—so French winemakers went to Spain and introduced their winemaking practices, which included aging in oak barrels. Instead of French oak barrels, Spanish winemakers chose American oak, which impart a stronger flavor to the wine.

Other Spanish Winemaking Regions

Spain has more vineyard acreage than any other country in the world. And regions other than Rioja are making names for themselves. Ribera del Duero, north of Madrid, is a relatively new "official" wine region, having been designated a DO in 1982. For the hundred plus years preceding that, wine production was dominated by one estate—Vega Sicilia. Today, wineries are springing up all over.

Penedés, Navarra, Rueda, and Rías Biaxas in Galicia are all coming into their own.

- Penedés is home to most of the Cava-producing (sparkling wine) wineries, which account for one-fifth of the vineyards. The companies also make still wines—mostly whites from the Xarel-lo, Macabeo, and Parellada grapes.
- Navarra used to offer easy-drinking Rosés but has traded them in for red wines from Tempranillo, Cabernet Sauvignon, and Merlot.
- Rueda has become famous for producing fresh and fruity white wines from the Verdejo grape—sometimes blended with Sauvignon Blanc.
- Rías Baixas is producing the much-acclaimed Albariño—the rich and complex white with high levels of acidity and alcohol.

Portugal

Portugal may be better known for Port and Madeira, but it's no newcomer to making table wines. Vineyards have flourished for centuries, and records show wine exports dating back to 1367. Portugal has an appellations system similar to other Old World countries, but it seems to be less important as a new generation of winemakers has produced wines with proprietary names not tied to regional dictates.

One of Portugal's notable exports is Vinho Verde. It's both a red and a white, but you're likely to see only the white. The reds are consumed mostly within Portugal's borders. Vinho Verde, which is the name of the appellation, means "green wine." It's so named because the grapes are picked early and the wine is drunk young. Its slight effervescence also qualifies it as a semisparkling wine. The better versions are made from the Alvarinho grape—the same one that makes Spain's Albariño wine. The Spanish and Portuguese districts are just across the border from each other.

Portugal is becoming a wonderful source for dry reds—particularly from the Douro and Dão regions. Barca Velha from Douro is a highly sought-after—and expensive—red that's made only in the better vintages. It's intense and full-bodied and needs time to age.

Austria

Austria has perhaps the most stringent wine production and labeling regulations anywhere—the result of a scandal in 1985. Because sweet, late harvest wines are so prized and expensive, a small group of unscrupulous producers adulterated ordinary wines with diethylene glycol (a substance related to antifreeze) to sweeten them. They labeled them late harvest and tried to pass them off as the real thing. The affair caused Austrian wine exports to plummet within the year to less than one-fifth of what they had been sending to other countries. The government stepped in, and new regulations were implemented to keep anything similar from happening again. Today, Austria is successfully exporting more of its wines than ever—dry whites in addition to the late harvest wines.

You might expect that Austria would produce wines more like its neighbor, Germany. But the Austrian style is dry—more like Alsace. Austria's most famous grape is Grüner Veltliner—a longtime favorite with Austrians and now making a big splash around the world. It produces wines that are typically dry, medium-bodied, and spicy. Austrian wines also rely on Riesling, Gewürztraminer, and Weissburgunder (Pinot Blanc). Reds, usually more difficult to find, are typically light.

Much like the German system of rating quality on sweetness, the quality levels are (in ascending order): Spätlese, Auslese, Ausbruch, and Trockenbeerenauslese.

CHAPTER 7

Wine Regions of the "New World"

"New World" was at one time a less than flattering term for the upstart winemakers outside of Europe. Since then, many of the philosophical borders between the Old World and the New World have eroded as Old World countries adapt to technological innovation and New World winemakers increasingly adopt traditional techniques. In winemaking, though, the effect of the land on the final product is paramount. And geography will always separate the two worlds.

Australia

For a country once known for its beer drinking, Australia sure has made a name for itself in the wine world. In fact, Australia has become the biggest wine exporter after Italy, France, and Spain. What makes it such an awesome feat is that 70 percent of Australia's land can't support agriculture of any kind. There are no native vines in Australia. And it was really European immigration to Australia that helped shape the wine industry.

The New Settlers

Beginning in 1788 England shipped off its felons to Australia—to exile them and to provide labor to create an infrastructure there. The "relocation" stopped in the middle of the nineteenth century when there were enough people to do the work.

The state of South Australia was the only "free" state—meaning that it was the only area not settled by British convicts. In 1836 the land was awarded to George Fife Angus, founder of the South Australian Company. He needed settlers to help develop the land, and he began to recruit them. It was ideal timing for European Lutherans who were fleeing the Continent because of religious persecution. They could buy land in South Australia for very little money in return for farming the land.

Many of the new immigrants came from Germany and left their imprint in town names, traditional foods—and wines. The area is still renowned for its Rieslings. By the 1890s the Barossa, Hunter, and Yarra Valleys were all producing wine.

Aussie Wines

Prior to the 1950s wine production focused on fortified wines. They were the most affordable wines during the worldwide Depression, and the added alcohol made them better for longer storage. The 1960s and 1970s saw a shift toward table wines—first the sweeter versions and, ultimately, dry styles.

While there's amazing diversity in Australian wines, they could be described as fun, bold, and affordable. Winemakers have been creative in their blends of Chardonnay-Sémillon and Shiraz-Cabernet. Probably the country's best reds are blends of Shiraz—recently with Viogner and other Rhone varieties as well as with Cabernet. Shiraz—the Aussie name for Syrah—is Australia's utility grape. It can be made lots of ways—big and oaky to go with a well-aged steak or light enough for summer sipping. Australia has been so successful in marketing their Shiraz wines that other countries have recently chosen to label their Syrah "Shiraz."

Vino Veritas

Australia was responsible in the 1970s for creating a phenomenon that's generating renewed interest today: wine in a box. Aussies have been drinking wine from a box nonstop since the '70s. Now it's catching on elsewhere as wine producers seek ways to package their wines to keep them away from corks and oxygen.

You can find some true treasures in Australia's dessert wines—nicknamed "stickies." Also of local interest is sparkling Shiraz—dark, dry, and slightly fizzy.

Australia's Wine Regions

Like the United States, Australia has a number of outstanding wine regions—fifty regions and subregions spread throughout the country. Many of them are clustered in southeastern Australia—particularly in the states of South Australia, Victoria, and New South Wales—and the more isolated maritime area of Western Australia.

- **Barossa Valley in South Australia**—This area is home to some of Australia's most famous wineries. Known for Riesling, Shiraz, and Cabernet Sauvignon.
- **Coonawara in South Australia**—This region is noted for its reddish-colored "terra rossa" soil. Popular wines are Shiraz and Cabernet Sauvignon.

- **Yarra Valley in Victoria**—This region is known especially for Pinot Noir and Cabernet Sauvignon.
- **Hunter Valley in New South Wales**—This region of Australia produces Sémillon and Cabernet Sauvignon among many others.

In addition to Cabernet, Shiraz, Pinot Noir, Riesling, and Sémillon (pronounced SEH-meh-lon Down Under), Australian wines include Merlot, Grenache, Chardonnay, and Sauvignon Blanc.

New Zealand

All was quiet on the New Zealand wine front when—BOOM—suddenly the country starts garnering prestigious wine awards. Who, outside of New Zealanders, even knew that grapes were growing there? Grapevines were first planted on New Zealand's North Island in 1816, but not much of note happened after that—until the 1980s.

In 1986 New Zealand took "best wine" medals three days in a row in international competition. The winning wine was a Sauvignon Blanc from the Marlborough region—and wine drinkers took notice. Sauvignon Blanc has become something of the country's goodwill ambassador to the rest of the world, but its other wines have as much to offer.

Savvy Sipping

New Zealand producers are turning their attention to another category of wines: aromatic whites—primarily Riesling but also Pinot Gris, Gewürztraminer, and Sémillon. They're all over the board in terms of sweetness levels. And there's usually no indication on the label to tell you.

A Land of Distinction

New Zealand has the distinction of having the most easterly vineyards—being closest to the International Date Line—and the world's most southern vineyards. The country's winemaking regions are located on the two large islands that comprise most of New Zealand. The warmer North Island has climatic differences from the cooler South Island, but both benefit from the cool ocean breezes. No location in New Zealand is farther than seventy-five miles from the water.

The emphasis is on growing grapes that suit cool growing conditions—mostly Chardonnay, Sauvignon Blanc, and Pinot Noir. These varieties make up 60 percent of the country's total vineyard area.

Regions and their Wines

The cultivated areas of New Zealand span 720 miles from north to south, and—except for the most southerly region—they all are on the eastern coastline. The development of vineyard land has roughly corresponded to population growth, which, in the twentieth century, started in the area around Auckland.

North Island

Auckland has a third of the country's population. While it produces its own wines, it's also a center of wine commerce where wines from other regions are vinified and blended. Gisborne produces over a third of the country's wine—most of it bulk wine. But it also has a reputation for fine wines and has been called the Chardonnay capital of New Zealand.

Hawke's Bay is one of New Zealand's older and best wine regions and often records the most sunshine hours. Chardonnay and Cabernet Sauvignon have been the most important varietals. Wellington is known for outstanding Pinot Noirs.

South Island

Marlborough's first vineyards were first planted in 1973. And by 1990, the region had become the largest vine-growing area with 40 percent of the country's total vineyards. Sauvignon Blanc is the most popular varietal, with Chardonnay second. Riesling is grown too—and, increasingly, Pinot Noir. Otago is the most southerly region where the vineyards are planted in hillside locations to minimize the danger of frost. The area is particularly known for its Pinot Noir and Gewürztraminer.

New Zealand Winemakers

One way New Zealand wines came so far so fast is that its young winemakers traveled to Europe during the Northern Hemisphere's harvest season to gain experience in the world's classic wine regions. What they learned they put into practice back home.

Without a long winemaking tradition in their own country, New Zealand winemakers are free to express their own styles—and they do.

South Africa

Most of South Africa's vineyards are clustered in the southwest in an area near the Cape of Good Hope that's become known as Cape Winelands. It has a Mediterranean climate—warm, dry summers and rainfall during the mild winter months. Perfect for growing grapes.

Message in a Bottle

Winemaking goes back to the early Dutch settlers. In fact, it was the Dutch governor who, in 1655, planted the first vines. Four years later the grapes were pressed into wine. But it was really the French Huguenots—fleeing religious persecution back home—who brought a serious tradition of winemaking to South Africa.

In the eighteenth century, the Cape established itself on the world wine stage with its Muscat-based dessert wine called Constantia. It was much in demand at all the royal courts of Europe. Napoleon, it's rumored, even ordered it from his exile on St. Helena.

In spite of the wild success of Constantia, the wine industry went into a 200-year decline. In 1918 a large farmers' cooperative (the KWV) was formed to control production and the market. It tended to put private wine producers at a disadvantage in favor of bulk grape growers—hardly a recipe for quality and innovation. Politics took their toll too. During the years of apartheid, international trade disappeared as sanctions were implemented.

Democracy Turns the Tide

With apartheid abolished in 1991 and sanctions lifted, the South African wine industry could turn its attention to improving its wines to compete in the world market. It imported better vine cuttings, expanded oak aging to commercial wines, and upgraded vineyard management, among other things.

South Africa has only 1.5 percent of the world's vineyards—ranking sixteenth in area planted. But with its large output, South Africa ranks seventh in production, representing 3 percent of the world's wine.

Chenin Blanc—called *Steen* in South Africa—is the country's most planted variety. It's made in a variety of styles including sparkling, late harvest, and Rosé. Following Chenin Blanc in production are Sultana, Colombard, and Chardonnay. White varieties account for about two-thirds of South Africa's grapes, but 80 percent of new plantings are red varieties.

Cabernet Sauvignon is the most planted red variety, followed by Pinotage and Shiraz.

Vino Veritas

Pinotage is South Africa's contribution to grape breeding. In 1925 a professor from Stellenbosch University crossed Pinot Noir with Cinsault (called Hermitage in South Africa, hence, the name). The first international critiques of Pinotage wines were unkind. But, over time, the wines have earned respect.

South Africa's most famous wine regions are:

+ **Stellenbosch.** Just east of Cape Town, it's home to many of the country's leading estates.
+ **Paarl.** Northwest of Cape Town, it's traditionally a white wine region—but is now concentrating on reds.
+ **Constantia.** It's the region closest to Cape Town (and home to the once-great dessert wine) where South Africa's first vineyards were planted.

Chile

Missionaries traveling with the conquistadors in the mid-1500s brought vine cuttings to Chile from their native Spain to produce wine for sacramental purposes. The wines were mostly rustic renditions of Spanish varietals—Pais and Moscatel. The grapes did so well that by the 1800s, Chilean wines were giving Spanish imports a real run for their money. And that was a problem, at least to the Spanish Crown. The Spanish government levied heavy taxes and imposed severe restrictions on winemaking—all of which took its toll on Chilean vineyards.

Following the wars of independence in the nineteenth century, the newly prosperous upper class of Chileans traveled to Europe, where they developed a fondness for French wines. Cuttings from the great Bordeaux varieties were imported, and the modern era of winemaking in Chile was underway.

Isolation Has Its Advantages

In the second half of the nineteenth century, the phylloxera epidemic wiped out the vineyards of Europe and North America. Chile was isolated by natural conditions. It has the Andes to the east, the Pacific to the west, and barren deserts to the north. Chile remained free of the disease while the rest of the wine world was decimated.

To this day, Chile remains the only country unaffected by phylloxera. Its vinifera vines are the only ones in the world still growing on their own rootstocks.

Carmenère: The Great Masquerade

Carmenère was an important grape of Bordeaux vineyards. When Chile imported vine cuttings from France, Carmenère was high on the list. Then came the phylloxera epidemic and the massive replanting of all the European vineyards. When Bordeaux was replanted, Carmenère was left out. Why? Compared to Merlot—which it resembled—Carmenère was too fussy. It doesn't flower when the springs are cold and wet. It ripens weeks after Merlot does. And it has lower yields than Merlot. It was an easy decision for French growers: Stick with the Merlot!

The climate in Chile, however, is perfect for Carmenère—so it grew happily for years alongside Merlot. Because they look so much alike, Carmenère lost its identity over the years and came to be called Merlot.

As Chilean wines gained popularity in recent years, more of it made its way into the world market. It didn't go unnoticed that Chilean Merlot tasted somewhat stronger and spicier than Merlots from elsewhere. Then in 1994, it was discovered through DNA testing that the Merlot was actually Carmenère!

Politics and Investment

The Chilean wine industry has had its ups and downs, in spite of nearly perfect conditions for growing grapes. In the 1940s Chilean wines grew in popularity—only to lose ground when the government nationalized many of the wineries and restricted production. Even when government regimes changed, civil war brought further instability to the wine industry—until, in 1980, almost half the country's vineyards were out of production.

Message in a Bottle

In 1995, under the new appellation system, Chile established the 75 percent rule. Seventy-five percent of the contents of a bottle of wine must come from the exact location, variety, and vintage specified on the label. Twenty-five percent is allowed for blending purposes. "Reserva" wines aren't as tightly controlled, and are required only to indicate a place of origin on the label.

With stability restored in the '80s, Chile was able to attract significant investment from companies in France, the United States, Australia, Spain, and Japan. Modern technology and replanted vineyards brought new life to Chilean wines. They became known, almost overnight, as excellent, value-priced varietals—with big plans for the fine-wines category.

Varietals

While Pais and Moscatel are still being turned into wine for the domestic market, the wine industry has invested heavily in high-quality reds for export. Cabernet Sauvignon, Merlot, Pinot Noir, Syrah—and, of course, Carmenère—are the focus. White varietals include Chardonnay, Sauvignon Blanc, Riesling, and Sémillon.

Argentina

Argentina's wines and wine history have always been tied to the country's economic and political circumstances. Spanish settlers first brought "work horse" vines to Argentina as early as the mid-1500s. Criolla (related to Chile's Pais grape) and Cereza were plentiful but didn't make wines of much character. The wines were made with an eye toward ensuring they were able to survive the harrowing shipping conditions to other South American countries.

The Ripe Stuff

How did the Spanish settlers grow vines so quickly in the desert?

The Huarpe Indians, and the Incans before them, had already established an irrigation system. The new settlers enhanced the system. Relying on the thaw of ice and snow from the Andes Mountains, they created a network of dykes and canals to channel the water to where it was needed.

Two waves of European immigration were responsible for introducing new varieties. In 1816 after Argentina's independence from Spain and again at the turn of the century, settlers from France, Spain, and Italy brought vine cuttings to make the wines they had enjoyed in Europe:

- Malbec, Cabernet Sauvignon, Merlot, and Chenin Blanc from France
- Torrontés and Tempranillo from Spain
- Sangiovese, Nebbiolo, Dolcetto, Barbera, and Lambrusco from Italy

Quantity vs. Quality

By the 1920s Argentina had become the eighth richest nation in the world. The Depression set it back, but, under Juan Perón, the country seemed to be recovering. In the mid-1950s Perón was deposed and a succession of military governments plunged the country into economic and political decline.

With a population that, frankly, drank a lot of wine (twenty-one gallons per capita per year), Argentina's winemakers focused on quantity rather than quality. Massive amounts of rustic "Vino de Mesa" were produced to satisfy domestic demand. In the late '80s and early '90s Argentina experienced runaway inflation—1,000 percent a year. Price controls were put on wine, forcing some growers to shift to crops other than grapes. For those who continued to grow grapes, a tax policy was established that rewarded the destruction of older vineyards of traditional grape varieties in favor or planting inferior, but high-volume, varieties.

Wine Exports

Argentina, one of the largest producers of wine, always had such an enormous domestic market for its product that it didn't worry too much about exports. But that scenario has changed. With competition from beer and soft drinks, the per capita consumption is now around eight gallons a year. While Argentines still consume 95 percent of the wine, exports are on the rise. Foreign and domestic investment has helped the wine industry to improve its product.

Message in a Bottle

Mendoza is Argentina's largest and best wine-producing region. It makes the country's top wines. When Spanish settlers brought vinifera vines to Argentina via Chile and Peru, they discovered that the best place to grow the grapes was at the foot of the Andes. They established the city of Mendoza there in 1561, and it remains the center of Argentina's winemaking industry today.

Malbec has emerged as the country's premier grape. The unheralded grape of Bordeaux has found a home in Argentina and has become the wine industry's signature export.

Canada

Oh, Canada . . . so often overlooked when it comes to wine. Winemaking in Canada goes back to the 1800s when European settlers tried to grow vinifera grapes in Ontario province. Like their neighbors to the south, the settlers were unsuccessful in their attempts. But the region's native grapes flourished. So, for the next hundred years Canadian winemakers used *Vitis labrusca* and *Vitis riparia* and American hybrids and crosses like Niagara, Concord, and Catawba.

By all reports, the wines weren't so great. But when they were made into fortified wines, they became a dependable and lucrative export to England.

The Turn of the Century

Around 1900 winemaking started in British Columbia, and *Vitis vinifera* vines were planted again in Canada. But something else was growing as well—a temperance movement that culminated in Canada's Prohibition in 1916. Unlike in the United States, wine wasn't banned and wineries stayed in business. Once Prohibition ended in 1927, the provinces took over control of production, distribution, and sale of alcoholic beverages.

Small wineries had proliferated during Prohibition, reaching sixty-one when Prohibition came to an end. Post-Prohibition, there was a period of consolidation. The bigger companies bought up the small ones so that, by 1974, there were only six wineries in the whole country.

A New Era

In 1974 the first winery license since Prohibition was awarded to partners Donald Ziraldo and Karl Kaiser who named their boutique winery Inniskillin. Their vision was to produce only the finest wines from traditional vinifera grapes. They were a model for other winemakers and brought Canada into a new era of winemaking.

At the 1991 VinExpo in Bordeaux, Inniskillin won the prestigious Prix d'Honneur for its 1989 Icewine. It was the first of many awards to come for Canadian producers.

Vino Veritas

The Canada/USA Free Trade Agreement of 1988 was a catalyst to the Canadian wine industry. The industry was going to have to compete in the world market without government protection. It rose to the challenge to produce premium wines. The growers of Ontario and British Columbia undertook a major program to replace native grape varieties with vinifera vines throughout their regions.

Weather Prevails

Canada can get cold . . . and stay cold. So much the better to produce ice wines, for which the country has become famous. In fact, Canada is the world's largest producer. Unlike in Germany (where ice wine originated) and Austria, Canadian winters are consistently cold from year to year—guaranteeing that ice wines will be made every year.

Canada makes its best-known whites from Chardonnay, Riesling, Gewürztraminer as well as Pinot Gris, and Pinot Blanc. Its reds are from Merlot, Pinot Noir, Cabernet Sauvignon, Cabernet Franc, and Gamay.

Message in a Bottle

Canada has an appellation system, Vintners Quality Alliance (VQA), similar to France's AOC system. It ensures minimum quality standards through tasting panel testing and by regulating winemaking techniques and grape ripeness. The VQA recognizes three Designated Viticultural Areas in Ontario (Niagara Peninsula, Pelee Island, Lake Erie North Shore) and four in British Columbia (Okanagan Valley, Similkameen Valley, Fraser Valley, Vancouver Island).

New Frontiers

There's hardly a significant area in the world that doesn't grow grapes for wine. To categorize some of these areas as "new" seems absurd because their winemaking histories go back centuries. China is a good example. Proof exists that its winemaking predates Europe's, but, in terms of modern production, it must be considered New World. China has about 100 wineries—although wines from vinifera varieties are still a fraction of their production.

Winemaking occurs in other seemingly unlikely places. Turkey is one. In spite of a largely Muslim population that consumes very little wine, Turkey has a strong winemaking industry. It has fifty wineries with total production not much less than Canada. And it surpasses in volume other, more expected, Middle Eastern winemaking countries like Israel and Lebanon. Tunisia, Japan, and Morocco are other examples. Their wines don't make much of a *blip* on the radar screen yet. But who knows what the future holds?

CHAPTER 8

Wine Regions
of the United States

The United States grows grapes and makes wine from sea to shining sea. Historically, grapevines were planted near large bodies of water, but now vineyards are located in mountains and valleys and plains. And every one of the fifty states has commercial wineries. For a country whose citizens drink so little wine (three gallons per person a year)—compared to places like Italy or France (fifteen gallons)—there sure is a whole lot of winemaking going on.

You're Not in France Anymore, Dorothy

Americans have always had their own ways of doing things. They've never been shy about declaring their independence. It's clear that attitude spills over into the world of wine. American winemakers produced entirely different styles of wines with the same grapes the Europeans used. And then, instead of naming the wines after the place they were produced as had been the tradition, they named their wines after the grape.

Until 1979 the United States had no coordinated system to designate or control geographical winemaking areas. France had made its AOC system into law in the 1930s, and it had become a model for other countries. It strictly regulates varieties that can be grown, yields, alcohol levels, and vineyard practices. Well, Americans weren't going to go for that. They wanted to retain the independence to make their wines using whatever grapes and methods they chose.

The federal government set up the American Viticultural Area (AVA) system as part of the Treasury Department—first under the auspices of the Bureau of Alcohol, Tobacco, and Firearms and more recently under the supervision of the Alcohol and Tobacco Trade Bureau. Unlike in the French and other European systems, the only requirement to use an AVA on the label is that 85 percent of the grapes used in making the wine come from the named region.

Vino Veritas

An AVA can be enormous or very small. The largest is the 26,000-square-mile, 16.5 million-acre Ohio River Valley AVA. It includes portions of several states: Indiana, Kentucky, Ohio, and West Virginia. The smallest is the Cole Ranch in California's Mendocino County which covers 150 acres and less than one-quarter square mile.

The term *AVA* doesn't appear on any label. But geographical names do . . . and those are the AVAs. There are AVAs within AVAs, and a producer will choose the smallest AVA possible that will meet its needs. A winemaker from Mt. Veeder in Napa will put "Mt. Veeder" on the label when 85 percent of the grapes come from there. If the winemaker buys grapes from its Napa neighbor in St. Helena to use, the "Napa" AVA must appear on the label. If the producer buys even more grapes from a Mendocino grower, the label will say "North Coast." The larger and less specific the AVA (like "California"), the more opportunity the producer has to blend grapes from various areas.

More than 170 AVAs exist—and new ones are approved every year. The cost to establish a new AVA starts at $15,000. Applicants have to provide proof of geographic and climatic significance, historical precedent for wine production, and boundary suggestion and mapping. As opposed to systems in other countries, AVAs don't assure quality. They only differentiate the growing areas.

California

California is, hands down, the wine state of the United States. It accounts for more than 90 percent of all the wines made in the country and 75 percent of all the wines consumed within its borders. The climate has a lot to do with California's pre-eminence. Not only is it ideal for growing grapes—it also has predictability because there's little variation from year to year. Getting enough sun every year to ripen the grapes is never a problem in California. The challenge is to find cool enough areas so the grapes don't ripen too early without full flavor development.

Wineries have popped up all over the state from the far reaches of the north to the Mexican border in the south. But the wine regions most conducive to producing wines are:

- ◆ **North Coast**—includes Napa, Sonoma, Mendocino, and Lake County
- ◆ **Central Coast**—the largest wine area of California (It stretches from San Francisco to Los Angeles. It includes Monterey, Santa Cruz, and Livermore in the northern part and San Luis Obispo and Santa Barbara in the south.)
- ◆ **Sierra Foothills**—on the western edge of the Sierra Nevada
- ◆ **Central Valley**—includes the vast San Joaquin Valley

"Wine Country"

The Napa Valley has almost become synonymous with the term *wine country*. It's famous for its expensive wines, rich history, and breathtaking landscapes. Inside the thirty-mile stretch, you can eat at elegant gourmet restaurants, get a bite at casual bistros (with a bottle of valley wine, naturally), or just experience the serenity of the valley floor as hot air balloons pass overhead.

Napa is like an amusement park for adults (with adult prices). And some of the wineries will give you a heck of a ride for your money. The Robert Mondavi Winery alone has ten different tours available. Critics say Napa is too pricey, too crowded, and too ostentatious. But no place else can compare.

Napa has fifteen distinct AVAs—with diverse microclimates. It's got cool breezes in the south where it meets the bay, and warms up as you move north. It's got ridgetop vineyards on Mount Veeder with different climate, soil, and exposure than the valley floor vineyards. And it's got well over 200 wineries to take advantage of all the valley's conditions. Some of the Napa AVAs that you'll probably recognize from wine labels are:

- Rutherford
- Howell Mountain
- Atlas Peak
- Mount Veeder
- Oakville
- Spring Mountain
- Stags' Leap District

Cabernet is king in Napa. And while many different varieties are grown, the most produced varietals are Chardonnay, Sauvignon Blanc, Merlot, and Zinfandel. And then there's Sonoma, California's oldest and second most famous "wine country." It's no Napa. And it doesn't want to be! That's not to say there aren't any wine powerhouses there. (Gallo and Korbel and Kendall-Jackson—all household names—have property in Sonoma.) But Sonoma has a more relaxed personality and more of the character of "Old California."

Sonoma is Napa's western neighbor. Because of its proximity to the Pacific coast, it has a very different climate than Napa. The fog rolls in . . . the fog rolls out. The days are warm, and the nights are cool. Sonoma has lots of AVAs and sub-AVAs. A few of the most notable:

- **Alexander Valley**—famous for its Cabs and Chardonnays
- **Russian River Valley**—produces Pinot Noir (thanks to its cooler climate); also known for Chardonnay and sparkling wine
- **Dry Creek Valley**—know for Zinfandel
- **Sonoma Valley and Sonoma Mountain**—produce Cabernet, Pinot Noir, and Chardonnay

The wine area of Carneros is a particularly interesting AVA. It's located partly in Sonoma and partly in Napa next to San Pablo Bay, the northern area of San Francisco Bay. It has a cool climate, making it an ideal area for growing Chardonnay and Pinot Noir. The grapes are used in the production of sparkling wines—although dry still wines are produced as well. Because of its climate, Carneros attracted a number of sparkling wine producers from France and Spain who have established wineries there.

Mendocino and Lake County

Do you remember (or at least remember hearing about) the hippies of the '60s? Many of them were drawn to Northern California, where free expression was accepted—and even encouraged. Since then, Northern California has had a reputation for residents who liked to "do their own thing." Mendocino and Lake County are California's northernmost wine-producing areas, and the winemakers there are open-minded and experimental about what grapes to grow. They've planted varieties that aren't traditionally associated with California. They're creating wines from Italian varieties like Fiano, Montepulciano, and Arneis and German and French varieties like Riesling, Gewürztraminer, and Pinot Blanc.

Of course, those varieties are in addition to the more traditional, cooler climate grapes of Pinot Noir and Chardonnay. Mendocino is credited with being in the forefront of sustainable agriculture and organic farming.

Sierra Foothills and Livermore Valley

The Sierra Foothills are Gold Rush country. It's mountainous with a cool climate. The most cultivated grapes are Syrah, Zinfandel, and Petite Sirah. But you'll also find Barbera, Sangiovese, and Mourvèdre.

About an hour outside of San Francisco to the southeast lies the Livermore Valley—a historic wine-producing area with a warm and windy climate. It's situated between the cool, marine air of the San Francisco Bay and the hot, dry air of the Central Valley. Sauvignon Blanc and Sémillon were first planted there by the French immigrants in the 1870s and 1880s. They remain and thrive. Other varieties include Chardonnay, Cabernet Sauvignon, Petite Sirah, and Zinfandel.

The Coastal Regions

The areas within the Central Coast AVA are numerous and disparate. Each one has its own distinctive qualities. Of course, the one with the most current celebrity is the Santa Ynez Valley, north of the town of Santa Barbara.

When you get an Academy Award nomination—like *Sideways* did in 2005—you can't help but become famous. The premise is two friends set off on a winetasting road trip and discover the pleasures—wine and otherwise—of the Santa Ynez Valley. There are a lot of wine pleasures to experience, from Pinot Noir and Chardonnay to Riesling and Sauvignon Blanc to the Vin Gris from Sanford Winery that the characters spent so much time analyzing.

Central Valley

No fine wine producer brags that its grapes come from the Central Valley. This huge expanse of inland vineyards produces the majority of California's bulk wine—accounting for three-quarters of the state's wine production. (It also grows table grapes and raisins.) But new facilities and technology have improved the wine's quality.

California Is Trendsetting

In the 1980s some progressive winemakers got tired of producing only Chardonnay and Cabernet Sauvignon. They wanted to express more of their creativity. In the vein of "everything old becomes new again," they looked to the Old World for inspiration. One group, dubbed the "Rhone Rangers," took their inspiration from southern France and concentrated on making wines from traditional Rhone varieties like Syrah and Viognier. The idea caught on, and more plantings of those grapes was the result.

Meanwhile, another group of Francophile winemakers wanted to express their creativity in blending—not making one-dimensional varietals. They looked to Bordeaux and its "noble" grapes. The result of their collaboration was Meritage wines and the Meritage Association.

Meritage wines have to blend at least two of the Bordeaux varieties, and no single variety can make up more than 90 percent of the blend. Meritage wines, both red and white, are now produced across the United States.

Vino Veritas

What's next? Because winemaking practices and the popular enjoyment of wine are cyclical, you can probably look to history for the answer. One trend seems to be the shift away from heavily oaked California wines. For twenty-five years California winemakers were fascinated with oak and used a lot of it. On another continent, the wine-producing regions of France—like the Loire Valley and Rhone—have always relied on the true taste of the fermented grape and have met with popular approval. Today, California winemakers are making the move to create softer, more fruit-driven wine—with little or no oak.

New York

New York is the second largest wine-producing state in the United States, but it often gets overlooked in the mind of the public—maybe because of the overwhelming presence of California. Until 1960, New York wines came from native American varieties like Concord, Catawba, Niagara, and Delaware and hybrid grapes such as Seyval Blanc and Baco Noir. The hybrids, in particular, are still produced, but the more popular vinifera wines have usurped their position.

The Finger Lakes

For years it was accepted that New York winters were too cold for vinifera vines to survive. Enter a Russian immigrant, Dr. Konstantin Frank. Dr. Frank had organized a collective farm and taught viticulture in his native Ukraine. When he came to the United States in 1951, he took a job at the New York State Agricultural Experiment Station, where he observed the lack of vinifera vines in the Finger Lakes area. When he asked why, he was given the expected answer. But Frank had already grown vinifera grapes successfully in the Ukraine where winters were much colder. So he set out to prove his point and, in 1953, succeeded in growing Riesling in Hammondsport, New York.

Today, the Finger Lakes region is an officially recognized AVA—whose Rieslings compare favorably with their European counterparts. The area encompasses 4,000 square miles and has 15,000 acres of vines. The area has more than seventy wineries of all sizes—including Constellation Brands (formerly Canandaigua), one of the world's largest wine suppliers. Finger Lakes producers do particularly well with Riesling, Chardonnay, Pinot Noir, sparkling wines, and ice wines.

Hudson River Valley

North of New York City along the majestic Hudson River is the historic Hudson Valley. It was a pioneering region for French-American hybrids such as Seyval Blanc and Baco Noir. These days it also grows Chardonnay and Cabernet Franc. The area has more than twenty wineries including the oldest continuously running winery in the country. Brotherhood Winery produced the first commercial vintage in 1839. It was able to keep its doors open through Prohibition by making sacramental wine.

Long Island

The Finger Lakes and Hudson Valley may have a rich past, but New York's Long Island has a bright future. It's the new kid on the block and quite a success story so far. In 1973 when Alex and Louisa Hargrave were looking for a suitable place to plant some grapevines, somebody suggested checking out Long Island. The maritime microclimate, it was said, was very similar to Bordeaux.

After researching and soil testing—but mostly because of intuition—the Hargraves put down roots on seventeen acres of the island's North Fork. Two years later they bottled their first wines and released them in 1977. Today, thirty-eight wineries are producing wines from grapes on 3,000 acres of land.

Long Island has been compared to Napa twenty-five years ago. And in some ways it's true. There's the proximity to a world-class city—Manhattan is to the North Fork as San Francisco is to Napa. And then there are all those celebrities buying up wine properties. Who knows? But Long Island—with its quality Merlot, Cab, Cabernet Franc, Chardonnay, and more—is off to a good start.

Oregon

Although wines were made in Oregon in the nineteenth century, Prohibition effectively wiped out the entire wine industry. Oregon's wine pioneers arrived in the 1960s. At the time no vinifera vines were planted. They brought enthusiasm, new ideas, and, in some cases, degrees from UC Davis.

Oregon's climate is marked by cool growing seasons . . . and plenty of rain. It presents challenges—but nothing Oregon's new winemakers didn't think they could overcome. They just had to be discerning about where and how they planted their vineyards. Unlike in California where sprawling vineyard tracts were the norm, Oregon vineyards were planted in small pockets to take advantage of the best weather conditions.

Pinot Noir Takes Root

Oregon's location along the 45th parallel, in addition to its maritime weather, make the growing climate very similar to that of Burgundy, France. One of Oregon's pioneers, David Lett of Eyrie Vineyard, was convinced that the traditional grapes of Burgundy could grow well in Oregon—and certainly grow better than they did in California. He planted the first Pinot Noir vines in 1965. A decade or so later, his Pinot Noir wines would put Oregon on the map of the wine world.

Message in a Bottle

In a 1979 Paris tasting with entries from 330 countries, the 1975 Eyrie Pinot Noir placed in the top ten. In a follow-up match in early 1980, it came in second to—and less than a point behind—the 1959 Drouhin Chambolle-Musigny. It was an international achievement! Since then Pinot Noir has become Oregon's flagship wine.

Oregon's Other Pinot

Pinot Noir's companion grape in Burgundy is Chardonnay, and it's no stranger to Oregon. But the real success story in the white wine category in Oregon in Pinot Gris. Again, thanks to David Lett, Pinot Gris was introduced to the region in 1965 and has since been adopted by winemakers across the state.

The style of Oregon's Pinot Gris has been compared to that made in Alsace, but subtle variations exist. And it's entirely different than the Pinot Grigio wines made from the same grape. In general, Oregon's Pinot Gris is medium-bodied, yellow to copper pink in color, crisp, with full fruit flavors. The wines from Alsace are medium- to full-bodied, slightly floral, and less fruity. Pinot Grigio—from almost everywhere—is light-bodied, light in color, and neutral in flavor.

Growing Regions

Oregon has nine officially recognized AVAs—three of them shared with neighboring Washington State—and six more in the works. Among them are:

- **Willamette Valley**—The largest and most important region. This fertile river valley is located directly south of Portland in the northwest end of the state. It produces primarily Pinot Noir, Pinot Gris, Chardonnay, and Riesling.
- **Umpqua Valley**—The site of Oregon's first winery, Hillcrest Vineyard. South of Willamette Valley, it has a warm climate and produces Chardonnay, Pinot Noir, Cabernet Sauvignon, Riesling, and Sauvignon Blanc.
- **Rogeue Valley**—This area is further south, with a dry, warm climate. Varietals include Pinot Gris, Riesling, Chardonnay, and Gewürztraminer.
- **Applegate Valley**—This region falls within the Rogue Valley. It produces Cabernet Franc, Sémillon, Cabernet Sauvignon, and Merlot.

Washington

Like Oregon, Washington was late getting into the wine business. Washington's two largest wineries—Columbia Winery and Château Ste. Michelle—planted the first commercial-scale vineyards in the 1960s. But even so, it wasn't until the '80s that most of the growth started. Today Washington has over 320 wineries.

Also like Oregon, the state is divided by the north-south Cascade Mountains. West of the mountain range the climate is cool with plenty of rain and vegetation. To the east of the mountains the land is desertlike: hot, dry summers and cold winters. Ninety-eight percent of the state's grapes grow east of the mountains.

Because of its northerly location, Washington gets lots of summer sun—two more hours of summer sunlight each day than in California regions. It's great for ripening the grapes. The cool autumn temperatures help the grapes maintain desirable acid levels as they reach maturity. In terms of volume, Washington produces more wine grapes than any state except California.

Wine Regions

Five of Washington's six official wine regions are in the arid east, where irrigation made commercial vine growing possible.

- **Yakima Valley**—Washington's very first AVA, it now has more than forty wineries. The most widely planted grapes are Chardonnay, followed by Merlot and Cabernet and significant acreage of Riesling and Syrah.
- **Columbia Valley**—The largest region in Washington, it represents a full third of Washington's landmass. Production of Merlot is followed by Cabernet, Chardonnay, Riesling, and Syrah.
- **Walla Walla Valley**—This AVA is shared with Oregon. It has more than fifty-five wineries and produces Cabernet Sauvignon, Merlot, Chardonnay, Syrah, Gewürztraminer, Cabernet Franc, and Sangiovese.
- **Red Mountain**—Located at the east end of the Yakima Valley, it's known for its red varietals: Cabernet, Merlot, Cabernet Franc, Syrah, and Sangiovese.
- **Columbia Gorge**—The newest AVA, part of the appellation is shared with Oregon. It produces Chardonnay, Gewürztraminer, Riesling, and Pinot Gris.

Vino Veritas

Lemberger. No, not the cheese. That's Limburger. Lemberger is a little-known German grape variety (*Blaufränkisch* in German) that's also grown in Austria. It makes a fruity but dry red. The wines are typically light-bodied—not unlike Beaujolais.

The sixth AVA is Puget Sound near Seattle. It has eighty vineyard acres of vinifera grapes and about thirty-five wineries. Many of the larger wineries are located in this area but obtain almost all their grapes from the Columbia and Yakima Valleys.

Most of Washington's wineries produce small quantities of their wines—so they may be difficult to find. Ste. Michelle Wine Estates produces about half of all Washington's wines. The company's labels include Columbia Crest, Snoqualmie, Northstar, Eroica, and Col Solare—a joint venture with Italy's Antinori.

Savvy Sipping

The "Other" 46

California, New York, and the Northwest may be the big wine players in the United States, but every state has its own unique wine story to tell. Take Missouri, for example. In the 1860s Missouri made more wine than California and New York combined! The influx of German immigrants to Hermann, an hour and a half west of St. Louis, on the banks of the Missouri River, made the area known as the Rhineland of Missouri. But the wines produced weren't made from German grapes. No Riesling in sight. Ageworthy reds are made from Norton and Cynthiana, and whites are made with Vignoles, Seyval Blanc, and Vidal Blanc.

Deep in the Heart of Texas

The Lone Star State comes in at number five in wine production—right after California, New York, Washington, and Oregon. Texas developed a close association with France during the 1880s phylloxera epidemic. A French scientist, Pierre Viala, from Cognac was sent to Texas to try to find a cure for the vineyard plague. He traveled to Denison, Texas, because the soil composition there was similar to that in Cognac and should have grape species capable of growing in both places. Viala was introduced to Thomas Volney Munson, a Texas scientist who knew Texas rootstocks were resistant to phylloxera. At Munson's suggestion Viala shipped the Texas rootstocks back to France where they were grafted to French vines. For his contribution to France, Munson was given the highest honor awarded to a foreign civilian, the Chevalier du Merite Agricole.

Vino Veritas

Archaeologists discovered a brick-lined wine cellar and intact wine bottles in Jamestown, Virginia—the first permanent English colony in America. The cellar, which dates back to the late 1600s, is one of the earliest wine cellars known in the United States. It's believed the cellar was part of a private home.

New Mexico Stands Proud

While every U.S. state can proudly boast of its wines—and rightfully so—a few states can claim top wine titles. New Mexico, a state not known for wine, can brag of its sparklings, particularly Gruet. The Gruet family produces six different sparkling wines. Their vineyards are located at 4,300 feet—some of the highest in the United States—which helps to produce grapes good for sparklings.

CHAPTER 9

Enjoying Wine: Tasting It and Talking about It

You walk into a wine shop, and the clerk asks if he can help you select a wine. You pause in thought, then turn in embarrassment and walk out the door. You know what kind of wine you like when you taste it, but you just don't know how to communicate that to the salesperson. Determining why you enjoy one wine over another and expressing yourself articulately are just a matter of practice and a few well-chosen words.

Why Wine Tastes Good: The Physiology of Taste

Taste is subjective—whether you're talking about art, fashion, music, or wine. Of course, with wine, there's also a physiological dimension to how we taste. No two people experience taste in exactly the same way. And because of our upbringing and cultural influences, we've learned to appreciate certain flavors.

Our own taste can change from day to day and from place to place. That incredible bottle of Chianti you shared over a romantic dinner didn't measure up when you drank it alone in front of the TV, did it? Your taste is affected by your mood, by your health, and by your environment. Try to enjoy a floral Viognier when you have a cold or when you're in a smoke-filled room. It will be quite a challenge.

What you taste is really a composite of four sensations: sight, smell, taste, and touch.

Vino Veritas

Individuals have genetic differences that determine their ability to taste. People can be divided into categories of "supertasters," "nontasters," and "normal tasters." Supertasters are especially sensitive to sweetness, bitterness, and the creamy sensation of fat. Apparently, they have more taste buds than everyone else—as many as a hundred times more than nontasters. About 25 percent of the population are supertasters . . . and two-thirds of all supertasters are women.

Sight

A wine's appearance influences your judgment. The color: Is it what you expected . . . or is it somehow "off"? The clarity: Is there any cloudiness that would indicate the wine is unfined? Or are there any tartrate crystals that might need decanting? In blind winetastings, participants are sometimes given black, opaque glasses so they're not prejudiced by what the wine looks like—even whether it's red or white.

Smell

Our sense of smell is our most acute—and a thousand times more sensitive than our sense of taste. You sense aromas either directly by inhaling through your nose or, indirectly, through the interior nasal passage at the back of your mouth. What we experience when we "taste" wine is actually 75 percent smell and only 25 percent taste. Wine is made up of over 200 different chemical compounds. Many of them are similar—or identical—to those in fruits, vegetables, flowers, herbs, and spices. So it's not surprising to hear someone say, "I smell peaches" over a glass of Riesling.

Taste

In contrast to the multitude of aromas the nose can identify, the tongue recognizes only four basic tastes: sweetness, saltiness, acidity, and bitterness. Saltiness doesn't come into play when tasting wine, but the others are critical. The tip of the tongue registers sweetness first. Acidity, in the form of a sour taste, registers along the sides of the tongue. And bitterness is recognized at the back of the tongue near the throat.

Sweetness and acidity are the yin and yang of the winetasting world. They balance each other. Think of lemonade. Lemon juice on its own is a mouth-puckering experience. The more sugar you add to the juice, the less you notice the acidity.

Message in a Bottle

A fifth taste, called *umami,* has been identified by food scientists. It has no flavor of its own and can be described as a flavor enhancer. It gives other flavors a completeness, or a delicious quality. Its action occurs in processes like ripening and fermentation.

Touch

Wines have texture that you can feel in your mouth. A wine can be thin—like water. Or it can be full—like cream. That's what a wine's "body" is all about. "Full-bodied" and "light-bodied" aren't value judgments . . . they're descriptions.

Your mouth distinguishes other sensations as well. Tannins, the elements responsible for a wine's ability to age, have an astringent, mouth-drying effect very much like the impression you get when you drink oversteeped tea. And the alcohol in the wine will give you a hot feeling at your throat and on the roof of your mouth.

Vino Veritas

Your perception of a wine's body—its texture and fullness—is due mostly to the amount of alcohol in the wine. The more potent a wine is, the more full-bodied it will seem. A big Zinfandel with a 14 percent alcohol content will have more body than a Riesling with 9 percent.

Winetasting Techniques from the Pros

There's nothing wrong with simply picking up your glass of wine and taking a swig. But for the full experience, you might want to copy what professional winetasters do. They employ certain techniques that can magnify the sensations—and the enjoyment—of the wine.

Swirling

You know how to swirl, don't you . . . just pick up your glass and whirl it around. The wine will rotate and spin and release its aromas into the air. (And you thought swirling was just some snobbish pretension!) Before the aromas escape and are lost, stick your nose right into the glass. Inhale deeply. Yes, it's much more than a sniff. Breathe it in.

And now, do it again. You can't possibly take in all the aroma nuances at once. Close your eyes. What scents are you detecting? You may smell something new each time.

And that's the fun.

Savvy Sipping

Don't even think about swirling with a full glass of wine! The glass should be no more than one-third full. There's got to be enough room between the level of the liquid and the top of the glass for the vapors to accumulate. Besides, any more than a third full and you'll have either a hefty dry-cleaning bill or a shirt you can't even give away.

Swishing and Slurping

Aromas, as seductive as they are, are still prelude. It's time to taste. Wine pros savor the moment. No quick swallow here. Swish the wine around in your mouth. Touch every surface of your tongue with wine. Hit every taste receptor.

You're not done yet. Purse your lips and draw in some air across the wine on your tongue. We know—it sounds gross. It's called slurping because, well, that's how it sounds. It aerates and oxidizes the wine so that you can smell/taste it through your rear nasal passage.

You're probably ready to swallow the wine right about now. Not so fast. Many professionals take this opportunity to spit. Yes, you heard right . . . spit. While most of us are loath to waste good wine that way, professional tasters have to keep their wits about them for the next wine (and there could be hundreds). So into the dump bucket goes a mouthful of wine. Amateurs, however, need not feel obligated to follow this step.

Message in a Bottle

If you're planning to taste several wines in a row, start with a light white. You can move on to more full-bodied whites, followed by light reds. Finish up with the heavy reds. That way, you won't have desensitized your palate for the more delicate wines.

Mastering the Lingo . . . Terms to Know

When wine lovers get excited about a new wine find, they want to share the experience. The only trouble is, words are so inadequate. But let's face it: Words are the best tools we have—short of handing out wine samples to everyone—to communicate our enthusiasm. Talking about wine has become intimidating, probably because wine snobs use words in such a way that it makes them mysterious and pretentious. Talk about wine any way you want in order to convey your meaning. If you want to compare a full-bodied wine to a Rubens painting, go for it. But there are some words used in wine descriptions that are good to know. Even if you never use them, you'll understand what's being said when other people use them.

- **Dry**—It's the opposite of sweet. When all the sugar in the grape juice has been converted to alcohol and carbon dioxide, the wine is said to be bone-dry. Of course, there's lots of room in the continuum between sweet and dry. If enough residual sugar remains to give the wine a slight sweetness, it's called off-dry.
- **Balance**—None of the wine's components is out-of-whack. The acid, alcohol, fruit, and tannins all work together so that one doesn't stand apart from the rest.
- **Finish**—A wine's aftertaste, or the flavor or aroma that lingers after you've swallowed the wine, is referred to as its *finish*. If it has one, it's considered a good thing. The longer the better. A "long finish" is a real compliment.
- **Complex**—Layers and nuances of flavor make a wine complex. A complex wine will continue to reveal itself as you sip it. This multidimensional quality is often achieved with aging. A complex wine is also said to have depth.
- **Fruity**—Fruit flavors—besides grapes—perceived in a wine make it "fruity." Blackberries, strawberries, and currants are just a few of the fruity flavors you can detect in wines. You notice them as the taste of the wine evolves. If they hit you—BANG!—as soon as you take the first sip, the term to use is *fruit-forward*.
- **Crisp**—A wine with good acidity and taste and no excessive sweetness is crisp. Think of an apple. The wine is relatively high in acidity, but the acidity doesn't overwhelm the other components.

In general some of the flavors you'll be able to discern from white wines are melon, apple, pineapple, pear, citrus, vanilla, caramel, flowers, herbs, grass, minerals, olives, and mushrooms. Some flavors from red wines are berries, peaches, currants, plums, cherries, oranges, flowers, earth, wood, smoke, chocolate, tobacco, leather, and coffee.

Many people confuse sweetness and fruitiness. They can't be blamed. Very often, wine labels describe sweet wine as fruity. If you have some doubt about what you're tasting, take a sip of the wine while holding your nose. If the wine is sweet, you'll taste its sweetness on your tongue—instead of sensing the aroma of the fruit.

Message in a Bottle

Recognizing "Flaws"

When you taste a wine you know if you like it. You can't always explain why. Maybe you don't even care about identifying the specific flavor characteristics that make the wine so tasty. You just want to sip and enjoy. But how about when you don't like the wine? You smell or taste it and . . . yuck! Is it just you? Are you particularly sensitive to a certain aroma?

Wines can be defective if they're not carefully made or if they're improperly handled or stored. Recognizing flaws isn't always black-and-white. There's no clear dividing line between good and bad wine. It's a matter of degree. Certain characteristics that make a wine flawed can actually, in small amounts, be considered by some people to be a plus. It's similar to adding garlic to food: A little bit enhances the dish, but too much ruins it. Recognizing flaws takes knowing what to look for. When you know the telltale signs, you'll know when it's bad.

Corks

Your wine smells of damp cardboard or musty basement. Whether the odor is pronounced or just slightly dank, it came from a cork tainted with a chemical compound called TCA. When the wine is damaged in this way, it's said to be corked. By industry estimates, 2 to 7 percent of all wines are corked. Cork processing improvements have been made to eliminate TCA production, but wineries are looking elsewhere—like to screw tops—for permanent remedies. When a wine is corked, it's bad.

Oxygen

The wine tastes dull, cooked, or a little Sherry-like. A white wine has an off color—brownish or dark yellow. These are all indications that the wine has been exposed to oxygen sometime during its life.

It could have happened while the wine was being made or when it was being stored. If wines are stored upright for long periods instead of on their sides, the cork can dry out and let air into the bottle. Wines with low acidity will smell cooked. Wines with high acidity will smell burned.

Perhaps your wine smells like vinegar or nail polish remover. This is an extreme case having to do with oxygen in the presence of a vinegar-producing bacterium called *acetobacter.* Acetobacter is everywhere—on grape skins, winery walls, barrels. By itself, it has no aroma or flavor. But when it meets oxygen in winemaking, it produces both acetic acid (the vinegar aroma) and ethyl acetate (the smell of nail polish remover). When this happens (it's called volatile acidity), the wine is bad.

Vino Veritas

Many people assume that when a wine gets too old, it turns to vinegar. More likely, it will become dull and take on a nutty taste. Thanks to Louis Pasteur and his groundbreaking work on fermentation, winemakers learned to keep wines out of contact with air and bacteria during the production process. As a result, a wine turning to vinegar has become a rarity.

Yeast

Your wine smells like a barnyard. It may be the result of a yeast called brettanomyces—brett, for short. Brett grows on grapes and in wineries and is next to impossible to get rid of. Winemakers use special filters to help reduce its growth. Some wine drinkers enjoy a low level of brett, maintaining that it adds complexity to the wine's aroma. But you know what they say about too much of a good thing. The wine is bad.

Sulfur Dioxide

Your wine smells like water from a sulfur spring. Winemakers add sulfur dioxide to preserve the wine. But too much and the odor is evident. You'll find this most often in cheap white wines. The wine is bad.

Heat

The wine is brown, and it smells like it's been cooked. In Madeira, this is a plus and part of the wine's essential character. In other wines, it's a flaw. It happens mostly to white and Rosé wines. The term to describe this condition is maderized. The wine has likely experienced severe fluctuations of temperature in a short period of time or been stored in heat. Sometimes the cork will be pushed up a little. The wine is bad.

Style Preferences

What you like in a wine, the next person might hate. Too much yeast? Too much oak? Too much acid? Personal preferences don't reflect a failure in the winemaking process. The fact that you don't like a wine doesn't mean it's flawed. It's not bad. Chalk it up to a bad choice.

Do Critics Know Best?

Wine ratings are like movie reviews. Just because a wine critic has anointed a bottle of California Cabernet with a perfect score of 100 doesn't mean that it will win an Academy Award at your house over dinner.

In your lifetime you've probably seen hundreds—if not thousands—of movies. You've developed a set of likes and dislikes. You like love stories, and you hate kickboxing movies. Based on your personal preferences, you decide what new movies you'll spend your hard-earned cash to see. So even if Roger Ebert gives a thumbs-up to the latest Jackie Chan flick, there's no way you're going to see it. You're confident about your movie choices because you have a basis of experience.

For many people wine is a completely different story. They haven't had the experience of tasting thousands of wines in order to develop a catalog of personal taste preferences. So they look to experts for guidance.

The Experts

Wine reviews come in all shapes and sizes, as do the delivery methods. There are individual reviewers, panel reports, and wine competitions. You can read them in newspapers, magazines, on "shelf talkers" and even on the back labels of bottles. Some are more helpful and reliable than others.

Without question, the wine world's most influential critic is Robert Parker. He first published his monthly newsletter, the *Wine Advocate,* in 1978 and introduced the 100-point scale for rating wines. The rating scale has been widely imitated ever since.

The Ripe Stuff

What does it mean when an expert talks about a wine's legs?

When you swirl a glass of wine, little streams of wine fall back down the sides of the glass. These are the legs. Some people draw conclusions from them about the wine's quality. But, bottom line: The "better" the legs, the higher the alcohol content.

Parker's influence is measurable. When he gives a wine a high score, the price goes up and availability goes down. Some producers in Bordeaux wait for Parker's scores before they set the release price of their wines. And his ratings have been instrumental in creating Napa's famous cult wines. The term *Parkerization* was coined to refer to wines that are made with the intention of earning Parker points by creating the kinds of wines he likes—rich, thick, ripe, and oaky. This underscores the importance of knowing a reviewer's taste preferences before following his advice. Not all reviewers are created equal. But, collectively, they've raised the public's consciousness about wine and its enjoyment.

Rating Systems

Robert Parker's ratings are based on single-blind, peer-group tastings, which means that the same type wines are tasted at the same time without tasters' knowledge of who the wine producers are.

Each wine automatically get 50 points—maybe just for the effort that went into making it. Color and appearance can earn up to 5 points. Aroma can get 15 points. Flavor and finish merit up to 20 points. And the overall quality can earn up to 10.

While other wine authorities such as *Wine Spectator* magazine also use the 100-point scale in their tastings, it's not the only one in use. *Decanter* magazine, an esteemed wine periodical in England, employs a 1-to-5 star rating. English wine writer Clive Coates uses a 20-point system. And Dorothy Gaiter and John Brecher, the much admired *Wall Street Journal* columnists, use simply, "Good/Very Good/Delicious/Delicious!" Some reviewers don't use a rating system at all, preferring narrative descriptions based on their tasting notes.

Another rating system—Quality/Price Ratio (QPR)—is becoming popular. It measures the correlation between what a wine sells for and its relative quality. A score of 100 percent means the price matches the quality. A score under 100 percent means you're getting a good deal for your money. A score over 100 percent means you're paying too much.

Savvy Sipping

Rating the Vintages

Not only wines get rated. Vintages get rated too. The years that the grapes are harvested get scores in the form of vintage charts. Wine-growing regions have different weather conditions every year—some with dramatic fluctuations—that affect wine quality. The charts direct you to the best years for each region or subregion.

Vintage charts range from basic to detailed, from one person's evaluation to a collective judgment, and from noted experts to your local retailer. Chart authors give each region a numerical score (as is done with individual wines) and map them on a grid to indicate the potential of that area's wine for that year. More comprehensive charts will tell you whether to hold the wine for aging or drink it now—or whether it's past its peak.

Even in the best years, a mediocre wine can show up. And in a so-so year, a talented winemaker can produce a very good wine. So instead of focusing entirely on vintage ratings, look at the track record of a winery over a period of years.

It Was a Very Good Year . . .

Wine critics have a grip on reality. They're not going to recommend wines that no one can afford (at least not all the time). Here are some wine suggestions from the experts:

- Bonterra North Coast Cabernet Sauvignon 2001 (Robin Garr)—$17
- Rudera Chenin Blanc 2002 (Tom Cannavan—*www.wine-pages.com*)—$22
- Carmen Carmenère-Cabernet Reserve Maipo Valley 2001 (*Decanter magazine*)—$14
- Villa Maria Reserve Marlborough Pinot Noir 2003 (Sue Courtney—*www.wineoftheweek. com*)—$45
- Porcupine Ridge Syrah 2003 (Jancis Robinson)—$13
- William Fevre Chablis 2002 (Jamie Goode—*www.wineanorak.com*)—$25
- Catena Malbec 2002 (*Wine Spectator* magazine)—$23
- Lamborghini Campoleone 1999 (Robert Parker)—$79

When it comes to enjoying wine—no matter what the vintage year, no matter what the critics say—it's ultimately up to you. Your personal preferences will guide you to make the right selections.

CHAPTER 10

Wine and Food

A century ago, life was simpler. Everyone just drank their local wine and didn't fret about the "perfect match" for a meal. Then wine snobs came up with rules. First, the rules were as simple as red wine with meat and white wine with fish. But food got more complex and so did the rules. The truth is food and wine pairing is highly subjective and inexact. There are certain principles that can guide you. In the end, though, it's your choice. So relax and enjoy the experimentation!

2nd Edition

The Dynamics of Food and Wine

Food and wine are like a couple of ballroom dancers. Each one affects the performance of the partner. Sometimes they're slightly out of step. Sometimes their footwork meshes seamlessly. On occasion, they move as one and transform a simple dance into a moment of magic. And even when both partners have two left feet, it's still a fun exercise.

Food and wine, whatever their individual personalities, influence the way the other one tastes. A particular food can exaggerate or diminish the flavor of a wine. A certain wine can overwhelm a food.

Message in a Bottle

When a food and wine combination has real synergy, the effect can be a third flavor experience that's greater than the two consumed separately. Admittedly, perfect unions are rare. And when they do happen, it's usually fate. So merely seeking two partners that are compatible is a reasonable strategy.

Wine as a Condiment

When wine geeks plan a meal, they choose the wine first and match the food to go with it. Most people start with the food and move on to the wine selection. Picking a wine is akin to adding a condiment. You'd hardly ask for a jar of mustard so you can slather some on your cheesecake. Matching wine and food is all about finding their common flavors and textures. You don't acquire that ability by memorizing a set of rules. You learn it through experimentation. Even though there are some matching principles that are good guides, everyone brings her own palate and taste preferences to the table.

If wine were a one-size-fits-all product, you could just pick food from column A of a chart and wine from column B. At fine-dining restaurants where wines are suggested for each menu item, the recommendations aren't just picked out of thin air. Before anything gets into print, the chef, the wine staff, and the wait staff all taste-test various wines with each course. They compare and discuss—and you can bet they don't all agree.

No one will know how the decisions are finalized. But the process exemplifies the fact that even professionals have different viewpoints.

Too Many Variables

It used to be you could order a steak and French fries and a glass of Cabernet. Now there's fusion food with sixty-three ingredients in one preparation. Which ingredient do you match the wine with?

Not only ingredients affect the way foods taste; cooking processes do as well. You can have your food baked, boiled, broiled, grilled, poached, sautéed, fried, marinated, pasteurized, tenderized, and liquefied. Whew!

Now consider the wine: thousands of grapes, endless blending combinations, a dry-to-sweet continuum, oak or no oak, high alcohol/low alcohol, aged or not aged. It's enough to make you want to throw your hands up in defeat and just order a cup of coffee.

Think back to the days before you drank wine. Did you ever sweat it when a restaurant only had Pepsi . . . no Coke? Did you worry that a 7-Up might be a better match for your grilled cheese? Almost any choice you make is okay. It's not likely to ruin your meal. You can drink more or less any wine with more or less any food—and enjoy the experience.

Matching Likes to Likes

There are some guiding principles that will point you in the right direction. The principles won't tell you *exactly* what to order, but they'll help you understand why some foods and some wines make compatible partners. The principles are based on the four tastes that the tongue can discern. And the idea is to match similar tastes in both the food and the wine.

A Sour Taste in Your Mouth

Foods that have a sour component are good matches for wines that are high in acid. A salad with a vinaigrette dressing and a fish fillet squirted with lemon both cry out for a high-acid wine. You're matching acid with acid. (Notice here that you're not matching the wine to the fish fillet itself or to the lettuce in the salad. You're taking into consideration the preparation.) Tomatoes, onions, green peppers, and green apples are examples of other high-acid foods. So, what wines are some potential high-acid wine partners? Sauvignon Blanc, to start. Also the northern French whites of Sancerre, Pouilly-Fumé, Vouvray, and Chablis. The wines of Alsace and Germany generally have high acidity. The acids in reds are often masked by the tannins, but safe bets are Italian reds. (Why do you think Italian wines go so perfectly with tomato-based pasta sauces?) The following whites are listed from low acid levels to high acid levels:

- Gewürztraminer (low)
- Pinot Gris/Pinot Grigio (low)
- Chardonnay (medium to high)
- Champagne (medium to high)
- Chablis (medium to high)
- Chenin Blanc (high)
- Riesling (high)
- Sauvignon Blanc (high)

Vino Veritas

Acidity is much more important in the taste and structure of white wines than red wines. In red wines, the taste balance depends on three components: alcohol, acids, and tannins—with tannins providing most of the structure. White wines have minimal tannins. So, there are only two components to consider: alcohol and acids—with acids providing the structure.

Sweet Thing

The sweeter the food, the less sweet a wine will taste. Say you're eating a slice of roast pork with a glass of off-dry Chenin Blanc. The sweetness of the wine will be obvious. Top your pork with a pineapple glaze and your glass of wine will taste positively dry.

When you get to dessert, the rule-of-thumb is to drink a wine that's sweeter than your food. Even a moderately sweet wine can taste thin, unpleasantly dry, and even bitter when you pair it with a sugar blockbuster. Some suggested pairings:

- Pear tart and Sauternes
- New York cheesecake and Muscat
- Bread pudding and late harvest Riesling
- Tiramisu and Port
- Dark chocolate mousse and Banyuls

The Ripe Stuff

Is there a way to tell how sweet or dry a wine is before you buy it?

Look at the percentage of alcohol listed on the label. Generally, the higher the alcohol level, the drier the wine. The lower the level, the sweeter the wine. That's because less sugar has been converted to alcohol during fermentation. This rule doesn't apply to fortified wines.

Don't Be Bitter

When you eat food with a hint of bitterness and drink a wine with some bitterness (from the tannins that have not yet mellowed), they cancel out each other's bitterness. It's like they knock each other out in the first round of a head-to-head fight—and you're the winner. The following red wines are listed from low to high tannin levels:

- Beaujolais (low)
- Tempranillo (low)
- Pinot Noir (low)
- Merlot (low)
- Sangiovese (medium)
- Zinfandel (medium to high)
- Syrah/Shiraz (high)
- Cabernet Sauvignon (high)

Salt of the Earth

Of course, you know there are no salty wines. But there are plenty of salty foods: ham, smoked salmon, oysters, teriyaki beef. The best wine accompaniments? Back to high-acid wines—especially sparkling wines. Acid cuts the saltiness—just like a squeeze of lemon does.

More Than Taste

There's more to wine (and matching wine to food) than the four perceived tastes. Wine has *power*—to a greater or lesser degree. So do foods. One can easily overpower the other if the matchup isn't comparable. Both food and wine have texture and flavor intensity that are part of the pairing equation. A big, brawny Amarone would overwhelm a dainty little broiled flounder at first sip. Conversely, a delicate Pinot Grigio wouldn't stand a chance of making an impression next to a fiery French pepper steak.

Alcohol is one of the contributors to a wine's sense of body and weight. The more alcohol, the more full-bodied the wine. So, even before tasting the wine, you can gauge its body by its alcohol content. A fuller-bodied wine will have more than 12 percent alcohol. Lighter-bodied wines will have under 12 percent.

Cutting the Fat

Maybe you've heard that tannic wines will "cut the fat." It's true—but not in the sense that they'll reduce the calories in that big, juicy steak. (Darn!)

Wine tannins are attracted to fatty proteins. As you chew your steak, your mouth is left with a coating of those fatty proteins. A sip of wine, and the tannin molecules attach themselves to the protein molecules—taking them along for the ride when you swallow. Now your mouth is refreshed and ready for the next forkful of meat.

Spice Up Your Life!

When you walk on the wild side with fiery dishes from Thailand or Mexico or India, choosing a wine can be tough. Your usual dry favorites somehow make the exciting heat of the food downright painful. Blame it on the alcohol. From a pain standpoint, you might be better off with a glass of milk—but, no, that's not an option. Wine it is.

A sweeter, lower-alcohol wine is a much more soothing match for spicy foods. Try a Riesling or Gewürztraminer or—gasp!—a White Zinfandel. With the heat turned down a notch, reds come into play. Pinot Noir and Beaujolais are definite candidates.

Message in a Bottle

It's not foolproof, but one way to estimate a wine's tannin level is by its color. The lighter it is, the less tannin the wine is likely to have. It stands to reason: The longer the skins stay in contact with the clear grape juice during fermentation, the more color and tannins they impart.

Wine and Cheese: The Classic Match

Black and white. Horse and carriage. Gin and tonic. Laurel and Hardy. Wine and cheese. Classic matches, all. Wine and cheese both date back to ancient times—although cheese is the newer kid on the block at about 4,000 years. Wine and cheese both reflect their terroir and continue to mature as they age. With so much in common, their matchup is a natural.

An old wine merchant's saying goes, "Buy on an apple and sell on cheese." It means that wine sipped with a sweet, acidic fruit will taste thin and metallic. The same wine drunk with cheese will seem fuller and softer. But that doesn't mean that all wines pair well with all cheeses. Certain wine and cheese pairings have become traditional, pleasing most of the people most of the time. Here are some of those matchups:

- Goat cheese and Sancerre
- Brie and unoaked Chardonnay or Pinot Noir
- Mozzarella and Chianti
- Parmigiano-Reggiano and Barolor
- Gouda and Riesling
- Chèvre and Gewürztraminer
- Sharp Cheddar and Cabernet Sauvignon
- Stilton and Port
- Roquefort and Sauternes

Wine and Cheese Pairing Guidelines

With the almost infinite number of wines and cheeses available, why stick to tradition? Experimentation is much more fun. These guidelines may help in narrowing your purchasing options.

- ◆ The softer the cheese, the more it coats your mouth—requiring higher acidity in the wine.
- ◆ The sweeter the cheese, the sweeter the wine should be. Some mild cheeses, especially, have a sweetness that requires an off-dry wine. Dry wines may be perceived as acidic.
- ◆ Strong, pungent cheeses need strong wines. Extreme flavors in cheese can be matched by big red wines, sweet wines, and fortified wines.
- ◆ The harder the cheese, the higher level of tannins a wine can have.

Warning: Bad Matches Ahead

A few baseball parks around the country have upgraded and expanded their concessions to include wine. Imagine having a hot dog with chopped onions, mustard, and sauerkraut and . . . well, sometimes you just have to order a beer. Some foods are difficult to match with wine—not *impossible*, but problematic. It's pretty much accepted that certain foods are less than ideal candidates for wine partnerships, such as:

Artichokes	*Olives*
Asparagus	*Spinach*
Chocolate	*Yogurt*

When "difficult" foods are part of the menu, there's a way to get around the food-wine clash (assuming the difficult one isn't the *only* food on the plate): a bite of something neutral, like rice or bread, between bites and sips.

Enemies of Food

On occasion, the wine is the difficult partner. There are some elements in wine that, when they're in full force, just don't taste good with food. Alcohol is one of them. It's a defining part of wine, but highly alcoholic wines are better drunk by themselves. More often than not, lower alcohol wines are more flexible with foods.

Oak can be another problem. The toasty or vanilla flavor is a pleasant taste and a popular style. But oak in abundance is no friend of food. There's nothing wrong with enjoying a wine for what it is—all by itself.

Fail-Safe Measures

Too much analysis can be exhausting! Sometimes you just want to kick back, not think too hard, and enjoy a meal with wine and friends. Yes, there are strategies for those occasions that require easy answers.

Back to the Home Country

You're eating ethnic—German, Italian, French, Spanish. The simple wine solution comes from the home country. Europeans never made a big deal about matching food and wine. They just cooked the way they wanted and made wines that went well with their foods. Globalization of wine notwithstanding, Europeans still produce wines that taste good with their traditional fare.

You're having paella? Bets are that a Rioja will be the best choice. Match your schnitzel and spaetzle with a German Riesling . . . or your osso buco with a Barolo . . . or your pot-au-feu with a Côtes du Rhone.

Of course, the system breaks down when the ethnic region of choice has no long history of winemaking—like Chinese, Thai, Cuban, and Indian. So, on to the next backup strategy.

Food-Friendly Wines

Some wines are just naturally friendly. They make ideal dining partners no matter what you eat. You can choose one of them in any situation with the confidence that it will make a good match. It's as simple as 1, 2, 3.

1. Champagne or sparkling wine
2. Riesling, if you're in the mood for white
3. Pinot Noir, if you feel like a red

Just-Plain-Friendly Wines

Some people have distinct wine preferences. Sure, maybe you think they need to walk on the wild side and try something new for a change. But the wine selection strategy that will be popular every time is to match the wine to the people.

Rarely has a meal been ruined by the wrong wine. If your friends drink exclusively Cabernet, or Shiraz, or White Zinfandel, make them happy by ordering their favorite. All right . . . you can't handle the White Zinfandel with your prime rib. That situation calls for two bottles of favorites.

Savvy Sipping

If the dish you're serving is overly salty and you can't repair the food somehow, the wine can come to the rescue. Serve a wine on the sweeter side—perhaps a Riesling or Muscat. It will make the food taste less salty.

Cooking with Wine

"I cook with wine; sometimes I even add it to the food." It's a funny line from W. C. Fields, but the underlying idea illuminates one of the surest ways to successfully match wine with a meal: Cook with the same wine you serve. The corollary to that piece of advice is don't cook with a wine that you wouldn't want to serve.

Wine Quality for Cooking

The best chefs and home cooks wouldn't be caught dead shaking powdered Parmesan from a can or making do with a mushy cucumber. No, they turn out magnificent meals because they use the finest and freshest natural ingredients. And they know not to skimp on the wine as an ingredient. They may not use a grand cru for their sauces, but the wines they add to a dish are flavorful and worthy of drinking.

Message in a Bottle

Wine left over from a meal is the perfect choice for cooking purposes. It's obviously worthy of drinking! You can easily keep it corked in the refrigerator for later use. Or you can freeze it. Pour the wine into a plastic ice tray. Once it's frozen, put the cubes into a plastic bag and store them in the freezer. Use as many—or as few—as you need.

You've undoubtedly run across bottles of "cooking wine" as you've cruised the supermarket aisles. You know . . . right above the vinegars. That should tell you something. Sure, they're tempting because they cost so much less than a real bottle of wine. But stay away!

For one thing, the wine they started out with wasn't so hot. On top of that, they contain salt as a preservative—which makes them undrinkable. If you can't sip as you cook, where's the fun? (Their undrinkability makes them exempt from alcoholic beverages taxes—another reason they're so cheap.)

Salt in wine is redundant for cooking. It's not that table wine has salt, but wine heightens the natural flavor of foods—making the addition of salt unnecessary. In fact, be judicious with the saltshaker when you're also adding wine to a dish because the wine intensifies salty flavors.

Rules for Cooking with Wine

Because wine has alcohol and acids and flavors all its own, it has certain cooking properties that you should be aware of. Some "rules" are hard and fast because they're based on chemistry. Others are just common sense.

- ♦ When using wine in dishes with milk, cream, eggs, or butter, add the wine first to prevent curdling.
- ♦ Add table wines at the beginning of cooking to allow the alcohol to evaporate and produce a subtle taste.
- ♦ Add fortified wines at the end of cooking to retain their full-bodied taste.
- ♦ To intensify a wine's flavor, reduce it. One cup of wine will reduce to ¼ cup when you cook it uncovered for about ten minutes.
- ♦ Using wine in a marinade will tenderize in addition to adding flavor.
- ♦ If you use wine in a recipe that doesn't call for wine, use it as part of the recipe's total liquid—not in addition.
- ♦ Unless the recipe specifies otherwise, use medium-dry to dry wines.
- ♦ Use white wine for light-colored and mildly flavored dishes and reds for darker-colored and more highly flavored dishes.

Message in a Bottle

A dash of wine can really perk up a familiar dish. Try a splash of dry Sherry in a cream soup . . . or a bit of leftover Sauvignon Blanc in the pan when you've finished sautéing chicken . . . or a cupful of Chianti to add a robust flavor to Italian tomato sauce.

The most important rule of all: Don't add too much. Save some for sipping!

CHAPTER 11

The Cost of Wine: What Goes into the Bottle

You're standing in front of a shelf of Cabernets wondering whether to buy the $10 bottle or the $50 bottle. Your wallet says go for the cheaper one; your palate wonders if the more expensive bottle is five times better. A bottle of wine acquires costs at every stage of its life from the vineyard to the table. Knowing all the costs won't make the $50 bottle any cheaper or the $10 bottle any better. But it will guide you toward realistic expectations and, ultimately, a reasonable decision.

Costs of Wine Production

The fact that one bottle sells for $10 and another for $50 isn't a matter of chance. Winemakers can choose whether they want to make their wines cheaply or expensively. There are lots of variables that go into pricing wine—but it all begins with the grapes.

Growing grapes takes land. Like any real estate, the watchwords for vineyard land are "location, location, location." Some properties are ideal for growing grapes: good soil, proper drainage, good breezes, the right sun exposure. Of course, not all vineyard land is created equal. Some properties, because of the cachet they acquire, command top dollar. The Napa Valley is a perfect example. In 1960 you could have bought an acre of vineyard land there for $2,000. Today, the average price per acre is $200,000. Not all vineyard land is that exorbitant. Elsewhere in the United States and certainly in areas like South America, you'll find affordable land for growing grapes. The cost of the vineyard land goes into your bottle of wine.

Vino Veritas

Winemakers who produce high-end wines like to brag about the low yields of their vineyards. It's not uncommon to hear about yields of less than a ton of grapes per acre. Contrast this to the grapes headed for the lower-priced wines. The yields can be from six tons per acre up to ten tons per acre. One ton of grapes produces about 740 bottles of wine.

How the grapes are grown affects price. It stands to reason that the more grapes you grow on an acre of land, the more wine you can make. On the other hand, it's generally agreed that lower yields produce better quality grapes and more concentrated flavors in the juice. So producers of high-quality wines seek to lower yields even though it will result in less juice. A winemaker who grows grapes in high-yielding vineyards will harvest the grapes by machine with minimum labor cost. To achieve lower yields, another winemaker will thin the vines—meaning she'll remove whole clusters of grapes—by hand. The cost of the bottle goes up again.

Buying Grapes

Winemakers who don't grow their own grapes buy them from other growers. The price they pay depends on the grape variety, the location of the vineyard and, of course, supply and demand. In 2003 Cabernet grapes from Napa Valley sold for about $4,000 per ton compared to about $1,200 for Cabernet grapes from Washington and about $300 for grapes from California's Central Valley.

Grape variety makes a difference. A less-in-demand grape will cost less. In the same year the Cabernet grapes from Napa sold for $4,000 a ton, other grape varieties from the same region had lower price tags. Chardonnay grapes went for $2,300, Pinot Noir grapes went for $2,200, and Riesling grapes sold for $1,800. That too is reflected in your bottle.

Turning Grapes into Wine

Pressing, fermenting, finishing, and aging all contribute to price. One winemaker might squeeze as much juice as possible out of the grapes and then ferment it in huge tanks—filtering and bottling after only a few weeks. Another producer might use minimal pressing, using only the free-run juice, and ferment and age the wine in oak barrels.

Oak is a major cost. American oak barrels sell for about $300, while French oak goes for $750. Barrels hold about 280 bottles of wine. So just aging in French oak could add more than $2.50 to what you pay for the wine. Barrels lose their potency with use, and they have to be replaced. Makers of high-end wines replace them every year.

A typical oak barrel holds sixty gallons and is about twice the size of a garbage can. It could take 150 barrels to accommodate the volume of a single stainless steel tank. And to hold all those barrels requires an enormous temperature-controlled warehouse.

Message in a Bottle

More Winemaker Decisions

Once the wine is produced, the question for the winemaker is whether or not to age the wine. And, if so, for how long. The longer the wine ages, the longer it sits without producing income . . . and the longer it will take for the winemaker to recoup her costs. It could be years down the road.

Packaging to Sell

When wines are ready for bottling, distinctive packaging is a must. The bottle itself can start at fifty cents and go up to $2 for a thicker, higher-quality version. Corks can cost anywhere from ten cents to $1.

The wine needs a label. First, someone has to design it. Then, the labels have to be printed—at twenty to thirty cents apiece. And before the wine goes out the door, it goes into a cardboard case, which can cost up to $7.

Establishing a Price

The winery has measurable production costs that it has to cover if it's going to stay in business. But, in setting a price for the wine, there are other matters to consider. One is the winery's profit. How does the producer allocate that on a per-bottle basis? It will depend on how many bottles it produced. The fewer bottles the winery has to sell, the more it has to charge per bottle. If the winery has lots to sell, the volume will make up for a smaller per-bottle margin.

Another consideration is the perceived value of the wine. The winery wants to position its wine at a price that's in line with other wines of the same caliber and stature. If the producer prices it too high, consumers will buy other wines instead. If the producer prices it too low, not only will the company lose money, but it will hurt the reputation of the wine as well. The winery's goal is to price it high enough to attract serious wine drinkers, but low enough to make sure it all gets sold.

Marketing Costs

If you were around in the '70s, you'll remember Orson Welles and his "Sell no wine before its time" television commercials. Today, the big, branded wines like Woodbridge, Turning Leaf, and Arbor Mist do significant advertising, but most wineries are small and can't afford the millions required to get results. In 2002 wineries collectively spent $122.4 million on advertising. That's a drop in the bucket compared to other industries.

Wineries have marketing expenses, of course, including tasting rooms, sales staffs, and promotions. The reality of how wines are sold—through distributors in each state—means that most of a winery's marketing efforts are directed toward building relationships with those wholesalers.

Message in a Bottle

The cost of a wine is not the best indicator of quality. Admittedly, many production and aging processes are expensive. But beyond a certain point, there are really no differences in the cost of production. If you shell out more than about $30 for a bottle of wine, you're paying for the prestige.

The Distribution System

After Prohibition ended, state and federal laws went into effect that separated the activities of the producers of wine (and all alcoholic beverages) and the activities of the sellers, namely the retailers. Enter the distributor or wholesaler—the middleman. This arrangement for conducting business is known as the three-tier system.

How It's Supposed to Work

Say a California winery (tier one) wants to sell its wine in Tennessee. It shops around for a wholesaler (tier two), chooses the one that provides the best deal, and starts shipping wine. The wholesaler sells the wine to retailers (tier three) and restaurants and pays the state the appropriate excise taxes. The retailer then sells the wine to the consumer.

In the process, the wholesaler:

- Ships the wine to its warehouse from the winery.
- Stores the wine in its warehouse.
- Sells the wine to stores and restaurants.
- Deliveries the wine to purchasers.

A wholesale operation requires people, buildings, and equipment. While markups will vary, a wholesaler will add about 30 percent to 40 percent to the cost of your wine.

State-by-State Variations

Every state has a different way of implementing the three-tier system. Some states have state-controlled liquor boards that act as wholesalers. Some states, like Pennsylvania, also assume the retailer role with their state-run stores. State laws may mandate price posting and specify markups, or prohibit quantity discounts and deliveries to retailers' distribution centers.

Savvy Sipping

States impose taxes on wine, and they go into the price you pay. The average state excise tax is sixty-four cents a gallon—the highest being Alaska at $2.50 a gallon and the lowest being Louisiana at eleven cents a gallon. And don't forget state and local sales taxes. With state budget deficits, many states are considering increasing taxes and fees on alcohol to supplement their income.

Some state laws regulate in-state and out-of-state wineries differently. Many states allow in-state wineries to sell directly to consumers but won't allow out-of-state wineries to do the same. Some states allow their own wineries to sell directly to retailers but, again, prohibit out-of-staters from taking part in the same activity.

These practices have been the basis in the last several years of litigation to open up free trade for wine between the states. A coalition of smaller, family-owned wineries has argued that the system prevents them from engaging in interstate commerce.

The Changing Landscape of Wine Distribution

A couple from New Jersey goes on vacation to California and visits wine country. While there, they find some wines they'd like to send home to enjoy when they get back. That's when they find out about shipping bans between the states. New Jersey is one of twenty-four states that prohibit direct shipment of wine to consumers.

Wineries have always objected to the direct shipping prohibition, but until the advent of the Internet, it was not much more than an irritant to wine drinkers. The power of the Internet to get online merchandise delivered to homes overnight has revolutionized the way people think about free trade and getting the best products at the best prices. These days, with thousands of Web sites selling wines that aren't available anywhere else, interstate shipping of wine has become a national obsession.

There are about 25,000 different wines that are available for sale to consumers in the United States. But only about 500 of them have access to the crowded distribution system and are sold through traditional stores. Online retail sales, which include wine, have grown at ten times the rate of store sales.

Vino Veritas

The Supreme Court Acts

In December 2004 a groundbreaking case went before the Supreme Court. At issue was the clash between the Twenty-first Amendment, which gives the states the right to regulate their own alcohol sales, and the Commerce Clause of the Constitution, which prohibits states from discriminating against out-of-state competitors. One of the reasons the Supreme Court will hear a case is to settle conflicting decisions by lower courts. In the domain of interstate wine shipping, two court decisions—one in Michigan and one in New York—came to opposite conclusions. Both states discriminated against out-of-state wineries in preference of in-state producers. The Michigan court ruled that Michigan's ban on direct shipping was permitted under the Twenty-first Amendment. The New York Court ruled that the shipping ban was unconstitutional. Whatever way the Supreme Court rules, it will take some time for consumers to feel the effects of the changes.

Savvy Sipping

In May 2005 the Supreme Court ruled that it's unconstitutional to grant preference to in-state wine shippers, opening the way for interstate shipment of wine. U.S. states must now allow shipment of wine from other states if they permit in-state wine shipments. But states that do not permit shipping wine at all may still continue to ban it.

Big Retailers Flex Their Muscles

Giant retailers like Wal-Mart and Costco have been able to offer their customers low prices in part because they negotiate large-volume buys directly from suppliers. Under the three-tier system in many states, the retailers can't buy from the producers and can't negotiate for lower prices.

Increasingly, the big-box retailers are looking to state courts for remedies, contending that state liquor regulations violate fair trade laws. Those retailers have a big stake in the outcome. While the court cases may take years to resolve, the decisions will affect what consumers ultimately pay for their wine.

Vino Veritas

Of the 2,700 wineries in the United States, only 350 have output of more than 10,000 cases per year. The wines from large producers are the ones you see most often in the stores because they're the ones that the wholesalers buy. Small wineries with small production rely on direct sales to consumers.

Demand for Wine

No one will ever know why Beanie Babies became such a craze in the 1990s. Tiny stuffed toys that cost pennies to produce—and people were paying fortunes to get them. Clever marketing was certainly involved. As each Beanie Baby was "retired," a scarcity mentality kicked in, and prices went through the roof.

Scarcity in supply determines wine prices as well. Consider the so-called "cult" wines of Napa Valley. Extreme examples, maybe. But these big, robust Cabernets with equally big reputations are made in such miniscule quantities that wine collectors are willing to pay incredible sums for them. It's a universal economic rule at work. When you have a small supply of a product, you can charge a higher price.

Message in a Bottle

Look at single-vineyard wines. The quantity of wine that can be produced in a single vineyard in a single year is finite. When it's gone, it's gone. A winemaker can't go buy more grapes elsewhere. As a result, the price of a winery's single vineyard wine will be more expensive than its others.

A Good Review Doesn't Hurt

Like with movies, a good review for a wine can drive demand. Retailers will tell you that every day of the week customers come into their stores holding a *Wine Spectator* score sheet or the most recent *Wall Street Journal* "Tastings" column. High-profile experts have a lot of power in spurring sales of wines they endorse.

For a lot of folks, the guy next door has even more influence. Word of mouth is powerful—particularly when the mouth belongs to someone whose opinion you respect. Unlike the movies where the price at the ticket window stays the same regardless of a movie's ratings, a wine's popularity has an eventual effect on price.

Price Influences Demand

Certainly, demand affects price. But it also works the other way around. Consider this revealing, perhaps apocryphal, story about Ernest Gallo, the founder of the giant American wine company. During his early years selling wine, he visited a New York buyer. He offered the buyer two samples of the same red wine. The buyer tasted the first one and asked about the price. Gallo told him it was five cents a bottle. The buyer tried the second wine and asked the price. This time Gallo said the wine cost ten cents a bottle. The buyer chose the ten-cent bottle. Sometimes, the more expensive the wine is, the more desirable it becomes. And, sometimes, the reverse is true.

A Price-Influences-Demand Case History

In the late 1990s the United States experienced a domestic grape shortage. In order to maximize their revenue American producers concentrated on making wines that sold for over $14 a bottle. That left a giant opportunity in the low-priced wine market. An Australian company was poised to take advantage of that opportunity.

Back in 1957 Filippo and Maria Casella arrived in Australia from Sicily. After several years of cutting sugarcane and picking grapes, Filippo bought a forty-acre farm. In 1969 he started producing wine. For the next quarter of a century the Casellas made wine and lived in the small, one-story house nestled in their vineyards.

In 1994 Filippo turned the business over to his son John, who expanded the capacity of the winery. By the late '90s the Casella winery was producing a low-priced, well-respected wine that, in its first year and a half, sold 19,000 cases.

In January 2001 John took samples of his wine to a New York importer. The importer liked the easy-drinking, fruity taste and the $7 retail price, although he had reservations about the kangaroo on the label. Well, they immediately introduced the wine into the American market, and in the first seven months, the Yellow Tail brand sold 200,000 cases. The American wine-drinking public jumped on the bandwagon. Three years after its introduction, sales of Yellow Tail reached 7 million cases.

"Hot" Wines Priced to Sell

The early years of the new century brought with them an oversupply of grapes to the wine business. Overplanting of vineyards in Northern and Central California led to a glut, and prices took a nosedive. It meant that producers could get inexpensive grapes and upgrade the quality of their wines at the same time. Similar to Yellow Tail's strategy, the domestic producers identified a price they would sell their wines for and tailored their production and marketing plans to make the price possible.

A number of these "market-driven" wines were introduced that combined above-average quality and prices in the $10 range.

HRM Rex-Goliath Cabernet, Merlot, Pinot Noir, and Chardonnay	$8
Castle Rock Winery Cabernet, Merlot, Pinot Noir, Syrah, Zinfandel, Chardonnay, and Sauvignon Blanc	$7 to $12
Jewel Wine Collection in nine varietals	$10
Three Thieves Zinfandel, Cabernet, Bianco in one-liter jugs	$7 to $10
Jest Red blend	$10
McManis Family Vineyards Cabernet, Merlot, Syrah, Chardonnay, and Pinot Grigio	$9 to $10

From Wholesaler to the Table

The tier-one folks (the producers) and the tier-two people (the wholesalers) have made the wine, packaged it, and delivered it to its selling destination—with their attendant markups. Now, it's on to tier three. First stop: your retail store.

Places that sell wine come in various forms. Depending on where you live, you can buy wine from a corner market, an exclusive wine shop, a supermarket, or a supersized discount warehouse. The similarity among the venues is an average markup of 50 percent over their cost—what the wholesaler charged them.

The other tier-three player is the restaurant. Three times the whole-sale price is the standard markup when you buy a bottle to accompany your meal. The markups can vary among restaurants. A "white table-cloth" restaurant probably charges more than a neighborhood joint for the same bottle.

Message in a Bottle

Charles Shaw wines, better known as "Two-Buck Chuck," introduced a new category of American wines—Super Value Wines—that sell in the $2 range. The winery took advantage of the California grape glut of 2000 and made an exclusive deal with Trader Joe stores to carry its varietals. It made wine cheaper than bottled water . . . and gave consumers a good reason to buy.

Markup variations occur also within a restaurant's own wine list. The least expensive bottles and the most expensive bottles may have higher markups than bottles in the midrange. Wines sold by the glass are marked up the most. While buying by the glass is a real convenience, you can be paying a four-time markup.

Now that you know what costs have gone into a bottle of wine, the choice is yours.

CHAPTER 12

Shopping for Wine

The world of wine changes every day. New vintages are released. New wineries spring up. Old grape varieties are rediscovered. As if those things aren't adjustments enough, the wine marketplace is going through its own dramatic changes. Do you buy bottles or boxes? Do you buy from a neighborhood wine store or stock up online? The savvy wine consumer explores all options.

Wine Stores

Depending on where you live, your wine shopping options can be abundant—or severely restricted. With every state on its own to set rules for wine sales, consumers have unequal opportunities to buy wine. At one extreme are the states that control all aspects of wine sales—from choosing the wines to put on the shelves, to posting store hours, to employing the clerks who bag your purchases. At the other end of the spectrum are states that freely allow sales in locations like supermarkets, discount warehouses, convenience stores, drugstores, and gas stations in addition to traditional wine shops.

Anatomy of a Wine Store

Wine specialty stores vary in size, selection, price points, and employee expertise. But they're the best place for the novice wine drinker to start. You have a good chance of finding someone knowledgeable about wine in general—and certainly knowledgeable about the store's inventory.

Message in a Bottle

If you want to track down wines that were recommended in a newspaper or magazine, by all means take the article with you to the store. Just be forewarned that, with the millions of wine available, your store may not stock the exact wine recommended in the paper. The wine merchant should be able to come up with acceptable alternatives.

In a store that's run by an owner or that has good staff training, the person behind the counter has likely tasted a lot of the wines the store carries. She can direct you to the types of wines you're looking for in your price category, suggest alternatives you might enjoy, or help you select a special-occasion or food-matched wine.

When you want to explore the wine shelves on your own, it's helpful to know a few things common to most stores:

Organization

Wines are often organized by country of origin. For classic regions like France, wines may be organized into smaller regions like Bordeaux, Burgundy, and the Rhone. Red wines and whites may be in separate sections. Other times stores will organize their wines by varietal. There's usually a separate section for sparkling wines. Rare and expensive wines are often located in a specially designated area—and, occasionally, an entirely separate room.

"Sale" Wines

At some point every store has to make room for new inventory and will put wines on sale. You'll often find them in special bins or boxes with case cards—large cardboard signs—describing the wines.

Cold Wines

You're on your way to a friend's house for dinner and need a chilled bottle to take with you. Most wine stores have a refrigerator full of wines just for you. You'll generally find best-selling whites along with (sometimes pricey) sparkling wines. If you're picking up a bottle to take to a tailgate, you may or may not be able to buy a corkscrew at the same time. Some states prohibit wine stores from selling wine accessories.

Take notice of a store's storage conditions. Wines parked in the sunlight or in the heat aren't being treated well. Most better wine shops have temperature-controlled areas for storage. They will also have their wines (except, perhaps, mass market wines that move quickly) lying in a horizontal position.

Savvy Sipping

Shelf Talkers

You've undoubtedly noticed little cards taped to the store shelves that describe individual wines and tell you how well this wine "pairs beautifully with chicken" and that wine has a "lovely finish." They're "shelf talkers." Can you trust them? *Hmm.* They're usually written by the wholesalers or the wineries that produced the wine. Hardly objective sources. They're probably of limited value. Other times the retailer writes them. The store could be steering you toward a good wine with good value. Or the store may have bought a lot of the stuff and wants to move it. Still other shelf talkers give you numerical scores. The question to ask yourself is, Do I know and respect the person or publication awarding this score? If the answer is "no," don't let the score influence your purchase decision.

In-Store Tastings

Some states allow in-store tastings. It's the ideal scenario for buying wine because you get to try it out first. Sure, you're only getting a tiny little taste—and probably out of a little plastic cup at that. And, yes, it might be a wine that the store or wholesaler wants to push. But it's a whole lot better than buying blind.

In areas where in-store tasting isn't possible, retailers often cosponsor winetastings with restaurants. They're inexpensive ways to sample a variety of wines. And, of course, you know where to buy the wines afterward.

Message in a Bottle

A reputable retailer will replace a bottle of wine if it's defective. Just stick the cork back in and take it back. It probably goes without saying that the bottle should be mostly full. Wine merchants who value their customers will often take back a bottle they've recommended if you're not happy with it. A happy customer is a repeat customer.

Discount Warehouses and Superstores

Everybody needs cheap wine at some point. Make that "inexpensive" wine. Who isn't cost-conscious—particularly when you're buying in quantity? The discount warehouse is where you're going to find lower prices. These stores have truly strong purchasing power. They buy single brands of liquor by the trailerload, and their wholesalers jump when they call to place an order.

Discount warehouses can buy for less and afford a lesser markup on their inventory (30 to 40 percent, rather than 50 to 60 percent) because of the volume of business they do. Some of the wines at these stores sell at prices below what the smaller stores pay wholesale for the same wines.

The downside of warehouse or superstore buying is you give up service and selection. It may be difficult to locate someone knowledgeable about the wines. And you don't have a big variety of wines to choose from. The wines are mainly large-production wines that can support the big advertising budgets that go into making them popular. Not that there's anything wrong with that! It's just that the superstores aren't the places to necessarily look for that special, limited production bottle.

Supermarkets account for 30 percent of U.S. wine sales. A combination of convenience and attractive pricing is pushing that number upward. Wine selection at supermarkets reflects the personality of the chain: mass market and highly advertised wines at mass retailers and more esoteric bottles at upscale markets.

Vino Veritas

What Are You Looking For?

The more wine buying and winetasting you do, the more you hone your skills for identifying a good deal. Whether you're a beginner trying to develop your tastes or a wine enthusiast searching for the "ultimate" bottle, the best basic advice is to get to know your retailer. He can give you more than recommendations. Once he knows your preferences, he can give you a heads-up about special arrivals and can give you advance notification of promotions and sales.

Knowing What You Want

With the millions of bottles you have to choose from, where do you start? You start small. First, become familiar with a certain grape. If you particularly like Sauvignon Blanc, start experimenting. Try Sauvignon

Blanc from California. Try Sauvignon Blanc from New Zealand. Try Sauvignon Blanc from different wineries. And, if you get the chance, try them side by side. The differences—and similarities—become obvious.

Get to know a region. If the Cabernet you like is from Alexander Valley, California, try a different Cabernet from that same region. Look for similar tastes that might be due to the climate and soil . . . the terroir.

Find a producer you like and try its other wines. If you like the Chardonnay from Château Potelle, take a chance and buy a bottle of the Cabernet and the Zinfandel and the Sauvignon Blanc. The wines are different, but the winemaker and the philosophy of winemaking are the same.

Strategies for Buying Wine

Maybe you've found a wine that you really like. It's comfortable. It's safe. You buy the same brand each time because you know what to expect. But there's a big world of wine out there. Experimentation, of course, has the potential to be both disappointing and expensive. But it's less of a risk when you have a strategy.

Look for Lesser-Known Varietals

Just as clothing goes in and out of fashion, grapes do too. One varietal can be hot, hot, hot for a time . . . then recede somewhat in popularity as another takes its place.

Message in a Bottle

When a varietal achieves a certain level of popularity, everyone starts to produce it to cash in on the craze. The inevitable result is an influx of mediocre wines. Merlot was a perfect example. Ultimately, though, the fad chasers move on to other varietals. There will always be quality Merlots.

Popularity determines price. It starts in the vineyards, and it extends to the marketplace. Cabernet and Chardonnay are still among the big sellers with the price tags to match. So cast a glance elsewhere for grape deals.

For reds, try:

- Malbec
- Mourvèdre
- Tempranillo
- Grenache

For whites, check out:

- Chenin Blanc
- Pinot Gris
- Gewürztraminer
- Viognier
- Pinot Blanc

Buy Wines from Less Prestigious Regions

Napa, Bordeaux, Burgundy, Tuscany . . . now, you're talking big bucks. Other wine-producing regions around the world with less-expensive real estate offer good wine value. If France is your objective, get a bottle from Provence, the Loire Valley, or Languedoc-Roussillon. If you're in the mood for Italian, look for wine from Campania, Calabria, Puglia, or Sicily.

Spanish wines have become exceptionally popular—with prices inching up as a result. But you can still find bargains from regions other than Rioja: Galicia, Rueda, Navarra, Penedès, and Priorato. You can say the same thing about South American wines. Both Chile and Argentina still are great deals.

Seek "Second Labels"

Wines that aren't quite up to snuff in quality to be bottled by a winery under its primary—and most prestigious—label may be bottled under a second label. It's not that the wine isn't any good. In fact, for wineries that have incredibly high standards, the rejected wine might be very good, indeed. Château Lafite is said to have started this practice in the eighteenth century, and other Bordeaux châteaus followed their example. In great vintage years, the gap between a winery's primary label and its second label is very narrow. Some second labels from famous Bordeaux châteaus:

- Carruades de Lafite from Château Lafite Rothschild
- Pavillon Rouge from Château Margaux
- Haut-Bages-Averous from Château Lynch-Bages
- Château Bahans-Haut-Brion from Château Haut-Brion
- Marbuzet from Château Cos d'Estournel

The United States has its second labels too. When wineries had excess wine that they couldn't sell under their flagship brands, they created second labels. Because the wine sells for less, it's a real value to consumers. Some of those second labels:

- Liberty School from Caymus Vineyards
- Hawk Crest from Stags' Leap Wine Cellars
- Decoy from Duckhorn
- Glass Mountain from Markham
- Bonverre from St. Supery
- Tin Pony from Iron Horse
- Pritchard Hill from Chappellet

Wineries with big budgets have taken second labels in a slightly different marketing direction. Instead of relying on a surplus of wine, they produce wines specifically targeted to the budget-minded. They blend wines from different regions that they can sell at low prices. Beringer produces Napa Ridge. Mondavi produces Woodbridge. Sebastiani produces Talus. And Fetzer produces Bel Arbor.

Unknown Producers in Great Years

Some years are safer than others to gamble on unknown producers. If a region has experienced a terrific vintage year, the wines from the major producers can get out of sight. But the smaller, lesser-known producers have produced wines under the same climatic conditions. The year 2000, for example, is considered an outstanding vintage in Bordeaux. Any 2000 Bordeaux will likely be pretty good.

Check Out the Bin End Sales

When a store is making room for new inventory and puts the "old" bottles on sale, you could run into some treasures. And in larger stores, they might be discounting whole cases. This is a bargain-hunter's paradise. Because you may not be able to tell at a glance which bottles are treasures and which ones are trash, it's prudent to buy just one and try it out first before investing in more.

Buy by the Case

Most retailers offer case discounts. You can mix and match and fill the twelve bottle slots with different wines if you want. The usual discount is 10 percent. Some wine merchants discount further if you buy a case of the same wine. You don't need to have an elaborate wine cellar to take advantage of case savings. It just makes sense if you buy wine on a regular basis.

Screw Tops Make the Big Time

It wasn't all that long ago that the click, click, click of a screw top instead of the pop of a cork meant someone was opening a bottle of cheap swill. My, how times have changed. With tainted corks ruining so many wines—disappointing consumers and costing winemakers millions in the process—it was time someone found an alternative. And there it was, right under everyone's noses. But the cork is sacred to many wine drinkers who enjoy the theater of opening the bottle. So winemakers looking for cork replacements turned first to cork look-alikes.

Plastic Corks

You've, no doubt, run into a plastic cork by now. Some may have looked, at first glance, like a real cork. Some producers wanted to win over cork traditionalists. But most have very un-corklike colors: red, purple, yellow, black. Synthetic corks are made from either medical- or food-grade plastic. They're designed to be inert—so they don't affect the taste of the wine—and seal the bottle efficiently so no air gets in to spoil the wine.

Wines in plastic-stoppered bottles tend to age faster—so you're not apt to see them in wines that require years of aging. Plastic corks are better suited to wines intended for early drinking.

Vino Veritas

Get out your "church-key" for these drink-me-now sparklers. Unlike other sparkling wines that keep the bubbles locked up with corks, Il Prosecco and Il Moscato from Mionetto Wines are topped with a crown cap. They're lightly sparking—*frizzante*, in Italian—and low in alcohol. And they're meant to be drunk right away.

The Stelvin Closure

The screw tops on wine bottles aren't the same ones you find on bottles of Miller Lite. After all, this *is* wine! The Stelvin screw top used on today's wine bottles was developed in the 1950s by a French manufacturer. When it was first introduced in the '70s, it was a complete marketing disaster because the public perception was that the wine inside was cheap and inferior.

In the '90s wineries in Australia and New Zealand adopted the Stelvin closure. It was a hit in their countries. In those days you could often buy an Aussie wine in the United States that had a cork . . . but the bottle had grooves at the mouth that were used back home for a twist-off cap. American wine enthusiasts, it was thought, would never adapt to screw tops. Then in 1997 screw tops got a lot of publicity when Gordon Getty, the owner of Napa's boutique PlumpJack Winery, announced he was going to use the twist-offs for his $150-a-bottle Cabernets.

Many other well-respected wineries have followed suit. Economics play a part because screw caps cost significantly less than corks. But the real issue is protecting the wine. And this time the wine-drinking public seems willing to accept the cork replacement. The tide toward alternative closures may have turned. There is some concern about the Stelvin's performance in long-term aging. But, so far, taste tests are generating optimism. And, with no necessity to keep the cork moist, you can store the bottles upright.

Some "Screwy" Recommendations

- Bonny Doon Ca'del Solo Big House Red and Big House White—$10
- Argyle Winery Merlot—$30
- Screw Kappa Napa—$13
- R. H. Phillips Shiraz—$16

Box Wines Come Out of the Closet

It used to be that wine in boxes was bought by beer-drinking party animals who thought they were doing their wine-drinking friends a favor. The wine was . . . well, not the best. But, with a five-liter capacity, there was a lot of wine inside the box. If you wanted to keep it for weeks, you could. And it wouldn't deteriorate into anything worse.

Message in a Bottle

The wine inside the box is actually contained in a vacuum-sealed plastic bladder. When the wine is dispensed through the attached tap, no air is allowed back in. And the plastic bag collapses. Without air contact to cause damage, the wine will stay fresher longer—a few weeks compared to a couple of days in a bottle.

Considering that the bag-in-a-box system works so well to preserve open wine, it's ironic that it has been used primarily for low-grade wines. Until recently. Some producers have put their premium wines into boxes, and the packaging—once thought to be gauche—is gaining respect. And it has a new name: cask wine.

There have been a few changes. The box is smaller. The popular three-liter box holds the equivalent of four bottles. And the technology for the valve system has been improved. It all makes sense: You can buy more wine for less money; the box is more portable and more easily stored than a bottle; and you can drink as little or as much at a time without oxidizing the wine.

The bag inside the box was invented in the 1950s as a container for battery acid. It caught on as a way to sell wine in Australia—where 55 percent of all wine is consumed in three-liter boxes. Now it's catching on in the United States. Wines that have received top ratings and won medals are going into boxes. A few of the new wines available in a box are:

- Black Box Chardonnay, Merlot, Cabernet Sauvignon, Shiraz—$25 (3 liters)
- Delicato Shiraz, Merlot, Chardonnay, Cabernet Sauvignon—$18 (3 liters)
- Jean-Marc Brocard Chablis Jurassique—$40 (3 liters)
- Banrock Station Chardonnay, Merlot, Cabernet Sauvignon, Shiraz—$16 (3 liters)
- Hardys Chardonnay, Merlot, Cabernet Sauvignon, Shiraz—$16 (3 liters)

The Ripe Stuff

If boxes are so popular, will cans be far behind?

They're here! Sofia Blanc de Blanc, a sparkling wine in a bold, pink single-serving can, is sold in a four-pack—straws included. It's named after Sofia Coppola, daughter of film director Francis Ford Coppola, who just happens to own the winery. It has become the drink of choice at many nightclubs.

Buying Wine Online

The Internet has opened up a worldwide marketplace for products. You can buy a sarong, a garage door opener, and a slab of granite with the click of a mouse. But because wine is a highly regulated product, it's not quite as simple to order it online. If you've already tried making a Web wine purchase, you've noticed that one of the first questions you're asked is where you live. Your state determines whether wine can be shipped to you.

For those U.S. residents who are permitted to ship wine into their states, the Internet is a virtual wine cellar. Selection is almost limitless. No longer confined just to brick-and-mortar stores, wine drinkers can purchase wines directly from their favorite producers or compare prices right at their keyboard.

Some states put limits on direct shipment of wine. Some states ban it outright. New Mexico residents, for instance, can receive up to two cases of wine a month—but only from states with reciprocity agreements. In Florida, Kentucky, Tennessee, and Utah, direct shipping of wine is a felony. Easing of state restrictions seems to be a trend. To check on the rules in your state, go to *wineinstitute.org*.

Savvy Sipping

After the dust settled from the dot-com crashes of the '90s, the online Web merchants who survived came back stronger. And new ones emerged. Today, you can buy wine from Internet-only sellers, from wineries, from traditional retailers, and from individuals.

Even with all the restrictions, online wine sales have risen.

It's possible to search for wine by region, type of wine, vintage year, price, producer, and name. And when you do, you'll get information about ratings, awards, suppliers, winemakers, release dates, latest news— among hundreds of other tidbits. Still, the Internet will never completely replace your local merchant. There's still the need to examine, touch, discuss . . . and drink it tonight!

Rare Finds at Auctions

You're not going to find your everyday wines at an auction. And you're not going to pay everyday prices. Whether an auction is conducted by a commercial auction house, accomplished online, or put on as a fundraiser for a charitable cause, the wines represented will be older, rarer wines. Getting a bargain isn't impossible, but don't count on it.

Many of the wines have been in someone's wine cellar and not on the open market for years. And therein lies a potential problem. You don't know how the wine has been stored. You reduce the risk when you deal with an auction house that has a good reputation and long history.

Vino Veritas

Some of the wines you read about in newspapers that are sold for astronomical sums at auction aren't even drinkable. The 1787 Château Lafite that sold at Christie's for $160,000 was acquired for collecting—not consuming. It had at one time belonged to the famous enophile, Thomas Jefferson.

With almost all auction houses, expect to pay a buyer's premium of 10 to 15 percent of your bid. And while the subject is money, the most important piece of advice for auctions is not to catch auction fever. You know . . . getting caught up in the excitement and the rush of adrenalin when you outbid a competitor. A smarter strategy is getting the catalog ahead of time, identifying the wines you want, and setting bidding limits for yourself. Of course, it's easier said than done—especially if the auction is benefiting a worthwhile organization that will put your money to good use.

Keeping Track of What You Like

If you drink wine, you want to remember whether or not you liked it. The good wine experiences you want to repeat . . . the bad ones you want to avoid. If you're like most people, you think you can remember what you liked and didn't like without writing anything down. This system doesn't work. If you write one sentence about each wine you try, you'll learn what your preferences are and avoid unnecessary disappointments.

If all varietals were created equal, remembering what you enjoyed wouldn't be so tough. But not all Chardonnays are the same, and no two Merlots taste alike. What happens to a lot of people is that they drink a bottle of a certain type of wine they like—maybe an Australian Shiraz—and they think they've found the red wine for them. They may, over time, come to realize that they really only like one Shiraz out of every three or four they try. Without record keeping, it may take a while to figure this out. Worst of all, it's easy to forget which ones you actually liked.

A Wine Journal

By keeping track of the wines you consume, you'll discover more than what wines you enjoy. You'll get a visual idea of the wines you've missed that you need to try. Here's some of the information to include in your journal:

- Name of the wine
- Name of the producer
- Country and region
- Vintage year—if it has one
- Price
- Where and when you tasted it (and with whom)
- Food you ate with it
- Color
- Aroma
- Taste
- Any other comments that may help you remember the wine later

One of the most helpful visual elements in remembering a wine is the label. Removing it can be frustrating, but there are products on the market that can simplify the task. One popular label removal system is a large adhesive strip that you lay over the label and then pull away from the bottle. It splits the wine label and removes only the printed surface, which you can adhere to the page of your journal.

Getting the label off without such aids can be a snap—or it can be problematic, depending on the adhesive the bottler uses. To test, use a razor to take up the corner of the back label. If the back of the label is sticky, fill the empty bottle with the hottest water you can and let it stand for a few minutes. Test the back label again by sliding the razor under the label to start it. It should peel right off.

If the back of the label isn't sticky, you've got more work to do. After you've filled the bottle with hot water, submerge the whole bottle into more hot water and let it soak for a few minutes up to a few hours. Then try removing the label, starting the process with the razor. Some people have more success when they add soap or ammonia to the soaking water. Good luck! The process might be more fun with a little wine.

CHAPTER 13

Entertaining at Home

Wine is certainly an everyday beverage. But it can take on a special significance when you're entertaining. The wine you choose and the way you serve it send a message to your guests. That doesn't mean exorbitantly expensive wines and pompous presentation. It means matching the wines to your friends and to the occasion—casual and formal alike—and taking care to show the wines at their best.

Choose Your Entertaining Style

Some men wouldn't be caught dead in a suit. Some women would never even consider going without pantyhose. Just as people have personal styles in dressing—some formal, some casual—they also have style preferences for entertaining. The great thing about wine is that it goes with all styles.

Your personality has a lot to do with the kinds of entertaining you're likely to enjoy. Consider whether you:

- Are outgoing—or more reserved
- Don't mind being the center of attention—or prefer the periphery
- Like to have detailed plans—or enjoy being "free-form"
- Are budget-minded—or don't have to worry about such things
- Are label-conscious—or oblivious

Look to your personality traits when you're planning to entertain at home. You want to be able to enjoy your own party—so choose a form of entertaining that you're comfortable with. That's not to say that you shouldn't "stretch" outside your comfort zone. But even if you're about to have a kind of party you've never hosted before (like a winetasting!), you have a variety of ways to make the event fit your style.

How would you describe the parties you like going to? Small, intimate dinner parties? Outdoor barbecues? Body-to-body cocktail receptions? Family get-togethers? Poolside festivities? Whatever the activities—whether the event is indoors or out, or large or small—there's always the opportunity to bump up the celebration with wine.

Glassware Basics

It's safe to assume that every wine drinker—regardless of snob level, income level, or age—has drunk (and enjoyed) wine out of a plastic glass. Was it their first choice? Hardly. But it proves that an imperfect vessel isn't going to completely ruin a wine. It may not show the wine at its best, but you know what they say: any port in a storm.

When you entertain in your own home, you have choices. One of them is what glassware to use for serving wine. Yes, *glass*ware. Glass, unlike plastic, is inert and doesn't affect the taste of the wine. What kind of glass?

- **Clean**—You might think that goes without saying, but there are all sorts of lingering "contaminants" that can make a wine taste off. Even if you've done your best in washing the glass but haven't rinsed it well, it will have detergent residue. If you've dried it with a dirty dishtowel, it'll have the telltale odor. Even dust will affect the wine's taste.
- **Clear**—Most wine enthusiasts will tell you it's important to see the wine—to check its clarity, to determine its age, or to just admire the color. A colored glass will not let you do any of those.
- **Thin**—Glasses with rolled rims can make the wine dribble into your mouth. A thin glass will present less foreign matter to come between you and the wine.
- **Stemmed**—The stem allows you to not hold the bowl of the glass in your warm hand and, by contact, warm the wine.
- **Tapered**—The bowl should narrow at the rim. It'll keep you from spilling when you swirl. And it will capture the aromas and not let them evaporate before you get your nose to the glass to sniff.

Buying Wineglasses

Do you need a different wineglass for each kind of wine? No. Do you want a different glass for each wine? Only you can answer that. It certainly depends on your interest, your budget, and your storage space. If you're just starting a glassware collection, it's helpful to know which ones to buy first, second, and third. This is a logical approach to purchasing stemware:

1. Start out with a twelve-ounce glass. You might think that sounds pretty big considering that a typical serving of wine is four to five ounces. But you want to leave plenty of room for swirl-

ing. You can use this as an all-purpose glass for either red or white wine.

2. A Champagne flute should be next on the list. Champagnes are the only wines that shouldn't be served from an all-purpose glass. The flute is tulip-shaped to keep the effervescence contained. The sherbet-style glasses let the bubbles dissipate too quickly.

3. Now it's time for another all-purpose glass—either larger or smaller. It depends on whether you want to use it for red wines (which traditionally are served in the larger glass) or for white wines. This decision will depend on your personal preference. If you want to choose whatever is in fashion, go with bigger.

4. Especially if you enjoy dessert wines and fortified wines, your next purchase should be a copita. It looks like a miniature version of the Champagne flute. The average serving size of a dessert wine is two to three ounces—so a smaller glass is called for.

Message in a Bottle

Once you move beyond the basics of stemware, other details might be important to you. Crystal, with an inherently rougher surface than glass, will create more turbulence when you swirl your wine—adding to the aromas. If you want different glasses for reds and whites, the one for reds should have a rounder bowl than the one for whites because reds are generally more aromatic.

Corkscrewing Around

Even though wine producers are increasingly turning to screw tops instead of corks as closures for the bottles, corks are still the traditional closure—and will probably be around for some time to come. So if you're going to drink wine at home, you'll need a corkscrew. There are hundreds—maybe thousands—of corkscrews available. But they fall into some general categories.

From the low-tech end of the spectrum are the "pullers." You probably have one in a drawer that some company gave you instead of a pen with the company logo on it. They take the form of a T-shape with a handle and a worm. And there are no moving parts—which is why it depends on sheer force (yours) to get the cork out of the bottle.

The two-pronged puller requires less force but more finesse. It has no worm but two blades that you wedge into the bottle to grip the sides of the cork and pull. Professionals like it particularly for older corks that are in danger of crumbling. It's known as the "Ah-So." And it takes some practice to use.

Lever-type corkscrews can take a variety of forms from something you can put in your pocket to something you can mount on the wall. The most ubiquitous lever type is the butterfly corkscrew. It has a worm and butterfly-wing handles for leverage. The simplest lever corkscrew is the "waiter's friend"—so-called because it's the favorite among restaurant servers. It's got either a dual or single lever. Then there's the popular "rabbit" corkscrew with gripping handles on the sides and a top lever handle.

What is a worm?

The Ripe Stuff

The worm is not something you find at the bottom of the bottle as you do in certain tequilas. It's the curly metal prong found on most corkscrews that bores into the cork for removal. To avoid getting cork pieces into your wine while you're extricating the cork, be sure the worm doesn't go completely through the cork.

Before you can insert any corkscrew into the cork, you have to remove the capsule that surrounds the cork end of the bottle. In days gone by the capsules were made of lead, but producers today use foil or plastic. Cut them off with a small knife or the foil cutter that comes with many corkscrews. To avoid wine dripping over the edge of the foil, be sure to cut it low enough on the neck of the bottle—under the second lip of the bottle.

Serving Tips

Wine seems so temperamental. Coffee you serve hot, lemonade you serve cold. Easy. No fuss. With wine, different styles require different temperature. Personal preference is a factor. Should a wine breathe or be poured the moment it's opened? What's an attentive host to do?

Serving Temperature

Serving wine too cold masks its aroma and flavor. Unless it's a wine you want to disguise, you don't want to overchill it. The cold also brings out any bitterness in the wine. On the other hand, serving a wine too warm will make it seem flat and dull and overly alcoholic.

The familiar rule for reds is to serve them at room temperature. But you have to take that advice in context. The rule was conceived when the "room" was in some stone castle with no central heating. Room temperature really means wine cellar temperature—somewhere between 50 and 55°F. Whites are served colder. Now, don't make yourself crazy with exact temperatures, but the following will give you some guidelines:

- *Sparkling wines and young, sweet white wines:* 40 to 50°F
- *Most whites:* 43 to 53°F
- *Rich, full-bodied whites:* 50 to 55°F
- *Light reds:* 50 to 60°F
- *Medium-bodied reds:* 55 to 65°F
- *Bold reds:* 62 to 67°F

Message in a Bottle

White wines stored in the refrigerator are often too cold to serve, and reds stored at room temperature are often on the warm side. To compensate, follow the Twenty-Minute Rule. Twenty minutes before you serve your wines, remove the white from the refrigerator to warm it up a bit, and replace it with the red to cool that one off.

Chilling a wine from room temperature will take from one to two hours in the refrigerator, depending on the final temperature target. You can reduce the time to about twenty minutes by submerging the bottle in a container of half ice and half water.

When to Let a Wine Breathe

Letting a wine breathe means exposing it to the air. The oxygen begins to age the wine. In young red wines with high tannins, the exposure "softens" the tannins much like a few years of aging will do. You'll notice that as you sip a wine from your glass over time, the taste will subtly change. Some say the wine "opens up." Not all wines benefit from breathing. Most whites and Rosés don't need to breathe. As a general rule of thumb . . . if a wine needs no further aging, it doesn't need to breathe.

Savvy Sipping

Oops! You somehow got fragments of cork into the bottle of wine. Or you discover, just minutes before serving, that your wine has sediment. There's no time to let things settle. You can filter the wine into a decanter through clean fabric such as muslin or through a paper coffee filter with no adverse effects.

Some people have interpreted "breathing" as simply uncorking the bottle in advance of pouring. The truth is wine can't breathe in the bottle. The neck is just too small to let enough air inside. Studies involving wine experts have demonstrated that no one can really tell the difference between a wine that's been breathing in the bottle for minutes versus one that's been breathing in the bottle for hours.

If you really want to aerate your wine, pour it into your glass, swirl it around, and let it sit for a while.

Decanting Your Wine

A wine can require decanting for two reasons: It needs aeration or it needs to be separated from sediment that has settled with aging. For breathing purposes, simply pour the bottle of wine into a decanter for serving. And if it *really* needs to breathe (like it's just too tannic to drink otherwise), pour it back and forth between two vessels a couple of times.

Decanting to remove sediment is a more delicate process. Stand the bottle upright. Let it stand that way as long as possible so the sediment falls to the bottom of the bottle. A couple of days is ideal, but even thirty minutes is helpful. Remove the cork without disturbing the sediment.

With a candle or flashlight standing next to the decanter, slowly pour the wine in a steady stream into the decanter. The light should be focused below the neck of the bottle. That way you'll be able to see the sediment the exact moment it appears. And that's your signal to stop pouring.

Serving Wine at Your Dinner Party

A dinner party puts you in control of events—barring any bad behavior on the part of your guests, of course. You orchestrate the meal—the courses, the ingredients, the preparation methods, the timing, the presentation . . . and the wine. Everyone will be eating the same foods—so you don't have to worry about matching the wine to six or eight or ten different dishes.

When you plan your food-wine matches, you can start either with the food or with the wine. If you're a particularly good cook—or if you have a special recipe that you want to showcase—that's the time to choose the wine based on how it will complement the food. If the food is to be the star, you'll want a wine in the "best supporting" role. If you have some exceptional bottles of wine that you've acquired and want to serve to an appreciative audience, you'll choose foods with some subtlety.

Wines in Sequence

A dinner party is like a staging a play. There's a sequence of events and a defined beginning, middle, and end. When your guests arrive, you can't just usher them into the dining room and make them eat. There's predinner chitchat that requires a light accompaniment. Why not start with sparkling wine with hot or cold hors d'oeuvres? An aperitif is meant to stimulate the appetite, and bubbly fills the bill.

Now, it's time for dinner. If you're serving more than one kind of wine with the meal, there's a general progression that works best for enjoyment. Serve white wines before reds, light wines before heavy ones, and dry wines before sweet ones. Yes, there are always circumstances that defy the rules. Say you have a light-bodied red and a full-bodied white. Which rule do you break? It's your choice. Or maybe you don't like red wines at all. There's nothing wrong with serving all whites.

In some circles, there's another rule: Drink lesser wines before better ones. The reasoning is that (like the play analogy), there's a big payoff at the end. It makes sense—but only to a point. After, say, the third wine, your guests will drink anything.

How Much Wine to Buy

How many bottles of each should you buy for your dinner party? With so many variables—your friends' passion for wine, the number of courses you plan to serve, if you plan to have a different wine with each course, the pace of the evening—there's no definitive answer. But there are guidelines. For total wine purchases, plan on one bottle of wine per person. Table 13-1 shows how it breaks down according to the number of guests.

13-1 Dinner Party Wine Purchase Plan

	BOTTLES OF EACH WINE				
Number of Wines	4 Guests	6 Guests	8 Guests	10 Guests	12 Guests
2	2 bottles	3 bottles	4 bottles	5 bottles	6 bottles
3	1 bottles	2 bottles	2 bottles	3 bottles	4 bottles
4	1 bottles	1 bottles	2 bottles	2 bottles	3 bottles
5	1 bottles	1 bottles	2 bottles	2 bottles	3 bottles

Dessert wines are a separate consideration altogether. You can serve them as an accompaniment to a dessert—or *as* dessert. The serving size is much smaller, and the bottle size is half that of a table wine.

The Gift of Wine

At some point, the tables will be turned, and you will be the one taking a bottle of wine to a dinner party. The important thing to remember is to let your host know that it is a gift and not necessarily meant to be served that evening. To get him off the hook, say something like, "This is for you to enjoy later."

If you would like to take a wine to be served at dinner, call the host ahead of time to let him know. That way you can take a wine appropriate for the food. And if you want your bottle oohed and aahed over, make sure the dinner will be a small gathering that will be properly appreciative.

Savvy Sipping

You've carefully selected your wines. You have a plan for which wine to serve with what food. As you greet your guests at the door, each one hands you a thoughtful gift of wine. What do you do? You say a gracious "thank you." You're not obligated to serve them—unless, of course, you want to.

Wine for Cocktail Parties

A cocktail party is any festive social event where people mingle and meet—reception, open house, mixer. "Cocktail" party implies that you'll be having . . . yes, cocktails with spirits and mixers and ice. In recent years, people have been drinking wine in place of cocktails—so it deserves a place at any cocktail party. The real question is whether you're going to offer a full range of drinks or whether you plan to limit the offerings to wine, beer, and nonalcoholic drinks.

The advantage to the latter is you don't have to worry about who's going to do all the mixing of drinks. But it's your choice. Now you have to determine what wines to buy and how much.

Choosing the Wines

Here you're walking a fine line between a good-quality wine that you'll be proud to serve and a budget that you've established for solid reasons. A discussion with your retailer can be of real help here.

Consider the wine drinking preferences of your friends. Are they mostly white wine drinkers? Or red drinkers? Or a mix? Or, do they predominantly fall into the blush wine category? Even when you know your friends' preferences well, there's no way to predict with any certainty what they'll actually drink. (The night of your party your best red-wine-drinking buddy has switched to white!) All you can do is take your best guess.

When you don't know your guests well enough to know their preferences, it's safe (and thoughtful on your part) to stock both a red and a white. Cocktail parties deserve wines that are easy-drinking and that will be acceptable partners to the foods you'll be serving. While wines can be made in wide ranges of styles, here are a few suggestions:

- ◆ Sauvignon Blanc or Pinot Gris for easy-drinking whites
- ◆ Riesling for food-friendly white
- ◆ Beaujolais for light, easy-drinking red
- ◆ Pinot Noir for food-friendly red
- ◆ Tempranillo or Côtes du Rhone for smooth, down-the-middle reds

Calculating Your Wine Purchases

The amount of wine you buy will depend on how many wine drinkers you expect and the length of the party. For ease of calculating, say you expect twenty wine drinkers for a three-hour cocktail party. Based on each person drinking a five-ounce glass of wine each hour, the equation looks like this:

20 (wine drinkers) × 5 (oz.) × 3 (hours) =
300 (Total Ounces) ÷ 25.4 (ounces in a bottle) = 11.8 (Total Bottles)

(Twelve bottles is a case. You get a case discount!) Is the equation absolute? Of course not. You may want to adjust the numbers if your guests are heavy drinkers—or light drinkers. If it's an open house, guests may not stay for the full three hours. Party planning is not an exact science. If you're going to err, err on the side of overstocking. If you've selected your wine wisely (meaning you like it), leftovers won't go to waste.

For large parties, consider buying wine in containers larger than the standard (750 ml) bottles.

Magnums, for example, can offer savings. And with better wines now available in boxes, they, too, are an option. Here's a chart to help you in your calculations for different size containers.

13-2 Contents of Typical Wine Bottles and Containers

Size	Ounces	5-oz. Servings	4-oz. Servings
187 ml	6.3	1	1
375 ml	12.7	2	3
750 ml	25.4	5	6
1 L	33.8	6	8
1.5 L	50.7	10	12
3 L	101.4	20	25
5 L	169.0	34	42

Winetasting Parties

Definition of winetasting party: solemn gathering of pompous individuals swirling, spitting, and uttering terms like "carbonic maceration" in reverential tones. Not! A winetasting party can be anything you want it to be. Start with your intention. Do you want your event to be educational in nature so that your guests come away having learned something new about wine? Would you rather assemble a bunch of different wines and let your guests learn something by guzzling the wines on their own? There's room for both of these approaches—and everything in between.

"Traditional" Winetastings

Traditional winetastings have a structure of sorts. And they need a leader—someone knowledgeable about the wines being served who can facilitate discussion and answer questions. If you're not comfortable in that role, it's not too difficult to locate someone who is. A phone call to a wine store or your favorite restaurant is usually all you have to do. (Make sure the person in the lead role has a sense of humor and is willing to go with the flow of your party.)

Who do you invite? Anyone—regardless of their wine sophistication—who has an interest in sampling and learning about wine. How many wines do you serve? As many as you want—but five or six wines work well.

When you're planning your wine purchases, remember that a "tasting" serving is much smaller than the typical four- or five-ounce glass of wine. About two ounces is the norm. You can get twelve servings from a standard bottle. Buy a little extra just in case one of your guests wants to come back for another taste.

Savvy Sipping

Seat guests at a table with empty wineglasses in front of them—one for each wine if possible. Not everyone has that much stemware, but you can rent glasses if you want to go that route. Or you can limit the glasses to one or two per person. If you'll be tasting both reds and whites, splurge and go for two per person. In any case, have a pitcher on the table to rinse the glasses between wines. And, of course, a dump bucket for the water (or, heaven forbid, a wine).

As with the sequence of wines for a dinner party, the general guidelines are white before red, light before heavy, and dry before sweet. In selecting the wines, you might want to consider a "theme." Consider these traditional options:

- **Vertical tasting**—You serve several bottles of the same wine from the same producer, only from different vintages. For example, you could serve a Silver Oak Cabernet Sauvignon from Napa Valley from 1997, 1998, 1999, 2000, and 2001. The objective is to identify the wine's traits that appear from year to year—or the differences from one year to the next.
- **Horizontal tasting**—No, not a tasting while everyone is reclining. You serve the same kind of wine from the same year from the same general area but from different producers—say Pinot Noirs from

Oregon's Willamette Valley from the 2003 vintage from different wineries.

♦ **Blind tasting**—You keep the identity of the wines secret while they're being tasted. That way no one is influenced by the reputation of a particular winery or region or vintage. Go ahead, include a jug wine in the tasting and see how it compares in the judging.

Message in a Bottle

Food has a place at a winetasting. It can be as simple as some unsalted crackers for guests to cleanse their palates between wines. At a structured tasting, you don't want the food to interfere. But an alternative "theme" would be a food and winetasting to see how certain flavors—salty, fatty, acidic—affect the taste of the wines.

Wine "Drinking" Parties

Informality suits some hosts (and guests) better than structure. But having a more casual winetasting party doesn't mean that everyone can't learn—or sample—something new. A straightforward (and economic) strategy is to invite your guests to bring a bottle of wine and be prepared to tell the group a little something about it. Depending on your guests, the background information might turn out to be serious wine geek stuff or less-serious information.

Allot one wineglass per person and place water pitchers and dump buckets around the party rooms. As different wines are being poured, call on the guest who brought it to describe the wine and explain why she chose it.

Themes create a fun atmosphere for these less formal tastings, where your guests bring a wine related to the theme.

♦ **Kentucky Derby:** Leaping Horse Merlot, Equus Run Vineyard Chardonnay, Two Paddocks Pinot Noir
♦ **Academy Awards:** Marilyn Merlot, Francis Coppola Diamond Series Syrah
♦ **Anniversary:** Iron Horse Wedding, Cupid Chardonnay

Holidays with Wines

Holidays present their share of challenges—completely separate from the challenges of family dynamics. Certain foods are traditional. They're not always the foods you think about pairing with wines. Fried chicken on the Fourth of July. Tacos al carbon on Cinco de Mayo. Black-eyed peas on New Year's Day.

Picnic Wines

Ever notice how many holidays involve eating outdoors? A serious Cabernet just doesn't taste right when you're out in the sun frolicking around a pool or running to catch an overthrown softball. No, it's time to drink something that can take a good chill.

- *Think white*: particularly a fruity white.
- *Think pink*: a chilled, dry Rosé is made for picnics.
- *Think light*: not all reds are big and bold (sure, chill the reds too).

Thanksgiving Wines

The problem with picking out a wine for Thanksgiving dinner isn't matching it to the turkey. It's all the other stuff. Every household has a well-established menu—with many of the recipes having been passed down for generations. You're not about to give up these foods anytime soon. Cranberry-walnut mold, sausage-apple stuffing, orange-praline sweet potatoes, pumpkin cheesecake. With all the competing flavors, it's hard to know what to match.

Sometimes it's best to not worry at all. Pick out a wine that you know you like. It may not go with everything on the table—but what would? If it turns out to be a horrendous match, eat first and drink the wine later. There's always a solution. If you're looking for more concrete wine recommendations, take a look at some popular Thanksgiving wines on the following page.

- ◆ Champagne
- ◆ Chenin Blanc
- ◆ Riesling
- ◆ Gewürztraminer

- ◆ Rosé
- ◆ Beaujolais
- ◆ Pinot Noir

Post-Party Tips

The party's over. Dirty dishes. Even more dirty glasses. Wine stains on the tablecloth. Leftover wine. What? Leftover wine? The best remedy for leftover wine is to drink it. But sometimes that's not the wisest move.

The wine has already started its inevitable decline. Its youth and vigor diminish with each passing minute. Oxygen and heat are the robbers. But even though you can't completely stop the premature aging, you can slow it down some. Recork the bottle and put it in the refrigerator. The cold will slow the chemical reaction that spoils wine. The advice goes for both white and red wines.

Wine bottles that are half full of wine are also half full of air. Removing the air is your goal, which you can accomplish with a set of marbles. Add them to the opened bottle until the level of the wine reaches the top. Recork and refrigerate.

Vino Veritas

There are devices on the market that pump the air out of the bottle, creating a vacuum, and others that replace the air with an inert gas. Some devices use nitrogen, which isn't completely inert. A system called Supremo uses argon gas and has been successful in keeping wine for a week.

But even with the best systems, you can't keep the wine forever. Usually, it's just days before the wine becomes dull and flat. Wines have different abilities to withstand the ravages of oxygen and time. For a wine to stay in relatively good condition once it's been exposed to the air, it needs to be capable of aging in the first place. High-tannin reds are the most durable because they were meant to age. Whites won't last as long.

The Big Cleanup

The morning after a party in the light of day you discover . . . red wine stains! The tablecloth, the carpet, your shirt. You'll find advice all over the Internet about ways to eliminate the stains, but your options for an effective resolution come down to two:

1. *Wine-Away:* It's a fruit-based formula in a spray bottle that you can use on carpet stains and as a presoak for laundry.
2. *A laundry presoak recipe from the UC Davis Department of Viticulture and Enology:* Mix equal parts 3 percent hydrogen peroxide and Dawn liquid dishwashing soap. Pour it on the stained fabric and launder as usual.

Now, on to cleaning your glassware. If you're washing the glasses by hand, use as little detergent as possible, the hottest water you can stand, and rinse, rinse, rinse. Sponges specifically designed for cleaning wine-glasses are available to make the job easier. If you use a dishwasher, wash glasses only (not dishes or pots and pans), and don't use any detergent. In addition to leaving an odor, detergent can etch the surface of your crystal. Crystal is more porous than glass and easily absorbs tastes and odors.

CHAPTER 14

Wine at Restaurants: You're in Charge

How many articulate, high-powered executives have been reduced to indecisive, gutless wimps when handed a restaurant wine list? Plenty! But that's not your style. Sure, choosing the perfect wine match may be intimidating. Sure, you've got a spending limit on your Visa card. Sure, all eyes are on you. But by the time you finish this chapter, you'll know what to order when, how to order it with panache and confidence, and how to do it within your budget.

A Restaurant's Attitude Toward Wine

Restaurants have "attitude." And you see their attitude in everything they do from the time they take your phone reservation to the moment they hand you the check. When it comes to wine, their attitude is just as obvious.

The Wine List

The first clue to a restaurant's wine personality—and to the kind of wine experience you're likely to have—is the "list." It can be as simple as a glass of red, a glass of white, and a glass of pink. No one is saying this is good or bad or right or wrong. You merely adjust your expectations accordingly. If you happen to be in a small ethnic restaurant offering some *vino bianco* from the homeland, this could be a wine night to remember.

At the other restaurant extreme, you might be handed a list with thousands of wines that requires weight training just to lift. The upside is that the establishment clearly has an interest in wine, and you can't help but find *something* to drink. The downside is too many pages and too little time.

Vino Veritas

More than 3,300 restaurants worldwide have received *Wine Spectator* Awards for their wine lists. The award criteria include such things as regions represented and thematic match with the menu. But size also matters. *Award of Excellence* winners have at least seventy-five selections, *Best of Award of Excellence* winners have 350 or more, and *Grand Award* winners have 1,000 or more.

A restaurant reveals its attitude not only by the number of wines it offers. Selection is another key. Some lists will give you household names—highly advertised, popular, everyday wines. Who could object to that? You know what you're getting: comfort and dependability. But where's the excitement?

Restaurants that really care about their customer's wine experience will offer a varied selection—some familiar names, some unknown—regardless of list size. You can decide for yourself whether you're in the mood for something tried-and-true or ready for an adventure.

The Server

Who presented the wine list to you? Was it your waiter or a sommelier? The sommelier is the restaurant's wine specialist (and not all restaurants have one) who creates the wine list and often serves the wine. Any restaurant with a sommelier (usually high-end places) cares about wine. Sommeliers have a reputation for being snooty. In reality, that's rarely the case. They're knowledgeable, well-trained professionals who can guide your wine selection based on preferences, food pairings, and price. Chances are, a sommelier will make your decision-making effortless.

Without a sommelier, next in line to answer your wine questions is the waiter. That can be a mixed bag. If well trained, the server will be acquainted enough with the wines to describe to you how they taste. If not . . . well, you're on your own.

Even if your server isn't equipped to provide a knowledgeable recommendation, he reflects the wine attitude of the restaurant in other ways. He may or may not be trained to present and pour according to long-standing wine traditions. He may or may not be attentive to you when your glass is empty. Or he may be overzealous in pouring by prematurely topping off the glasses so you run out of wine before your entrée is served—necessitating another bottle, of course.

Glassware

If you went to a restaurant and ordered a $30 steak and then got plastic utensils to eat it with, you'd be plenty mad. But that's the kind of treatment most of us have come to accept when we order wine: a pricey Cabernet served in cheap glasses.

The typical glassware is either too small or too thick. Sometimes the glasses have no stems—which may be acceptable for a theme restaurant—but an eatery that makes wine a priority shows its wine-drinking customers respect by using appropriate glasses.

Wine by the Glass

What a concept! Wine by the glass has made it so easy—and relatively inexpensive—to throw caution to the wind and experiment with new and unfamiliar wines. But watch how a restaurant treats its opened bottles.

As soon as a bottle is uncorked, the wine begins to deteriorate because of contact with the air. So proper storage is paramount. There's a big difference in attitude between a restaurant that has an expensive preservation system that keeps wine fresh and a restaurant that's content to leave an opened bottle sitting on a counter until tomorrow's lunch crowd charges through the door. Of course, there's ample room in between these extremes for careful handling of opened wine.

Message in a Bottle

One of the advantages of ordering by the glass is that a restaurant is usually willing to give you a "taste" before you buy. More than likely, the bottle is already opened. The restaurant pleases a customer, and you get the chance to either confirm your first choice or change your mind.

When you order a wine by the glass, it's perfectly acceptable to ask your server when the bottle was uncorked. If the wine has been hanging around for a day or two, you might be well served to make another selection.

Deciphering the Wine List

How wines are presented and described on the list can be helpful in your decision-making—or not. There's no way of predicting what you'll find—except, of course, for the prices. Wine lists come in all shapes, sizes, degree of description, and degree of accuracy.

Basic Classifications

Most often, wines will be listed under general headings of red, white, sparkling, and dessert. This presentation is limited in its usefulness. But it does come in handy for unfamiliar Old World wines—the ones that are named after geographical locations with no mention of grape variety. Like Château Canon La Gaffeliere Saint-Emilion. (It's red.) Or for varietal wines made from grapes you've never heard of. Like Lemberger. (It's red too.)

This generic-type wine list will occasionally include after-dinner drinks in its dessert wine section. So, in addition to Sauternes and Ports, you may find liqueurs and single-malt Scotches.

Listing by Country or Varietal

More detailed lists may be subdivided by country, region, or varietal. In this scenario, wines might be listed under French Reds, Italian Reds, and American Reds or specified further by Bordeaux, Campania, and California. With varietal listings, likely headings in the white wine section are Chardonnay, Sauvignon Blanc, and Pinot Grigio.

"Stylish" Wine Lists

Words like *big, full-bodied, fresh, oaky,* and *dry* may be more meaningful than geographical and varietal headings to someone not acquainted with a particular wine. And that's why a lot of wine lists are organized according to their style. Under a white heading of "Dry and Crisp," you could find a Pinot Grigio alongside a Sancerre and Chablis. A short but descriptive "Big Reds" might include a California Cabernet and an Italian Barolo. When you have no clue about a wine's grape heritage or region of origin, you'll get the general idea of taste from this sort of listing.

Progressive Lists

Some lists will put wines in some sort of progressive sequence—like from lightest in style to richest. In such a list you could expect to see a Beaujolais at or near the top, perhaps a Chianti in the middle, and a Cabernet at the end. Another "progressive" technique is listing the wines by price—either cheapest to most expensive or the reverse. This is helpful to the cost conscious and the status conscious. Really—who wants to be seen ordering the cheapest wine when it's so glaringly listed at the top?

The Ripe Stuff

How much wine should I order for a group?

The rule of thumb is about a half bottle per person—although that could go way up or down according to your group's drinking profile. For a group of three or more whose wine preferences you don't know, it's always safe to order both a red and a white.

Strategies for Choosing a Wine

When was the last time your restaurant meal was ruined by a bad wine selection? Probably never. Sure, some matches may not have been exactly ethereal, but, chances are, you were able to enjoy the meal anyway. In the worst case, you might have had to "enjoy" the food and wine separately. So, first piece of advice: Don't sweat it. Now . . . on to specific strategies.

Strategy #1: Keep It "Friendly"

Certain wines are known to be food-friendly. For whatever reason, they can pair equally well with pompano and peanuts. It only makes sense, at a restaurant when everyone at the table will be ordering something different, to choose a wine that will go with everything.

Among the food-friendly wines are Pinot Noir and Riesling. One red, one white. That's all you have to remember. How easy can you get? The group wants red? Order a Pinot Noir. You'll find terrific Pinots from Oregon and California. And, of course, the Burgundy region of France. The group prefers white? Try an exceptional Riesling from upstate New York, Canada, Germany, or Alsace.

Message in a Bottle

Ordering a Riesling has challenges. Rieslings range in overall character from bone-dry to supersweet. Dry Rieslings can usually be identified by "dry" on American labels and "trocken" on German labels. Rieslings are sometimes listed with other names. Johannisberg Riesling, Rhine Riesling, and White Riesling are all "real" Rieslings. Riesling Italico and Riesling-Sylvaner are different grapes altogether.

Strategy #2: Get a Sneak Preview

The one sure-fire way to choose a wine with confidence and impress your dining partners with your knowledge and sophistication is to have an advance copy of the wine list to study. In the quiet and comfort of your own home, you can decide what varietal, what winery, what vintage, and what price are best. And you can also learn to pronounce Pouilly-Fuissé (poo-yee-fwee-SAY).

A lot of restaurants today have Web sites—and a good share of those have their wine lists (in whole or in part) available there. The next option is a fax. Most restaurants will be pleased to send you the list, provided you're not calling them during their peak business hours. And the old-fashioned way still works: Make an in-person visit a day or two ahead of your reservation.

Savvy Sipping

Be careful about ordering older vintages. They can be risky choices. First of all, they're expensive. And being older could mean they're more fragile. They're on the list for a reason, of course. But that could be because no one else was sucker enough to buy them.

Strategy #3: Ask for Help!

There's no shame in asking for help. In fact, it shows a good deal of self-assurance. The person to ask is the sommelier.

If you're imagining the sommelier is a seventy-year-old tuxedoed Frenchman looking down his nose at you, you're behind the times. Today's sommeliers are often younger, hipper, and just as likely to be a woman as a man.

Vino Veritas

The sommelier of yore had a silver cup hanging around his neck on a ribbon. Called a *tastevin* ("taste wine" in French), it dates back to the cellar masters of Burgundy who used them to sample wines in near-dark cellars. The dimples in the metal reflected what light there was and made it possible to check the wine's appearance.

They're more like tour guides than professors. They'll ask you a bunch of questions about the kinds and styles of wines you like, what you might be ordering to eat, how open you are to try something new and different. And during your conversation, the sommelier will probably get a feeling for how much you plan to drink and how much you want to spend.

Sommeliers know their wine lists intimately . . . because, in most cases, they've created them. They have chosen the wines, negotiated the purchases, overseen the storage, written the descriptions, and trained the staff to serve the wines. Sommeliers are enthusiastic about sharing their wine finds. Sometimes they've been able to buy bottles that aren't available in any retail store. This could be your night to sip something truly remarkable.

Wine Etiquette

For a beverage that dates back thousands of years, you'd expect there would be some traditions that go along with its consumption. Nowhere is that more obvious than inside a restaurant.

Presentation of the Cork

Way back when before wine bottles had labels, there was no real proof that a particular bottle of wine came from the winery it was attributed to. Human nature being what it is, some unscrupulous restaurateurs would pass off common French wine as having come from the famous châteaus. To maintain their good reputations, the châteaus began branding their corks. And restaurants began presenting them to customers to verify the wine's origin.

The practice continues to this day long after the need to do so has passed. So, what are you, the diner, supposed to do with the cork once the waiter has plopped it down in front of you? Anything you want. Ignore it. Examine it if you prefer. Sniff it if you feel like it. Slip it into your pocket to take as a souvenir. The cork won't tell you anything that won't be evident in the glass.

Savvy Sipping

Corks that are either dry and crumbly or completely wet are a clue that air may have crept into the bottle and spoiled the wine. A taste will tell you. Occasionally, harmless tartrate crystals form at the end of the cork that had contact with the wine. They have no effect on taste.

Presentation of the cork will become less of an issue as more and more wineries opt for screw top closures. Unless there's a winning sweepstakes number inside the cap, the screw top probably won't be presented for inspection.

The Tasting Ritual

You've seen the winetasting dance dozens—if not hundreds—of times. The *pas de deux* of wine server and wine sampler. What's all the fancy footwork about? Back in the days before modern winemaking methods, wine would often go bad—so patrons were offered the opportunity to sample their wine before drinking it. That's still the reason for the ritual. It's not merely to see if the wine meets your expectations. It's not to test your wine knowledge and show you up as a rube. It's simply to make sure you're getting the wine you ordered and that the wine is in good condition.

Here are the steps in the routine. The waiter presents the bottle for you to visually inspect. You check that it's the same wine and same vintage that you ordered. If not, speak up. If the wine you ordered isn't available, your server should make a recommendation for a similar wine *in the same price range*.

The waiter cuts the capsule and removes the cork. He puts the cork on the table in front of you. You've already mastered this step.

The waiter pours an itsy-bitsy, teeny-weeny bit of wine into your glass. You admire it. Study the wine against a white or light background—like the tablecloth or napkin.

If the wine's color and clarity have met with your approval, it's time to swirl. Really get that wine moving around the glass. Now stick your nose right into the glass . . . and breathe deeply. *Ahh!*

Assuming the aromas have been pleasing, take a sip. Hold the wine in your mouth. Roll it around on your tongue before you swallow.

Now to the big finish. The wine is acceptable, and you nod to the waiter. That's his signal to pour for the group.

That's all there is to it. Take a bow.

Message in a Bottle

When you order a second bottle of a different wine, the waiter brings clean glasses. And you repeat the ritual. When the second bottle is the same wine, the waiter brings one clean glass and offers you the opportunity to taste again. It's up to you. The restaurant is under no obligation to bring clean glasses for everyone, but it's a nice gesture.

Sending a Wine Back

Whew! You took a whiff of the wine. No fruitiness there. It smelled more like a damp basement. You tasted it. You know there's something wrong. It's time to send the bottle back.

"I'm afraid this is a bad bottle, and I'd like to send it back." That's all you have to say. A waiter who knows wine will probably smell it for himself and cart off the offending bottle. He'll return with a replacement. Even if you're the only one who perceives the flaw, the waiter will most likely replace the wine anyway.

You don't have to feel bad that it's a financial hardship for the restaurant. The restaurant will, in turn, send the bottle back to the distributor for replacement.

Sample Before You Order

The tasting ritual is all about the condition of the wine—not just whether or not you're happy with your selection. But wouldn't it be nice to know ahead of time that you were going to like the wine you ordered?

A restaurant isn't about to open a bottle of wine just for you to taste. It would be too wasteful—and expensive—if you didn't like it. But if the bottle you're considering is also available by the glass, it's a different story. Chances are, your waiter will give you a small sample to try. And if he doesn't, you can always buy a glass to try. Then again . . . there's something very bold about venturing into the unknown.

BYO Restaurants

Some of the best restaurants for enjoying wine have no wine lists at all. That's because you "Bring Your Own." You can pick out something special from your cellar or stop at a wine shop on the way and pick up something from the closeout shelf. You don't pay restaurant markups at BYOs. But you can expect to pay a corkage fee—for wine service and use of the restaurant's glassware. The fee is usually a per-bottle charge and can vary dramatically.

Wine enthusiasts with extensive collections and individuals who just have a special bottle will, occasionally, want to drink their wines at a restaurant over dinner. Restaurants with wine lists who permit this form of

BYO obviously lose out on a wine sale. That's why they charge high corkage fees.

There are some rules of etiquette to follow when you want to take a bottle to a wine-serving restaurant. Never take a bottle that is already on the restaurant's wine list. Call in advance to check. In fact, calling ahead is always a good idea. When you explain that you've been saving this special wine for ten years to drink in celebration of your tenth anniversary, what restaurateur won't be charmed?

At tipping time, don't forget to do the right thing: Tip your waiter according to what the bill would have been had you ordered the wine from the restaurant's list.

Getting the Most for Your Money

Let's face it—money is often a top priority when you choose a wine. If you had unlimited financial resources, you could order anything that struck your fancy. And if you didn't care for it—what the heck, you could order something else. *Time for a reality check.* The goal is to get the best possible wine for the dollars you plan to spend—in other words, the best value for your money.

Savvy Sipping

Mozart made you do it . . . spend more on wine, that is. A British study has shown that when restaurants play classical music, their customers buy pricier wines. Apparently, Beethoven, Mahler, and Vivaldi make people feel more sophisticated and more willing to pay for the pleasures of the grape.

How Restaurants Price Wines

Pricing policies are as different as the restaurants themselves. But here's a general rule of thumb. If the wholesale price of a bottle of wine is $10, a retail wine shop will charge $15. A typical restaurant will charge $20 to $30 for the same bottle.

The markups vary from wine to wine—the biggest markups being at the low and high ends of the list. At the low end, the wines are cash cows. Some customers want their wine and they want it cheap—and they're not too picky about what they get. And the restaurant makes a killing.

At the other end of the list, you have a different scenario. The restaurant is selling either to the extremely well-heeled or to expense account diners who are indifferent to what the wine costs. Ka-ching! At the middle of the list, the wines usually have lower markups. And that's where you'll find the best value.

Some restaurants—especially those committed to the wine drinking public—have another approach. Their objective is to get their customers to drink more and higher-quality wines, and they achieve this through a pricing strategy of adding about $10 to the retail price of the wine. Even with these modest markups, the restaurant still makes money—and attracts faithful customers.

Vino Veritas

Flights of wine are small tastes of wine (about two ounces apiece) served by a restaurant as a series. The four-to-six offerings are often based on a theme—Italian reds, for example, or whites with oak or wines with funny names. The purpose is to present wine lovers an opportunity to experiment with new wines at a reasonable cost.

More Tips for the Value-Conscious

No one wants to be regarded as a cheapskate. But common sense says that if you maximize "value," you can order more bottles for less money. Here are some ways to do that:

- *Unless you're familiar with the "house" wine, skip it in favor of something else.* The restaurant probably bought it on the basis of price and gave it the highest markup.
- *Buy by the bottle.* A standard bottle contains four to six glasses of wine—depending on the size of the pour. Once you've purchased three wines by the glass, you've paid for a whole bottle.

- *Choose a wine from the same region as the restaurant's food specialty.* A good Italian restaurant, for example, will have a creative—and usually value-priced—selection of Italian wines.
- *Look for varietals that aren't all the current rage.* Chardonnays, Cabs, and Merlots have been hot sellers in the past and have commanded higher dollars. Cast your eyes elsewhere for, say, Chenin Blanc or Pinot Gris or Malbec.
- *Experiment with wines from parts of the world where the land itself is less expensive (and, hence, the end cost of the wine is less expensive), like South America.*

CHAPTER 15

All Things Bubbly

Champagne rings in each new year, launches mighty ships, and celebrates newlywed vows. Bubbles are consumed to commemorate auspicious occasions—from royal coronations and corporate mergers to the birth of a child. Sparkling wine is synonymous with celebration. And, more and more, it's become the partner to everyday events too. Bubblies come by different names, in lots of styles, and from places far removed from France. The informed wine drinker knows how to choose the right one for any occasion.

Champagne vs. Sparkling Wine

What's the big deal? Who cares whether you call it Champagne or sparkling wine? The French do! They've protected the name Champagne by international treaty—which means, technically, only sparkling wines produced in the Champagne region of France can bear the name on the label. The treaty, by the way, doesn't apply in the United States.

The term "*champagne*" has become generic in the United States to mean all bubblies. A hundred years ago Korbel used "champagne" on its labels. And so have others. It's been only in the last few decades that France has actively sought to protect the name. So, American marketers, with a century of tradition behind them, continue to call their product champagne. And most people—wine geeks included—do the same.

Making the Bubbles

Champagne is more than a name. It's a universally adored beverage whose bubbles are created in a time-consuming and labor-intensive process. The technique, *méthode champenoise*, has six basic steps:

1. Grapes are fermented for about three weeks to produce still wines.
2. The producer blends his still wines according to what style he wants to achieve. This base wine is called the *cuvée*.
3. The wine is bottled and laid down. During the next nine weeks or so, a second fermentation takes place inside the bottle—producing carbon dioxide in the form of bubbles.
4. The wine is aged—anywhere from nine months to several years—according to the producer's specifications.
5. The bottles are rotated from a horizontal position to a vertical, upside-down, position. This allows sediment to collect in the neck of the bottle close to the cork so that it can be removed easily and quickly. Rotating the bottles is called *riddling*.

6. The neck of the bottle is frozen and the sediment (in the form of a frozen plug) is removed—called *disgorging*. At this point, sugar is added (a process known as *dosage*)—the amount dependent on how sweet the producer wants the final product. And the bottles are recorked.

Another sparkling process, the transfer method, is similar to *méthode champenoise* except that, instead of riddling and disgorgement, the wine is transferred after the second fermentation to pressurized tanks and filtered. You have to read the fine print on the label to know. "Fermented in *this* bottle" means traditional method. "Fermented in *the* bottle" means transfer method.

Savvy Sipping

Cheap Bubbles

The traditional method of producing bubbles is expensive. The price you pay is a reflection of that. You can bet that when you buy a $5 bottle of sparkling wine, it was produced another—cheaper—way. The Charmat method (also known as bulk method, tank method, and cuve close) was likely used. It involves conducting the second fermentation in large, closed, pressurized tanks. With this process, you can produce a lot of wine in a short period of time—so the sparkling wine is ready to drink not long after harvest. Maybe only a few weeks. Here's what happens:

1. Still wine is put into closed, pressurized tanks, and sugar and yeast are added.
2. Fermentation takes place, and carbon dioxide forms in the wine—producing a sparkling wine with an alcohol content higher than the base wine.
3. The wine is filtered under pressure to remove any solids.
4. Sugar is added to adjust to the sweetness level desired, and the wine is bottled.

An even less expensive technique is sometimes used that simply injects carbon dioxide into the wine—like a carbonated soft drink. If that's the case, the label on the bottle will say "carbonated."

Savvy Sipping

The bubbles will tell you something about what method was used. *Méthode champenoise* produces tiny bubbles that float upward in a continuous stream. Cheaper bubbles are large and random and don't last as long. Bubbles from carbonation aren't integrated into the wines like in Champagne—so they'll quickly disappear, much like the bubbles in your can of Coke.

Grapes Matter

To be "real" Champagne, only three grape varieties are allowed: Pinot Meunier, Pinot Noir, and Chardonnay. Pinot Meunier contributes a youthful fruitiness. Pinot Noir gives Champagne its weight and richness and is responsible for its longevity. Chardonnay adds lightness.

One of the most important decisions a Champagne-maker has to make is how to blend these grapes to make the base wine. Wines from the different varieties and vineyards are kept separate. The producer then blends the wines (including wines from past years) in varying proportions to create its distinct cuvée. This is what distinguishes the ultimate taste of one producer's Champagne compared to others.

For sparkling wines produced by other methods, there are no such strict rules regarding grape variety. Generally speaking, tank-fermented bubblies tend to be fruitier than their Champagne counterparts.

History of Champagne

Until the mid-1600s, Champagne as we know it didn't exist. The region produced still wines, which were very popular with European nobility. But Champagne had yet to be "discovered." The Champagne region in northern France has a cold climate, posing problems for growing grapes and winemaking. Cold winters and short growing seasons mean that grapes had to be harvested as late as possible to get them as ripe as possible. That meant just a short time for fermentation because the cold temperatures of winter would put an end to the process. So the wines were bottled before all the sugar had been converted to alcohol.

Then spring would arrive, and fermentation would begin again—this time in the bottle. When the bottles didn't explode from all the pressure that had built up from the carbon dioxide inside, the wines had bubbles. To the winemakers of the time, bubbles were a sign of poor winemaking.

Dom Pérignon, the Benedictine monk who's often called the inventor of Champagne, was one of those winemakers. He spent a good deal of time trying to prevent the bubbles. He wasn't successful, but he did develop the basic principles used in Champagne making that continue to this day:

- He advanced the art of blending to include different grapes and different vineyards of the same grape.
- He invented a method to produce white juice from black grapes.
- He improved clarification techniques.
- He used stronger bottles to prevent exploding.

When Dom Pérignon died in 1715, Champagne accounted for only about 10 percent of the region's wine. But it was fast becoming the preferred drink of English and French royalty. A royal ordinance in 1735 dictated the size, weight, and shape of Champagne bottles as well as the size of the cork. Two historic Champagne houses came into existence: Ruinart in 1729 and Moët in 1743. By the 1800s the Champagne industry was in full swing.

Vino Veritas

Madame Clicquot, a young widow who ran her husband's Champagne house after his death in 1805, was the first to solve the sediment removal problem. She cut a series of holes in her dining-room table so that the bottles could be positioned upside down at 45-degree angles. After several weeks of turning and re-angling the bottles, all the sediment collected in the neck.

Champagne Houses

Unlike other French wines that are named after growing regions, Champagnes are named for the houses that produce them. The houses, in turn, produce various brands of Champagne—called marques. The largest and most famous of the houses are known as Grandes Marques. You guessed it: big brands! Twenty-four of them belong to an organization that requires they meet certain minimum standards. Some of the more recognizable members are:

- Bollinger
- Charles Heidsieck
- Krug
- Laurent-Perrier
- Moët et Chandon
- G. H. Mumm
- Perrier-Jouët
- Pol Roger
- Pommery & Greno
- Louis Roederer
- Ruinart
- Taittinger
- Veuve Clicquot-Ponsardin

Beginning with Moët et Chandon in 1974, a number of French Champagne houses opened up shop in California. They produce sparkling wines the traditional way using the same grape varieties as in France: Pinot Noir, Chardonnay, and Pinot Meunier. The French-American productions include Domaine Carneros (owned by Taittinger), Domaine Chandon (owned by Moët et Chandon), Mumm Cuvée Napa (owned by G. H. Mumm), Piper Sonoma (owned by Piper-Heidsieck), and Roederer Estate (owned by Louis Roederer).

Vino Veritas

Madam Lilly Bollinger, a young widow who took control of the esteemed Bollinger Champagne house, had this to say about bubbly: "I only drink Champagne when I'm happy and when I'm sad. Sometimes I drink it when I'm alone. When I have company I consider it obligatory. I trifle with it if I am not hungry and drink it when I am. Otherwise I never touch it—unless I'm thirsty."

"Grower" Champagne

While some of the major Champagne houses have sizeable vineyard holdings, they still buy most of their grapes from the 20,000 or so small growers in the Champagne district. The small growers, who collectively own about 90 percent of the vineyards, are increasingly making their own Champagnes. About 130 of these grower Champagnes are available in the U.S. market (out of the 3,747 sold in France). You've probably never heard their names (they can't afford to pay for promotion and advertising like the big guys), but they offer high quality and bargain prices.

How do you recognize a grower Champagne? It's on the label. In the lower right-hand corner of the front label are two letters followed by some numbers. The letters that will tell you it's a grower Champagne are either "RM" or "SR." Here are all the possible letters and what they mean:

- NM (*Négociant-Manipulant*)—The term means merchant-distributor. These are the big houses. They buy grapes in volume from independent growers.
- RM (*Récoltant-Manipulant*)—The term means grower-distributor. This is a grower that makes and markets its own Champagne.
- SR (*Societe de Récoltants*)—This is basically the same as grower Champagne. Two or more growers share a winemaking facility and market their own brands.
- CM (*Cooperative-Manipulant*)—This is a cooperative of growers who bottle their product together—although these wines can include purchased grapes.
- RC (*Recoltant-Cooperative*)—This means a grower sends its grapes to a cooperative to be made into wine. The grapes can be blended with other wines in the cooperative.

Choosing a Champagne

A Champagne house establishes its reputation based on a particular style. Many factors influence the style—grape varieties, vineyards, blending choices, tradition. The objective of each house is to provide consistency from one year to the next. When you find a Champagne that you like, you can be sure it will have the same characteristics year after year.

Vintage Years

Champagne is produced every year. But "vintage" Champagne is only produced in the best years. Like in all other regions, some grape harvests in Champagne are better than others. In exceptional years, a house will decide to make its bubbly using only the grapes from that harvest—and will date the bottle with that year. In the years in between, the house blends wines from multiple years. It's termed *non-vintage* (NV). Blending across years is one reason you can expect uniform quality.

Vino Veritas

For a Champagne to qualify for a vintage date, at least 80 percent of the grapes used in producing it have to have been harvested that year. The other 20 percent can come from reserve wines from other years. A vintage Champagne has to age for three years before its release but can be, and often is, aged longer.

Nonvintage Champagne represents most of a house's production—80 percent or more. They're usually lighter, fresher, and less complex than their vintage counterparts.

From Dry to Sweet

If Champagne were like most other wines, the grapes would be picked when they're perfectly ripe. They'd have plenty of natural sugar to be converted to alcohol. But, alas, that's not the case. The grapes are less than ripe. So the winemaker has to add enough sugar so the yeast will have adequate fuel to convert into alcohol. How much sugar is up to the winemaker. And, needless to say, adding more sugar will make the

Champagne taste sweeter. Then, there's another addition of sweetness at the end of the process right before bottling. Sweetness levels of Champagne are important parts of their styles. Progressing from dry to sweet, these are levels:

- **Extra Brut (also called Brut Sauvage, Ultra Brut, Brut Integral, Brut Zero)**—driest of all but not a common style
- **Brut**—the most popular style and considered to be a good balance of sweetness to dryness
- **Extra Dry (or Extra Sec)**—dry to medium-dry
- **Sec**—medium-dry to medium-sweet
- **Demi-Sec**—sweet
- **Doux**—*very* sweet

Variations on a Theme

Pink Champagne! The accompaniment to romance! Rosé Champagne gets its pink color in one of two ways. The winemaker can leave the skins of the grapes in brief contact with the grape juice during the first fermentation . . . or add a little Pinot Noir wine to base the wine blend. People sometimes think of Rosé Champagne as sweet (maybe because they associate it with sweet blush wines), but it's definitely dry. It's available both as a vintage wine and as nonvintage.

Blanc de noir has a hint of pink, too. In wine terms, *blanc de noir* means "white wine from black grapes." This Champagne is made from just one of the permitted grapes: Pinot Noir or, less often, Pinot Meunier. It's fuller than Champagnes with Chardonnay in the blend. *Blanc de blanc* is another one-grape bubbly. It's Chardonnay all the way. It's lighter and more delicate than Champagnes that also include Pinot Noir.

Name Your Size

Have you ever noticed those superlarge Champagne bottles on display at wine stores and restaurants? Well, they're not just some marketing tool. They're real. Champagne is bottled in ten different sizes, shown in Table 15-1.

Table 15-1 Champagne Bottle Sizes and Names

Measure	Size Equivalent	Servings	Popular Name
187 ml	quarter bottle	1	split
375 ml	half bottle	2	half
750 ml	standard	4	fifth
1.5 L	2 bottles	8	magnum
3 L	4 bottles	17	jeroboam
4.5 L	6 bottles	24	rehoboam
6 L	8 bottles	34	methuselah
9 L	12 bottles (1 case)	50	salmanazar
12 L	16 bottles	68	balthazar
15 L	20 bottles	112	nebuchadnezzar

Only the half bottle, standard bottle, and magnum contain Champagne that's undergone the second fermentation in the bottle. And the three largest sizes are rarely made anymore. How many people must it take to pour from them?

Savvy Sipping

Champagne "splits" are handy because of their size—about a serving and a half. But, even though they are corked just like their bigger brothers, they don't keep as well. So drink them up right away before they lose their freshness.

Champagne by Any Other Name

The fact that a sparkling wine is produced outside of the Champagne region of France doesn't mean that it's inferior. It's just a little different. Some sparklers are made with the exact same grapes employing the same traditional method. They'll be different because of the terroir—the taste the earth has given to the grapes—and the blending choices of the winemaker. But even some experts have failed to recognize the difference between well-made bubblies from inside and outside the Champagne region.

French but Not Champagne

Even in the Loire Valley (so close to Champagne) they can't use the Champagne name on the labels of their sparkling wines. The region known, in part, for its use of Chenin Blanc grapes in Vouvray uses the same grapes for its bubblies. The effect is refreshing and creamy.

The eastern regions of France, including Alsace, are known for blending Pinot Noir, Pinot Blanc, and Pinot Gris for their sparkling wines. The bubblies turn out crisp. French sparkling wines produced outside of Champagne are labeled "Vins Mousseux."

Spanish Bubbly

It used to be called "Spanish Champagne." Then in 1970 the European Union banned the use of the term outside of Champagne. From then on Spanish sparkling wines have been known as *Cava*. The word is Catalan for "cellar," referring to the underground cellars where the wines are aged.

To qualify as a Cava, the sparkling wine has to be produced in the traditional method using specified grape varieties. The list includes Chardonnay and Pinot Noir, which are used in the best wines, but producers still use the "big three" indigenous grapes: Macabeo, Xarel-Lo, and Parellada.

Using atomic spectrometry to measure metal concentrations in the wines, researchers at the University of Seville in Spain correctly identified bottles of Champagne versus bottles of Cava 100 percent of the time. The measurements reflected the trace metal content in the soils where the grapes were grown. This technique could be used in the future to detect wine fraud.

Vino Veritas

Cavas are usually light and crisp and inexpensive. Look for:

- Freixenet Cordon Negro Brut—$10
- Segura Viudas Aria Brut—$12
- Mont-Marcal Brut—$12
- Codorniu Brut—$12
- Paul Cheneau—$10
- Fleur de Nuit—$7

Italy Sparkles

Oh, so many bubblies to choose from in Italy . . . starting with Prosecco. It's made from the grape of the same name in the Veneto region of northeastern Italy. Prosecco comes both fully sparkling (*spumante*) and lightly sparkling (*frizzante*). They're crisp and dry and inexpensive. They've become very popular, and you see more and more of them on restaurant wine lists.

Then there's the more familiar Asti (in the past known as Asti Spumante) made from the Muscat grape. Its second fermentation takes place in pressurized tanks in a modified version of the charmat method, and its taste is semisweet to sweet. Asti's cousin is Moscato d'Asti. It differs from Asti in that it's *frizzante* instead of fully sparkling, sweeter, lower in alcohol, and is corked like a still wine. Both should be drunk young and fresh.

Lambrusco is another Italian option. Most Americans know it as pink, semisweet, and *frizzante*. But it's also made white and dry.

Vino Veritas

Germany may not be known for sparkling wines, but it produces a whole lot of it. Most of it is consumed within its own borders. It's called *Sekt*, and it's made using the charmat method. Riesling is used for the better wines. If the bubbly has been made using just one variety, the grape name will be on the label.

Domestic Sparkling Wine

Sparkling wine is made almost everywhere still wine is made—the two largest producing states being California and New York. In California, particularly in the cooler climates of Sonoma and Mendocino counties, many wineries produce excellent bubblies. And not just the ones with ties to France. Names to look for: Gloria Ferrer, S. Anderson, Iron Horse, Schramsberg, to name just a few. While California gets most of the attention, sparkling wine has been a mainstay of New York winemaking since before the Civil War when French Champagne-makers were recruited there by local wineries.

Some sparkling wine recommendations from around the United States:

- Château Frank Brut (New York)—$28
- Argyle Brut (Oregon)—$40
- Gruet Brut (New Mexico)—$14

Storing and Serving Bubbly

You never know when you'll need a bottle of Champagne. A friend drops in to say she's gotten (pick one): engaged, divorced, promoted, a raise, a diploma, a puppy. You need an appropriate way to celebrate: Champagne. Or you get home after a long day of arguing with your boss. You need an effective mood enhancer: Champagne. It's the universal beverage. Keeping a supply just makes good sense.

How to Keep It When You're Not Drinking It

Champagne is sensitive to temperature and light. Like other wines, it does best stored in a cool, dark place without big temperature fluctuations. You don't need an expensive cooling unit—a 50°F basement usually works fine. Champagne is ready for immediate consumption as soon as it leaves the Champagne house, but if you provide the right conditions for your bubbly, it'll last for three to four years—if you haven't drunk it by then.

And don't be afraid to keep it in the refrigerator. A couple weeks in the cold isn't going to hurt it.

Message in a Bottle

Bubbly is best served around 45°F. It will take three to four hours in the refrigerator to cool a bottle. But you can quick-chill your Champagne in about twenty minutes by immersing the bottle in ice water. It's faster than ice alone. Half ice and half water in an ice bucket is the way to go. No bucket? The kitchen sink will do.

"Popping" the Cork

First word of advice: Popping the cork wastes bubbles. The cork should be removed so the sound you hear is a soft "sigh." Removing the cork in this slow manner also reduces the risks of killing someone in the room. (After all, there are 70 pounds-per-square-inch of pressure in that bottle!) Here's a checklist for how to safely open your bottle of Champagne:

1. Remove the foil covering.
2. Stand the bottle on a counter for support. (It's safer than holding the bottle in your arms and possibly pointing it at someone.)
3. Get a towel. Keep one hand over the top of the cork with the towel between your hand and the cork. Untwist the wire cage. Remove the wire.
4. Keep the towel on top of the cork with one hand and put your other hand on the bottle at a point where you have a good grasp.
5. Turn the bottle—not the cork. You'll feel the cork loosen a bit. Keep a downward pressure on the cork as it completely loosens and finally releases.
6. Hold the cork over the opened bottle for a few seconds to ensure the Champagne doesn't escape.
7. Pour!

Pour slowly. Because of the bubbles, the liquid rises quickly . . . and you can end up with overflow (and wasted Champagne!) before you know it.

Drinking Vessels

You've undoubtedly seen the sherbet-style glasses that were popular in the 1950s. Now that "retro" is so chic, the glasses are everywhere. Buy them if you want . . . but don't use them for Champagne. Long-stemmed flutes are the glassware of choice for sparkling wines. The elongated shape and slight narrowing at the rim enhance the flow of bubbles and keep them from escaping.

There's no need to chill the glasses. If you do, they'll just fog up and cloud your view of the bubbles.

Vino Veritas

Because of its rougher surface, crystal produces more bubbles than ordinary glass. If you want the effect of crystal without the expense, do what restaurants do. Lightly scratch an X in the bottom of the inside of the glass with the tip of a knife. This gives the bubbles something to cling to—just like the crystal.

A couple more words about glasses. If there's soap residue on the glasses, you may experience lots of foam that doesn't subside—caused when the carbon dioxide meets the detergent. To prevent this always rinse the glasses thoroughly when they're washed. And dusty glasses will destroy the bubbles.

Champagne Leftovers

On the rare occasions that the bottle of bubbly hasn't been emptied, your main objective is to save the bubbles for another day. Your best bet to preserve the effervescence is a Champagne bottle stopper. It's made of metal with a spring and special lip to grab the rim of the bottle. They're available

Champagne Recipes

Champagne is divine all on its own. The aroma is captivating. The flavor is delicious. The texture is creamy. The bubbles are exciting. The finish is . . . sparkling. The only other ingredient you really need to enjoy Champagne is a glass. But Champagne also works in combination with other ingredients to make some really fun cocktails.

If you have a bottle of inexpensive bubbly that's just too sweet for your taste, you can rescue it with a lime. Squeeze a few drops of juice into your Champagne glass and top with the bubbly. It will add some needed acidity and make the taste less sweet.

Classic Champagne Cocktail

Sugar cube, Angostura bitters, Champagne

Place the sugar cube in the bottom of a Champagne glass. Add two dashes of bitters and fill the glass with Champagne. Garnish with a lemon peel.

Bubble Bubble Toil and Trouble

½ ounce black vodka, ½ ounce pear nectar, Champagne

Pour the vodka and nectar into a Champagne glass and fill with Champagne.

Tropical Rain Champagne

½ ounce melon liqueur, ½ ounce coconut rum, Champagne

Pour the melon liqueur and rum into a Champagne glass. Slowly fill the glass with Champagne by tipping the glass so that the green melon layer is on the bottom. Garnish with a cherry.

Campaign Trail Champagne Cocktail

¼ ounce grenadine, ¼ ounce blue Curacao, Champagne

Fill a Champagne glass with dry Champagne. Pour in the grenadine, allowing it to sink to the bottom. Gently float the blue Curacao on top.

in most kitchen stores and in wine stores in states that allow them to sell wine accessories. A good backup procedure is to wrap the bottle opening with two layers of plastic wrap and secure it with a rubber band.

Message in a Bottle

For quality Champagnes, you can usually stick the uncorked bottle back in the refrigerator overnight and still have bubbles in the morning. What happens is that inert and heavy carbon dioxide gas from the bubbles forms a protective layer on top of the wine, preventing oxidation and containing the bubbles below. But a day—maybe two—is about as long as the protection will last.

Alas! You open the refrigerator door, and all the bubbles have disappeared. There are still last-ditch efforts you can make to try to revive the patient. One is to put a raisin in the bottle. Another is to put a paper clip into the bottom of each glass before you pour the Champagne into them. It's always worth a try. Remember, even without bubbles, Champagne makes an excellent cooking wine!

Leftover Champagne Trivia

You never know when you'll be on *Jeopardy!* and have to answer a Champagne question for the big win. Some facts—and some near-facts—may come in handy. It's your responsibility to put the following in the form of questions:

- ◆ A bottle of sparkling wine has 49 million bubbles.
- ◆ The average diameter of a bubble is 0.5 mm.
- ◆ Way back when, the foil wrapped around the outside of the cage was lined with lead to prevent mice from eating the cork.
- ◆ The indentation at the bottom of a Champagne bottle is called a *punt*.

Now, go ahead. Impress your friends with your knowledge of all things bubbly.

CHAPTER 16

Dessert Wines and Fortified Wines

To paraphrase Shakespeare, "A dessert wine by any other name would taste as sweet." In the United States "dessert wine" means fortified wines—both sweet and dry. In Australia dessert wines are called "stickies." Elsewhere in the world, dessert wines refer to sweet wines in general. By whatever name, they've recently become the darlings of the wine world—with prices to match.

Sweet Wines in History

The popularity of sweet wines has gone through cycles. One day they're on top of the heap, next day they're out of favor. Some of them were almost accidents of nature. Others were more accidents of commerce. Whatever their origins, they've had a resurgence in popularity of late.

Sweet wines go back to ancient times. The most acclaimed wines in Rome were sweet and white. The ancient winemakers let the grapes raisin on the vine or they dried them on straw mats to concentrate their flavors. The resulting wines were sweeter and stronger—and more durable to withstand transportation to outlying areas.

Vino Veritas

Not all wines that start out with the grapes being dried on mats are sweet. Far from it! Recioto della Valpolicella Amarone—better known as just "Amarone"—is made in the same way except that it's fully fermented to produce a completely dry wine. The name *Amarone* translates to "strongly bitter."

In the Middle Ages Venice and Genoa made sweet dried-grape wines that they exported to northern Europe. Sweet wines appeared in other parts of the world too. Tokaji from Hungary and Constantia from South Africa were highly prized sweet wines that were on every royal table in Europe.

Late Harvest and Noble Rot

Legends, by definition, aren't totally reliable. But here's one version of the creation of late harvest sweet wines: In 1775 a messenger was sent to Schloss Johannisberg in Germany's Rheingau region to give the official order to start harvesting the grapes. He was robbed on the way and delayed. By the time he got to the wine estate, the grapes had begun to raisin on the vine. They were picked anyway and produced astonishingly delicious sweet wine. There's evidence that sweet late harvest wines had already been produced throughout Europe in the previous century. But it makes a colorful story.

Late Harvest Wines

The term *late harvest* means that the grapes were picked late into the harvest season when they were ripened past the sugar levels required for ordinary table wine. The extra ripening time—which can be weeks—adds sugar but also adds significant risk from rain, rot, and birds. The high sugar content of the grapes can translate into a wine that's sweet or a wine high in alcohol—or both.

Late harvest wines are known for their rich, honeyed flavors. Riesling grapes (the variety of most late harvest wines) have the ability to develop high sugar levels and, at the same time, maintain their acidity. That's why they can be unbelievably sweet without being cloying. The acidity also helps these white wines to age as well as they do. Late harvest wines aren't limited to Riesling. They're also made from Sauvignon Blanc, Gewürztraminer, Sémillon, and even Zinfandel.

Noble Rot

While the Germans have their legend for "inventing" late harvest wines, the French have their own legend for the famous Sauternes wines. It seems a château owner told his workers not to pick his grapes until he got back from a trip. By the time he returned, the grapes were infected with a fungus that shriveled them. Despite their disgusting appearance, the grapes were picked and turned into wine. The taste was so exquisite that the owner declared his grapes would thereafter always be picked after the fungus had arrived.

The friendly fungus of the legend is *Botrytis cinerea*, known affectionately as noble rot. It helps the water in the grape evaporate and causes the grape to shrivel, leaving a more concentrated sweet juice.

Botrytis is a finicky fungus. Under the wrong conditions, "gray rot" forms instead and spoils the grapes. If the weather is unremittingly hot and dry, the fungus won't develop at all. The result is a sweet but much less complex wine.

Savvy Sipping

A wide range of grapes can benefit from the positive effects of noble rot—Riesling, Chenin Blanc, Gewürztraminer, Sauvignon Blanc, Sémillon, and Furmint among them. Three areas in particular are historically famous for their botrytized wines.

- **Sauternes**—The wine by the same name is made mostly from Sémillon but usually includes some Sauvignon Blanc and sometimes Muscadelle. The sweet Sauternes aren't necessarily made every year. If the grapes don't ripen properly and if *Botrytis* infection doesn't set in, the winemakers may decide to produce dry wines instead and label them as Bordeaux.
- **Germany**—German winemakers use Riesling to produce their Beerenauslese and Trockenbeerenauslese wines.
- **Hungary**—Tokaji (also referred to as Tokay) comes from an area around the town of Tokaj. They're made primarily from Furmint grapes.

Vino Veritas

Château d'Yquem is in a class all by itself in the world of Sauternes. Because of the selective process of making their wines, only one glass of wine per vine is produced. The harvesting of the grapes alone can last eight to nine weeks because only the perfectly ripe ones are picked. Now you know, in part, why those Sauternes are so coveted—and expensive.

Ice Wines

Who ever would have thought up the idea of making wine from frozen grapes? It was one of those divine accidents. The "discovery" of ice wine dates back to the winter of 1794 when producers in Franconia, Germany, had frozen grapes on their hands and decided to go forward with the pressing. When they finished, they were startled by the high sugar concentration of the juice.

When grapes freeze, the first solid to form is ice. As the grapes are crushed, the ice is left behind with the other solids—the skins and seeds.

To give you an idea of how concentrated the juice is: If the sugar content of the juice was 22 percent when pressed normally, it would be 50 percent or more after freezing and pressing.

In order for the grapes to freeze, they have to be left on the vine well into the winter months. Waiting for them to freeze can be risky business. If the weather doesn't cooperate and the grapes don't freeze, a grower can lose his entire crop. Harvesting takes place by hand in the early (and necessarily cold) morning hours when acidity levels are at their highest. Pressing produces only tiny amounts of juice—one reason for the extremely high prices of ice wines.

Who Makes Ice Wine

Germany and Austria were the traditional producers of ice wine (*Eiswein* in German), but in the last ten years Canada has taken over as the largest producer. Canadian winters are much more predictable. The Canadian versions use a variety of grapes besides Riesling, including some lesser-known varieties like Vidal Blanc and Vignoles.

In Canada—as in Germany and Austria—the making of ice wines is strictly regulated. There are standards for sugar levels, temperature at harvest, and for processing. Ice wines are produced in the United States—particularly in Washington State, New York's Finger Lakes region, and states around the Great Lakes like Michigan and Ohio. No such strict standards exist for domestic ice wines.

Some producers use an alternate method for making ice wine: They stick the grapes in the freezer before pressing them. The lower prices for these ice wines reflect the easier production.

Serving Ice Wine

Ice wines and sweet late harvest wines come in small (375 ml) bottles with big price tags. It isn't unusual to pay $60 to $200 for a half bottle. Fortunately, you serve less of them—two to three ounces—than you would a table wine. They're best served chilled and in stemware.

Port

The origins of Port—the great fortified red wine—goes back to the seventeenth century trade wars between England and France. The British had developed a real affection for the wines of Bordeaux, but import bans and high taxes forced the English merchants to look elsewhere for their red wines. The "elsewhere" was Portugal. They found wines to their liking inland along the Douro River. To make sure that the wines arrived back in England in good condition, the merchants added brandy to stabilize them before shipping them.

Then in 1678 a Liverpool wine merchant sent his sons to Portugal to search out some wines. They ended up at a monastery in the mountains above the Douro where the abbot was adding brandy *during* fermentation—not after. The alcohol stopped the fermentation process, leaving a sweet, high-alcohol wine. And that, as legend has it, was the beginning of Port as the world has come to know it.

What's in a Name

English merchants set up trading companies in the city of Oporto to ship the wines to England. That's one reason so many of the Port producers have English names.

The Ripe Stuff

What are the top Port producers?

The quality Port producers that are of British descent are Cockburn, Sandeman, Croft, Taylor, Syington, Dow, Graham, and Warre. The "Grand Dame" of Port is Ferreira. Equally good Port houses are Fonseca and Quinta do Noval.

The wine became known as Porto—and, to this day, that designation on the label means that the contents are authentic Port.

Kind of like the rules about the name *Champagne,* to be called *Port* the wine has to come from a specific place—the Douro region of

Portugal. Port-style wines are made all over the world, but they're not true Port.

The regulations governing Port's production allow eighty different grape varieties to be used. In practice, though, it really comes down to a handful. The most important ones are:

♦ Tinta Roriz (the same as Spain's Tempranillo)
♦ Touriga Nacional
♦ Tinta Barroca
♦ Tinto Cão
♦ Touriga Francesca
♦ Bastardo
♦ Mourisco

Ports come in a head-spinning number of styles. Most of them are red and sweet. But not all. The style varies according to the quality of the base wine, how long the wine ages in wood before it's bottled, and whether the wine is from a single year or blended with wines from other years.

Port is aged in large wooden casks over a number of years. It reacts with oxygen through the surface area and through the wooden stoves. The aging process in bottles is much slower because there's almost no oxygen. Ports are either wood Ports or bottle-aged Ports—except when they're a little bit of both. Is all this becoming perfectly clear?

Top of the Line: Vintage Port

A Vintage Port is aged in the bottle for most of its life. It spends only two years in cask. When it's bottled at the age of two, it hasn't had a chance to shed its harsh tannins. That's left to happen in the bottle, which—without oxygen—is going to take a *very* long time. It requires at least twenty years of aging and can continue to improve for decades after that.

What really distinguishes a Vintage Port from all the others is that the grapes come from the best vineyard sites in a singularly outstanding year. And that doesn't occur every year. On average a Vintage Port will be made three years out of ten. The wines that are produced in the off years (the *undeclared*) years go into the other types of Port.

Vintage Port is bottled unfiltered and unfined—so, once opened, it requires decanting to remove the sediment that's accumulated. The wine should be consumed in one sitting.

Vino Veritas

Single Quinta (meaning vineyard property) Vintage Ports emerged in the 1980s and have become very popular. They're made from grapes from single-vineyard sites, and they're usually produced in undeclared years. The producer has deemed the quality of the wine from that location to be exceptional.

Late-Bottled Vintage Port (LBV)

LBVs are probably the next best thing to Vintage Port. They're vintage dated and made from a producer's best grapes, but they come from undeclared years. LBVs spend from five to six years in cask to speed up the aging process. They're ready to drink when they're released.

Tawny Port

Tawnies are aged in wood for years—as long as forty—until they fade to a tawny color. They're a blend of wines from several years and are ready to drink immediately. Once opened, they can retain their vitality for a few weeks.

A Tawny Port will often be categorized by age, which appears as "10 Year Old," "20 Year Old," "30 Year Old," and "40 Year Old" on the label. The number is really an average age because older, more complex wines are blended with younger, fruitier wines. Colheita Ports are Tawny Ports from a single year (*colheita* is Portuguese for "vintage").

Ruby Port

Ruby Port is one of the least expensive Ports. It's bottled while it's still young—with only two to three years in wood. It retains its dark ruby color and has a limited shelf life. "Reserve" or "Special Reserve" indicates it's been aged longer.

Message in a Bottle

Vintage Character Ports are Ruby Ports made from higher-quality grapes. They're blended from several years. You won't see the term *vintage character* on the label. These wines are given proprietary names like Bin 27, Six Grapes, and Boardroom.

White Port

White Port is produced just like red Port except it's made from white grapes—principally Malvasia and Donzelinho. Producers sometimes make a drier style by lengthening the fermentation period. The drier whites are typically served as an apéritif.

Sherry

Say "Sherry," and you immediately think of England. But Sherry—the underrated and misunderstood fortified wine—comes from Spain. It's produced in the Jerex region from three main grape varieties: Palomino for the dry Sherries and Pedro Jimenex and Moscatel for the sweet wines. Making Sherry involves a number of steps and many twists and turns.

Relying on a Finicky Yeast

Once the base wine is made and put into barrels, a yeast called *flor* forms on the top of the wine. Not all the wines in the barrels are susceptible to the yeast, and the yeast will only grow with proper temperature and humidity. The flor does a couple of things. If influences the flavor—adding a tangy character to the wine—and it creates a protective layer like a crust on top of the wine so no further oxidation can occur. How well the flor develops determines the style of the Sherry. When the flor fully forms, the wine will be dry and crisp. These will be *fino* Sherry.

Occasionally—and mysteriously—the flor will begin to form and then stop. This may happen in one out of every hundred barrels. The dry and complex Sherry that results is called Palo Cortado.

Wines that don't form the flor at all are the *olorosos*, which have a rich, raisin flavor. They develop with full exposure to the air.

Fortifying and Blending

The next step is to fortify the wines with a clear Brandy, which boosts their alcohol content—and then onto one of the most fascinating blending operations in all of winemaking, known as the *solera system*. Because most Sherries aren't vintage dated, there is the need to make the wines consistent from year to year. To achieve this, wines from many years—and sometimes wines from as far back as a hundred years—are blended together.

Imagine rows and rows of casks all stacked on top of each other—up to fourteen tiers. The oldest wines are on the bottom and the youngest on top. Producers remove about a quarter to a third of the wine from the bottom barrels and bottle it. They replace what they just removed with a wine from the next oldest, one tier up. This cascading of Sherry from the younger to the older continues all the way to the top. By blending all these wines together, you get a product that's consistent and homogenous.

Vino Veritas

Manzanilla is an extra-dry fino Sherry. It's light and delicate with a slightly salty flavor derived, more than likely, from the seaside town where it's aged. Amontillado is an aged fino that's rich, almost amber in color with a nutty flavor.

Sherry to the nth Power

Sherries start out as either a fino or an oloroso (with the very few exceptions of the Palo Cortado). Then it gets complicated. Sometimes aging will change the character of a Sherry so it no longer fits into its initial category. And sometimes the Sherries are sweetened, producing still different styles.

Among the sweet Sherries are:

- **Paul-Cream**—a lightly sweetened fino
- **Cream Sherry**—a heavily sweetened oloroso
- **Brown Sherry**—an extremely sweet and dark oloroso

Madeira

Madeira is just about indestructible. While almost all other wines can't take heat and motion and won't last more than a couple of days once the bottles are opened, Madeira can survive all those things. In fact, Madeira thrives on heat. That's how it's made.

Madeira is a Portuguese island off the coast of North Africa. It was perfectly situated in the Atlantic to become a thriving port for ships traveling to South America and around Africa to Asia. Ships loaded wine onboard for the long journeys. The only problem was that the wines were undrinkable by the time the ships arrived at their destinations. So alcohol, distilled from cane sugar, was added to stabilize the wines.

After enough trips, it was discovered that the wines tasted better after the voyages than before. And, further, that Madeira that had made a round trip was better than Madeira that had traveled only one way.

Shippers began putting wine in the holds of ships for the sole purpose of developing their flavors. It eventually got too expensive—so winemakers had to come up with other ways to simulate the journeys. Subjecting the wine to heat did the trick.

Madeira usually starts out as a white wine. After fermentation it spends at least three months in heated tanks or rooms—or exposed to the sun. As the wine bakes, sugars become caramelized to an amber color, and the wine is oxidized. The term is *maderized*.

The different styles of Madeira are named after the grapes they're made from:

- **Sercial**—the driest style, tangy with high acidity
- **Verhelho**—medium-dry with nutty flavor
- **Bual (or Boal)**—rich, medium-sweet with raisin flavor
- **Malvasia (or Malmsy)**—sweet and concentrated

Sercial and Verdelho are appropriate as apéritifs. The sweeter two are dessert wines. When grape names don't appear on the label, the style will be indicated in a more straightforward fashion: dry, medium-dry, medium-sweet, and sweet.

CHAPTER 17

Establishing a Home Wine Cellar

"Wine cellar" conjures up thoughts of damp caves and monks—or mansions, millionaires, and label-obsessed snobs. But a wine cellar can be anywhere you collect and store wine for future use. You determine the size, shape, and location. You decide what bottles to buy, how many, and what to spend on them. Your wine cellar should reflect your lifestyle. A wine drinker who can't plan more than a week ahead will have a different cellar strategy than someone who plans to "invest" in wine. With the options explained in this chapter, you'll be able to create a wine cellar adapted to your personal needs.

Why Do You Want a Wine Cellar?

Ninety-five percent of all wines produced are meant to be consumed the year they're released. And, in practice, most of those are actually drunk within nanoseconds of their arrival at home. Obviously, no one needs a cellar for those bottles. But if you buy more wine than you drink—and especially if some of those wines are part of the 5 percent that can age—a cellar might be in your future. The point of having a cellar (in any form) is not so much how many bottles you accumulate as it is about your appreciation of wine and making sure your stash is in prime condition when you get around to drinking it.

Why do you think you need a cellar? Look at the top six reasons people say they want a wine cellar. Do any—or all—of them apply to you?

- **Saving money**—A cellar will let them stock up on ageworthy wines while they (the wines) are still young and relatively inexpensive.
- **Convenience**—They won't have to run out to the store every time they want to open a bottle wine.
- **Selection**—They can retrieve a bottle suitable for every occasion.
- **Knowledge**—They'll learn more about wine as they collect bottles from around the world.
- **Status**—A cellar will impress their friends.
- **Investment**—They can make financial gains if they buy wisely.

Assessing Your Buying and Drinking Habits

The fact is you may already have a wine cellar without knowing it. If you're holding wine somewhere for drinking later, you've got a cellar. But before you take the next step (meaning, spend money) to ensure your bottles are adequately housed, it's helpful to take a look at how and why you make your wine purchases. Here are some questions to ask yourself:

- What kinds of wines do you buy? Easy-drinking whites? Long-lived reds? Both?

- Do you drink a special bottle of wine as soon as you get it home? Or do you save it for a worthy occasion?
- Do you like to scout out wine stores in search of promising discoveries? Or would you prefer someone else do the footwork for you?
- Do you buy wines for your personal enjoyment . . . or is your enjoyment predicated on sharing wines with others?

The answers will be a guide to the kind of cellar you choose.

What Does a Wine Cellar Look Like?

A wine cellar can be an elaborate imitation of underground cave conditions—or as ordinary as a hall closet. The common denominator (whatever the outward trappings) is they all provide optimum conditions for storing and aging wine.

Storage Conditions

Temperature is your number one consideration when storing wines—with 55°F being the ideal. Cool temperatures slow the aging process. Higher temperatures cause wines to develop prematurely. Subjected to heat, wines will—at the very least—reach their peak in one year instead of several. At worst, red wines will become "cooked," and white wines will become brown and taste oxidized.

Colder temperatures aren't as harmful to wine. However, drastic temperature swings have an adverse effect. When the wine warms up, it expands and can push the cork out slightly. When the wine cools, the wine contracts and draws air (gasp!) into the bottle.

A refrigerator is not the best place to store your wine over time because the wine will be subjected to wide variations in temperature every few minutes or every few hours. A refrigerator is just not designed to maintain temperature within a narrow range of a few degrees. On top of that, the compressors cause lots of vibrations.

Savvy Sipping

Light is a no-no for good wine storage because it can alter the bio-chemistry of bottle aging. It's most damaging to white wines in color-less bottles. Adequate humidity prevents moisture inside the bottle from migrating through the cork and eventually evaporating into the air. Avoid lots of vibration. It can cause wines to throw off their sediment too soon. Because wine breathes through the cork, avoid strong odors.

Bottles with cork stoppers should be stored on their sides to maintain contact between the cork and the wine. Without the contact, the cork may dry out, shrink, and let in air.

Wine Refrigerators

If you have room for a fifteen-inch computer monitor, you have room for a basic countertop wine storage unit. With a modest investment of a hundred or so dollars and access to a standard wall electrical outlet, you can pamper your wines with ideal temperature, humidity, and posi-tioning. Compact units only hold a few bottles—like six to twenty—but, hey, it's a place to start. Moving up as your wine collection grows is always possible. As you can imagine, freestanding units can get pret-ty fancy-shmancy—and pricey. For a few thousand dollars, the options are many: 700-bottle capacity, mahogany racking, digital cooling system, French doors. The advantage is that you can take them with you when you move.

When space is at a premium and household construction is not an issue, there are built-in units. Some people would gladly give up their dishwashers for an undercounter wine fridge.

Custom Wine Cellars

So you have some space and think you want a custom cellar? There's no shortage of wine cellar consultants to help you. You can turn your extra space into an efficient storage area for a modest collection or into an expansive and architecturally distinctive tasting and storage room—or something in between. Whether you plan to hire someone to build the cellar or do it yourself, here are some tips from people who've "been there":

- Invest in a wine-cooling unit that cools without removing the moisture that's essential to maintaining the integrity of the corks. Standard refrigeration systems and air-conditioning equipment aren't adequate.
- Use the highest-quality wood for racks that won't warp from the humidity and won't need staining. Redwood is preferable.
- Use racks with open sides that allow for airflow around the bottles to help maintain even temperature.
- Install one central light instead of multiple fixtures to prevent warming the wine.
- Install shelves that can accommodate big bottles such as magnums and jeroboams. Likewise, make room for cases.
- Install moisture-resistant flooring. Brick, tile, and stone are good choices.
- Use an exterior-grade, insulated door with complete weather stripping.
- Use a vapor barrier to prevent the higher humidity in the wine cellar from migrating to the lower humidity outside the room.

Low-cost, prefabricated (or "little assembly required") wine racks are available in stainless steel, wire grids, and wood. The metal materials are cheaper but less desirable than wood because they more readily transmit heat and cold. While hardwoods are the ideal choice for racks because they don't warp or emit any odor, softer woods—like pine and Douglas fir—are easier on the budget.

Message in a Bottle

Cellar-less Storage

If you happen to live in an English castle, you have a *passive wine cellar*—a place that stays damp and very cool, where you don't have to do anything to change the surroundings to properly store wine. Or maybe you have a basement with the same environment. Lucky you! Even if you don't have a passive cellar, you can still try to manage a space in your home to store your wine with little or no investment. It's risky, of course. But there are ways to reduce the risk of damage to your wine over time:

- Choose wines that are ageworthy to begin with. If you're planning to hold onto them for several years, pick wines that are meant for aging—particularly big, tannic (but well-balanced) reds.
- Keep the temperature constant and cool. A constant 65°F in your basement is fine. A bedroom that goes from 65°F in the morning to 80°F in the afternoon is not. And just forget about the kitchen.
- Avoid areas that are wet. Humidity levels between 55 percent and 75 percent are good. Beyond 95 percent, you're asking for mold and deteriorating labels.
- Avoid showing off your wine collection in bright, high-traffic areas.

Vino Veritas

If you think your wine might be evaporating through the cork, look at the *ullage*—the space in the neck of the bottle between the wine and the cork. If it's growing, you've got evaporation. This could be an indication of not enough humidity in your storage area. A simple solution could be to buy a small home humidifier.

No matter what form your wine cellar takes, the most important piece of advice is to overestimate your future wine purchases and plan for a storage capacity that you can grow into.

Starting Your Wine Collection

Few people wake up in the morning and say, "I think I'll start a wine collection today." No, wine collecting usually happens inadvertently. You find a wine you like and decide to stock up. Or you discover a knockout wine while visiting a winery and have a case of it shipped home. Or you acquire some very prestigious bottles that you're saving for a special occasion. However it starts, you end up with your own version of a wine cellar. So . . . since you have the right conditions and some extra space, you might as well fill it up with more wine.

Where do you go from here? It's good to have a wine-buying strategy. Sure, you're going to deviate from it—just like your New Year's resolutions. But your strategy will at least give you a framework to work within and a set of goals to achieve. It will also allow you to set aside a certain amount of money for your newfound pastime.

"Time" Management Strategy

Pretend you've assembled a couple hundred bottles of wine. Now imagine that they're all "drink-me-now" wines. Wow! You've got a lot of wine drinking to do in a short period of time. That's not altogether bad . . . but you'll be depleting your cellar in that little amount of time as well.

That's why it's important to plan your purchases for short-, medium-, and long-term aging. Short-term wines are those you might have on hand as your "house" wine—the ones you look forward to at the end of the business day. Short-term wines are good for casual get-togethers and for spur-of-the-moment uncorking. They're ready to drink today and aren't meant for aging. On a per-bottle basis, they're probably the least expensive of your collection.

Instead of curing a wine's problems, aging can exacerbate them. If a wine is fat and flabby in its youth, bottle aging won't bump up its acidity and structure. Likewise, a wine that's extremely oaky won't "soften" after it's spent a few years in your cellar. You're still not going to taste lively fruit.

Savvy Sipping

Medium-term wines are ones that have aging potential for three to ten years. They're perfectly fine to drink now, but you might enjoy them even more a couple of years down the road. You probably won't serve them quite as casually as you do the short-term wines because you likely paid more for them.

Long-term wines are the ones that actually need time in the bottle to show their best stuff. You can get relative bargains when you buy them as soon as they're released. But these will undoubtedly be your most expensive per-bottle investments.

Wines Worth Cellaring

Not all wines age gracefully. Some are the drink-me-now kind of wines that will only decline over time. This is not to say that you won't want to include young-drinking wines in your collection. Just put them in an obvious location so you'll remember to drink them before it's too late.

Savvy Sipping

For advice about aging specific wines, ask the salesperson at the time of your purchase—or go to the winery's Web site, which may contain cellaring information. Aging wine is not predictable with any precision. However, consider some general tips on aging for these popular varietals and categories.

Cabernet Sauvignon

Cabs are meant for aging. Just how long depends on the quality of the wine. Cabs from Napa and Bordeaux can improve over decades. Check out the best vintages because, frankly, a mediocre wine at the time of release isn't going to develop into a better wine no matter how long you keep it. The softer, more easy-drinking Cabs will cellar nicely for a couple of years. The sky's the limit for serious, collectible Cabs.

Merlot

Not all Merlots are soft, fruity, and simple. Remember, this is one of the "noble" grape varieties. It has the potential to be every bit as big, powerful, and robust as the noble Cab—if in a more velvety style.

Drink inexpensive Merlots soon after you bring them home. A high-quality Merlot can age from five to twenty-five years. Maybe more.

Nebbiolo

Nebbiolo-based wines—particularly Northern Italy's Barolo and Barbaresco—hold up well for long-term cellaring. Age releases their complexity. Barolos will age for fifteen to forty years. Barbaresco, somewhat less.

Pinot Noir

Pinot shows its finicky personality all through its growing and production stages. Predicting its ageworthiness with any precision is no picnic either. Fine Burgundies have been known to evolve into real beauties over several decades. But Pinots from California, Oregon, and New Zealand, for example, are probably at their peak at seven to ten years.

Syrah/Shiraz

Syrah/Shiraz, as a varietal on its own or in blends, has maturing potential. In wines of the Rhone, Syrah is the principal grape. Côte Rôtie can easily age for ten years or more. And Hermitage, intense and tannic in its youth, can age fifteen to forty years.

Riesling

Of all white wines, Riesling is the longest-lived. The best German Rieslings have a history of tasting delicious after decades of aging. In fact, the young ones can be austere and benefit from cellaring. The ageability of Rieslings from other parts of the world varies. But a general guideline is from two to ten years.

Chardonnay

Chardonnays are all over the map in terms of longevity—although great Chardonnays outlast most other whites. With Chardonnays, you can pretty much determine ageability by price. Drink less-expensive ones soon after purchase. Higher-priced ones will improve for two or three years.

Dessert Wines

Dessert wines, particularly fortified wines, are long-lived. Vintage Ports—with their high alcohol, good acid, and plentiful tannins—have been known to outlive their owners. It's not unusual to hear about Port lasting 100 years. White wines with a lot of sweetness—like Sauternes, ice wines, and late harvest Rieslings—can age gracefully for many years.

Message in a Bottle

Only after tasting a wine do you really know if it needs further aging. So what are you supposed to do if you have only one bottle? A quick and easy (although not fool-proof) method of deciding what bottles to age is by price. If you paid more than $30 for the bottle, hold onto it. If you paid less, drink up!

"Balanced" Choices

The wines you choose for cellaring—just like the ones you choose for immediate consumption—should be balanced. It's especially important for aging considerations because whatever is out-of-whack with a wine will become more pronounced over time. A few things to consider:

♦ **Alcohol**—If a wine tastes of too much alcohol now, it will only taste more so later.
♦ **Acid**—Acid gives wine backbone, but it doesn't diminish with age. Over time when fruit and tannins fade into the background, the acidity remains intact and will be more pronounced.

- **Oak**—Oak doesn't mellow either. It can overpower the other elements after long aging.
- **Tannin**—Tannin is definitely tamed with age. But if the tannin is overbearing to start, it might outlast its fruit partner.

Expanding Your Wine Collection

What you put in your cellar will depend on your personal taste and your pocketbook—both of which can (and probably will) change over time. The most sensible way to start a collection is to buy what you like to drink. No one knows your taste better than you. It may sound obvious, but be sure to taste a wine before you invest in a case of it. More than one collector has been caught up in the excitement of wine shopping and lived to regret a case purchase.

Then there's always the question of how much to buy. The truth is, once you get "hooked" on wine collecting, you tend to buy more than you had planned. One the one hand, you'll want to buy enough wine to satisfy your everyday consumption habits and your need for special-occasion bottles. On the other hand, you don't want to overbuy for the amount of storage space you have.

Geographical Strategies

As your tastes evolve and as you seek out different and better wines, you might decide to adopt a geography-based strategy. Think "global." Wine-producing areas around the world are known for specific wines. By tasting a variety of Riojas from different producers, you get an idea what the Spanish beauty has to offer. Or, by tasting Rieslings from Germany, Alsace, and New York, you may come to appreciate both the similarities and differences according to location.

If you already know what areas of the world produce wines to suit your palate, you might choose a regional strategy. Italy or Burgundy (with its hundreds of appellations) or California could easily keep you collecting, experimenting, and learning for a lifetime.

"Vertical" Strategy

A wine drinker interested in how wine changes from vintage to vintage would be well served to collect ageworthy wines from specific appellations over a period of years. Whether you buy Cabernets from Napa or Barolos from Piedmont, collecting in this manner will enable you to compare both vintages and producers.

Taste one producer's wine over several vintages and discover the effect of the environment. Taste several producers' wines from the same year and discern winemaker influences.

Where to Buy Collectible Wines

How often have you read about some collector spending an outrageous fortune for a bottle of wine? Well, you can bet the bottle wasn't just pulled from a retailer's shelf. Yet, when you're acquiring wines for your cellar, your retailer is the first place to start.

Savvy retailers keep tabs on what's new, what's good, and what it costs. They can help you locate a hard-to-find wine when it's not in their own inventory.

And—like doctors—they specialize. Not all of them. But a lot of them. If you're interested mostly in Italian wines or French wines, for example, there's a retailer out there with the same focus that can offer you good variety.

Wine Auctions

When wines are old and rare, you'll find them at auctions. These are wines that have been out of circulation for years. Auctions specialize in these rarities and cater to a well-heeled crowd. But make no mistake about this audience: They are just as susceptible as mere mortals to auction fever. That's one reason auction houses prefer a live audience to absentee bids by phone, fax, and e-mail.

Wine auctions can be treacherous territory for novice bidders, but doing your homework can reduce the risk. Find out what the wine you want is really worth. Beware of bargains that are "too good to be true." And make sure you're dealing with a reputable seller.

Vino Veritas

The number of "live bodies" at commercial wine auctions has dwindled. That means no flurry of skyrocketing bids. Auction houses have reacted by offering incentives: extravagant lunches at four-star restaurants, wine samplings from the sale inventory, complimentary Champagne. It seems to work.

The Internet has made wine auctions more accessible. Some of the major wine auction houses and Web sites include:

- Morrell & Company (*www.morrellwineauctions.com*)
- Acker Merrall & Condit (*www.ackerwines.com*)
- WineBid.com (*www.winebid.com*)
- Christie's (*www.christies.com*)
- Sothebys (*www.sothebys.com*)
- Brentwood Wine Company (*www.brentwoodwine.com*)
- Chicago Wine Company (*www.tcwc.com*)
- MagnumWines (*www.magnumwines.com*)
- Bonhams & Butterfields (*www.butterfields.com*)
- Zachys Wine Online (*www.zachys.com*)

Message in a Bottle

Just like when you buy something on eBay, some auction items will have reserve bids. If they're not stated up front, be sure to ask. The same goes for disclosures of shipping, insurance, and liability conditions. Reputable houses—online or offline—will offer this information openly.

Winery-Direct

You don't have to visit a winery to buy direct (assuming, of course, that your state allows direct shipping of wine). Getting on a winery's mailing list will get you all the information you need to order. The exclusive cult wines that emerged in the '90s made mailing lists status symbols. Acquiring a bottle of one of those limited production wines was possible only by paying a high price at a restaurant or through the mailing list. Even when you got on the list (which was no easy feat), you could get only your allotment.

Buying wine futures from a winery or through a store is another option. You buy wine before it's bottled at an agreed upon prerelease price. When it's ready for sale, you take delivery. One advantage is that you buy the wine at a discount . . . you hope. Sometimes the price at release is the same as you paid—only you've had your money tied up for a year or more.

The real benefit of buying futures comes when the wine is so popular and made in such small quantities that it could be sold out before it even reaches the store. Futures are most often associated with the wines of Bordeaux and California Cabs.

Savvy Sipping

You'd think that, without all the middlemen, buying wine directly from the producer would offer a cost savings. Not so. Wineries are reluctant to jeopardize their relationships with other sellers of their wines by undercutting them on price. In fact, you can often spend less at a discount warehouse.

Wine Consultants

Imagine the luxury of having someone come into your home, design and build the ideal cellar, assess your wine tastes, and then acquire the wines of your dreams. That's what personal wine consultants are all about. Some specialize in cellar construction. Some focus on your collection and utilize their own contacts and databases to secure hard-to-get wines. They bring their expertise to your project so you can sit back and let the pros do the work.

For most people, hiring a wine consultant is only a fantasy. But a more modest option is a wine-of-the-month club, where you can make regular wine purchases at your own price level. You can focus on specific regions or experiment with global selections.

Research

Regardless of your method of purchase, knowing the real market value of the wine you're about to buy is essential. Otherwise, you could overspend big time. Research is as easy as going to the Internet.

Wine Spectator (www.winespectator.com) publishes a quarterly Auction Index that lists average prices paid for commonly traded wines. It also provides high/low price comparisons and percentage changes from quarter to quarter. In addition to being a guide for your auction bidding, it can help you determine fair retail market value for older vintages.

Wine-searcher.com is an online resource for wine retail availability and pricing. You type in the wine, producer, or vintage you're looking for, and you get the names of retailers that have it and the prices they're charging. Wine-searcher has two services—one free, the other a paid service. For the free service, search results are limited to Wine-Searcher retail sponsors. The paid version locates the best prices and shows all the suppliers (from their 4,000+ list) that have your wine.

Wine as an Investment

Most wine collectors don't buy to own . . . they buy to drink. They never make any money from their collections because they keep depleting the resource and have to regularly replenish the cellar. But because some wines show such a dramatic increase in value over time, investing (and reaping the profits) is tempting. While it's true that great wines from outstanding vintages produce above average investments, almost anything less in quality performs below average.

Say you bought a bottle of wine from a renowned French château in 1970 for $10. In 2005 you sold it for $200. Not bad: an 8.9 percent return on investment! Of course, that doesn't take into account your expenses in maintaining the wine over thirty-five years—or the sad lost opportunity of not being able to drink the wine yourself.

There are real risks to your wine investments that you can't control. A low score from a famous critic could devalue your collection. Or a power outage could ruin it.

Managing and Maintaining Your Cellar

Your wine collection changes every time you drink a bottle and add a bottle. It's easy to lose track of what's in your cellar. Some kind of organization is essential. And a little record-keeping wouldn't hurt either.

Message in a Bottle

Give your cellar a regular physical checkup. For $25 or less, you can buy a minimum/maximum thermometer that will display the high and low temperatures your cellar reaches. Monitor it for a week. If the temperature swing is more than 5° to 8°F, you need to make some changes.

Organization

Drink your wines before they get too old! You don't want to discover a case of drink-me-now wines five years after their prime. Put wines you're likely to drink soon where you'll see them. Out of sight, out of mind.

Tag your wines with drink-by dates as a reminder. Inexpensive bottle tags are available anywhere wine accessories are sold.

As your collection grows, an inventory system becomes more important. Start simple: a notebook where you can log in new purchases, record prices, keep track of consumption, and maybe even include tasting notes. Computer technology is also here to help you. Inexpensive, downloadable software programs are available just for wine cellars. And there are several software packages for PDAs to make it even more convenient.

Restocking

Every time you drink a bottle of wine, you deplete your inventory. A restocking plan for maintaining your cellar should be based on how much you consume. If you drink three bottles a week, you'd need to buy roughly a case a month to restock. Five bottles a week would be closer to two cases.

A wine enthusiast can easily buy more wine than she actually drinks. That's why friends were made.

CHAPTER 18

Wine and Health

Wine has been associated with good health for thousands of years. Clay tablets dating back to 2100 B.C. show wine being used as medicine. In 450 B.C. Hippocrates recommended wine to relieve fevers, disinfect wounds, and supplement nutrition. In 1680 the doctor for Louis XIV urged the king to regularly drink Burgundy to maintain his health. And in the nineteenth century, European wine drinkers escaped the ravages of cholera, scientists believe, because the wine wiped out the bacteria causing the disease. And today, researchers are trying to find out just how wine interacts with the human body.

The French Paradox

It was a Sunday evening in November 1991 when 33.7 million Americans turned on their TVs to watch *60 Minutes* and saw Morley Safer report on an odd phenomenon in France. The French people, he said, ate high-fat, cholesterol-laden foods—like cheese, butter, eggs, organ meats—yet they had a much lower rate of heart disease than supposedly healthier-eating Americans. He went on, "Obviously, they're doing something right—something Americans are not doing. Now it's all but confirmed: Alcohol—in particular red wine—reduces the risk of heart disease."

This phenomenon became known as the French Paradox and, within four weeks of the television show's broadcast, U.S. sales of red wine soared by 40 percent. The report prompted a change in thinking of wine as a toxin to wine as a potential healer. And it encouraged research projects to investigate how wine consumption affects our hearts, lungs, brains, bones—and our overall health.

Does the French Paradox still stand up? While the research is ongoing, studies conducted around the world seem to confirm that wine and other alcoholic beverages—consumed in moderation—reduce the risk of coronary heart disease by 20 to 40 percent.

Wine vs. Beer and Spirits

With all the research analyzing the effects of wine, beer, and spirits on various parts of the body, the jury is still out on whether the health effects are due entirely to the components in wine or to alcohol in general. Some studies have shown wine to have influence independent of alcohol. Still other studies have produced the same results regardless of the source of alcohol.

The impacts on health resulting from wine and other alcoholic beverages may differ, researchers believe, because of the way they're consumed—not necessarily their inherent properties.

- ◆ Wine enthusiasts tend to drink wine with meals rather than on empty stomachs.

- Wine drinkers tend to sip more slowly.
- Wine drinkers tend to spread their drinking out over an entire week rather than binge on weekends.

The upshot is that, for wine drinkers, the alcohol may be absorbed more slowly and over a longer period of time. And the resulting health effects might be different.

What the Studies Say

It's hard not to be confused by all the scientific studies that are released every day. The information is often complicated, incomplete, or even contradictory. What is universally accepted is that excessive consumption of alcohol creates serious health risks—liver damage and hypertension among them. At the same time, evidence is emerging that moderate wine consumption can be beneficial in a number of areas.

The Ripe Stuff

What is "moderate" consumption?

. . . .

The U.S. government defines it as no more than two drinks a day for men and one drink a day for women. One drink is the equivalent of five ounces of wine, twelve ounces of beer, or one shot (about 1.5 ounces) of spirits like scotch or vodka. Other countries define "moderate" more liberally.

. . . .

Heart Disease and Stroke

Individuals who drink alcoholic beverages in moderation have a lower risk of coronary heart disease than heavy drinkers or abstainers. It doesn't seem to matter whether the alcohol comes from an expensive Bordeaux, a Bud, or a dirty martini. The alcohol increases the level of "good" cholesterol (HDL) in the body. HDL acts like a detergent, removing excess fat in the blood and carrying it to the liver where it's metabolized.

Much the same holds true for preventing strokes. In addition to increasing the level of good cholesterol, the blood is prevented from clotting—which reduces the risk of ischemic strokes.

Diabetes

Observational studies indicate that diabetes occurs less often in moderate drinkers than in abstainers. The Harvard School of Public Health conducted a study of 100,000 women over fourteen years. The women were divided into three levels of alcohol consumption. After factoring for family history of diabetes and smoking, the results showed that the women who drank moderately and regularly had a 58 percent lower risk of developing diabetes than abstainers. Women who drank more or less still had a 20 percent lower risk than nondrinkers. Results applied to both wine and beer drinkers—but not spirits drinkers.

Alzheimer's Disease and Dementia

Studies from different areas around the world have shown that moderate drinkers are less likely to develop dementia. Research on elderly participants have documented that the moderate drinkers performed better on memory and cognitive tests than nondrinkers.

In a Danish study designed to screen for signs of mental decline, researchers found that participants who drank at least one glass of wine a week were much less likely than those who drank no wine to develop dementia. Beer and spirits failed to produce the same results.

Bone Mass

It was once accepted that alcohol lowers a woman's bone mass, leading to osteoporosis. However, a couple of recent studies have indicated otherwise. One study was conducted to determine the effect of alcohol consumption on the bones of elderly women and how that might differ from the use of estrogen-replacement therapy. Moderate drinkers, it showed, had the greatest bone mass followed by light drinkers and followed, finally, by nondrinkers.

In a study of twins in England, it was determined that moderate-drinking individuals had significantly greater bone mass than their infrequently drinking twins.

Longevity

The American Cancer Society conducted a survey of a half million people over nine years to examine "total mortality"; that is, the risk of dying of any cause. The risk was greatest among abstainers and people who drank six or more alcoholic beverages a day. Moderate drinkers (who had one-half to two drinks a day) had a 21 percent lower risk than nondrinkers.

Patterns of Consumption

Current thinking is that the health effects of alcohol consumption depend on both how much you drink and your drinking patterns. Because many of the biological effects of alcohol are short-lived (lasting only twenty-four hours), the best advice seems to be, if you're going to drink, do it moderately every day. Don't save it up for weekend partying.

Drinking alcoholic beverages is always inappropriate at certain times—like when you're going to be behind the wheel of a car. Or when you're pregnant. While fetal alcohol syndrome is caused only by heavy drinking, the conservative approach is to avoid drinking during pregnancy.

Savvy Sipping

A recent University College London study of civil servants found frequent drinking was more beneficial for cognitive function than drinking only on special occasions. Research on hypertension at the Worcester Medical Center in Massachusetts determined that men who drank monthly had a 17 percent lower risk of cardiovascular disease than non-drinkers. Weekly drinkers had a 39 percent lower risk. And daily drinkers had a 44 percent lower risk.

Although the explanations have yet to be conclusively determined, consuming alcoholic beverages with food seems to be beneficial as well.

Health Components in Wine

Wine in some cases goes beyond just the alcohol in producing health benefits. Recent research focuses on identifying the specific components in wine that are responsible and explaining how they work. Much of the emphasis is on antioxidants. Oxidation of cholesterol in the blood has been linked to clogged arteries, blood-clot formation, and tumor growth. Antioxidants inhibit that oxidation.

Vino Veritas

The antioxidants found in wine come from the grapes. But the antioxidants aren't exclusive to grapes. The same ones are also found in allium vegetables—onions, leeks, garlic, shallots—and broccoli, spinach, blueberries, strawberries, tea . . . and chocolate!

Antioxidants

Antioxidants in wine come in the form of phenolic compounds such as tannins and flavonoids. The flavonoids in red wine are especially powerful—more than twenty times more powerful than those in vegetables.

The antioxidant that's getting most of the attention these days is resveratrol. Resveratrol is produced in the skins of grapes in response to fungus attacks and stress. Because red wines are fermented in contact with the skins, they acquire more resveratrol than white wines and carry more potential benefits than either white wines or other alcoholic beverages.

Grapes from cold, damp climates that have to "fight" harder to survive produce more resveratrol than those in warm climates. And grapes that are more sensitive to growing conditions—like Pinot Noir—seem to have more resveratrol than their hardier counterparts—like Cabernets.

Wine and Weight Loss

Confusion reigns when it comes to the effect of wine (and other alcoholic beverages) on weight loss. Wine has plenty of calories—about 100 calories a glass. So it would just seem logical that if you cut out wine, you'd lose weight. But there's no evidence that giving up wine on your diet will necessarily help you shed the pounds. In fact, a major U.S. study revealed that dieters who gave up their alcohol lost no more weight than those who kept drinking.

Wine's calories come primarily from the alcohol. Most of the sugar was converted to alcohol during fermentation. The exceptions are fortified dessert wines that have both high sugar *and* high alcohol content. You may notice, too, that even some slightly sweet wines—like White Zinfandel and Riesling—have more calories than fully dry table wines.

Message in a Bottle

Calories in wine are directly related to the alcohol content. To determine the number of calories in a glass of wine, multiply the percentage of alcohol (found on the label) by the number of ounces you pour into the glass, and multiply that by 1.6. Example: *13 (percent alcohol) × 5 (oz.) × 1.6 = 104 total calories*

There are numerous variables that affect how wine will fit into your weight-loss regimen:

- ◆ Whether you use wine to replace food or drink it in addition to food
- ◆ How much wine you consume
- ◆ How your body is genetically predisposed to process alcohol
- ◆ What foods you eat
- ◆ How much exercise you get

Wine and Carbohydrates

Wine labels are now allowed to include calorie and carbohydrate counts. Low-carb diets have been so popular that some wine companies were quick to jump on the bandwagon of "low-carb" wines. Wines, of course, are inherently low-carb. The residual sugar left over after fermentation determines the number of carbohydrates. Compare the amounts to other beverage choices.

Table 18-1   Carbohydrate Counts in Selected Beverages

Beverage	Amount	Carb Grams
Red Wine	1 glass	0.4–2.3
White Wine	1 glass	0.8–1.0
Dessert Wine	2-oz. glass	7.0
Beer	1 bottle	9.0–12.0
Light Beer	1 bottle	3.0–8.0
Spirits	1.5-oz. shot	0–0.1
Coca Cola	1 can	40.0
Diet Coke	1 can	0.3

Too Much of a Good Thing

So it was one drink too many? The queasy tummy, the shaking hands, the pounding headache . . . the can't-keep-your-balance and oh-my-gosh-I'm-gonna-be-sick kind of feeling? Yes, you overdid a good thing. Right . . . it'll never happen again. Well, just for the sake of science, take a look at how your body reacts to ingesting alcohol.

How Wine Moves Through the Body

Once you take a sip of that incredible Amarone, it goes into the stomach, where 20 percent of the alcohol is absorbed. The rest moves on to the small intestines, where most of the rest is absorbed. The alcohol is delivered to the liver, where enzymes break it down. Now, the liver can only process a limited amount of alcohol at a time—about one drink an hour. When you consume more, the alcohol is in a holding pattern—in your blood and body tissues—until the liver can metabolize some more.

Vino Veritas

The alcohol that remains unmetabolized can be measured in breath and urine as "blood alcohol concentration" (BAC) or "blood alcohol level" (BAL). BAC peaks within thirty to forty-five minutes after consuming a drink. BAC is measured as a percentage. In most states, .08 percent is considered legally drunk.

Men and Women Process Alcohol Differently

Some physiological differences between men and women are obvious. Others are less apparent. The ways their bodies process alcohol are different—even when they're the same size:

♦ *Women have less body water—52 percent compared to 61 percent for men.* The man's body will be able to dilute the alcohol more readily than a woman's body can.
♦ *Women have less of the liver enzyme (dehydrogenase) that breaks down alcohol.* So a woman will metabolize alcohol more slowly.
♦ *Hormonal factors have an impact.* Premenstrual hormones cause a woman to get intoxicated more quickly. Also, birth control pills and estrogen medications will slow down the rate that alcohol is eliminated from the body.

The Hangover

A hangover is the body's reaction to alcohol poisoning and withdrawal. It starts from eight to twelve hours after your last drink. The severity may vary from one person to the next—but, fundamentally, it's based on how much you consumed. The symptoms might be as mild as thirst and fatigue—or as acute as headache, depression, nausea, and vomiting.

Savvy Sipping

Heavy drinking causes brain shrinkage. Yikes! Overindulging has more lasting effects than hangovers. The brain shrinks as a natural part of aging, but excess alcohol speeds it up and causes damage to the brain's frontal lobe—the part that controls cognitive functions.

There are few things you can do to cure a hangover. Time and water are your best friends at that stage. But there are some measures you can take to prevent a hangover. (Drinking less goes without saying!)

- Before you start drinking: Eat something high in fat. It will delay absorption of the alcohol.
- While you're drinking, drink a glass of water between each glass of wine. It will keep you hydrated and minimize intoxication.
- While you're drinking, snack, snack, snack.
- Before you go to bed, eat something salty to replenish what the alcohol has flushed out of your body. And then drink *more* water.

Headaches

Here it goes again. You're sipping a perfectly exquisite Cabernet, appreciating its maturity and its velvety texture and—WHAM! The throbbing starts and doesn't abate. Where did that headache come from?

You've heard all the rumors about sulfites. Surely, they're the culprits. They must be evil. After all, the label on the wine bottle has a bold, cautionary warning: "Contains sulfites"!

Relax . . . or relax as much as you can while you're experiencing excruciating pain. You're going to have to find another scapegoat. Chances are, your headache derives from something other than sulfites. Only 1 percent of the general population is actually allergic to sulfites—usually individuals with asthma or those on steroid medications. If that's you, you'll more than likely develop rashes, abdominal pain, or extreme breathing problems from the wine.

Message in a Bottle

Sulfites are present in lots of foods—and at usually higher concentrations than in wine. They're contained in dried fruits, jams, baked goods, canned vegetables, frozen orange juice, bacon, dried noodles, and pickled foods. Where's the bold warning on those labels?

The Sulfite Story

In wine, as in other foods, some sulfites are naturally present. Sulfur is abundant in various forms in all living things. In winemaking, manufactured sulfites are added to wine to prevent bacterial growth and to protect against oxidation. The practice of using sulfites as a preservative isn't new—and it's done by winemakers worldwide. Only when their wines are sold in the United States do they have to be labeled with the sulfite warning. Same wine—different label.

The amounts of added sulfites are small—measured in parts per million (ppm). The legal limit for some foods goes as high as 6,000 ppm. For wine the maximum allowed is 350 ppm, but most wines contain much less—typically from 25 to 150 ppm. In general, the less expensive the wine, the more sulfites it will have. And whites will have more than reds.

The law says that if a wine contains 10 ppm or more total sulfites, the label must carry the sulfite warning. To be labeled a "no sulfite wine," it can contain no more than 1 ppm. Because those wines are very perishable, they should be drunk soon after release.

More sulfites are added to white wines than to reds. White wine grapes are fermented after their skins have been separated. Red wines are fermented in contact with their skins. In addition to imparting color, the skins pass on tannins during fermentation, which act as a natural preservative.

The Blame Game

Okay, don't blame it on the sulfites. But the headache isn't just your imagination. So what causes it? There are plenty of suspects, but it's not so easy to pick out the exact one.

- ◆ **Histamines**—These are chemical substances found in aged and fermented foods like wine, cheese, and salami and found naturally in eggplant. Histamines can dilate the blood vessels in your brain. Red wines usually have a higher level of histamines.
- ◆ **Tyramines**—These are chemical substances found in cultured foods such as cheese and yogurt; fermented foods like wine, dark beer, and soy sauce; and chocolate, vanilla, nuts, and beans. Tyramines can constrict the blood vessels in the brain.
- ◆ **Congeners**—These organic compounds are the by-products of the fermentation process that give wine its characteristic flavor. There are hundreds of them present in wines in varying amounts depending on the type of wine. When congeners enter the bloodstream, your immune system recognizes them as poisons and releases cytokines (the same molecules that fight off the flu) to eliminate them. Generally, darker beverages (red wine, bourbon) have more congeners than lighter ones (white wine, vodka).
- ◆ **Prostaglandins**—These are naturally occurring pain-producing substances in your body. Dilation of the arteries triggers their release. They're also thought to be responsible for migraine headaches.
- ◆ **Sensitivities to elements in wine production**—Some people have a sensitivity to woods. The soil where the grapes are grown contains various types of chemicals and could be a factor. That's why you might be able to drink a Cab from Napa, for example, without any negative effect—yet get a headache from a Cab made in Australia.

Wine-Health Challenges

Real wine enthusiasts, rather than casual drinkers, look for ways to keep wine as part of their daily lives—in spite of occasional "challenges." Headaches are major challenges, but life presents others that are more easily managed.

Purple Teeth

You may not be a professional wine taster who samples a couple hundred wines in a day's time, but you're not totally immune to the discoloring effects of red wine. The stains usually aren't permanent and disappear when you brush your teeth. But if you're really into reds big time, you may notice that the purple color doesn't completely go away. A trip to the dentist for a professional whitening procedure is the best answer. However, there are some measures you can take to prevent and fix the situation.

- ♦ Wait an hour or so after drinking wine to brush. The high acidity in wine can leave your teeth sensitive to abrasion. Brushing prematurely could damage your tooth enamel.
- ♦ Drink water between sips of wine. It will help eliminate the acid.
- ♦ Before brushing, rinse with a little bicarbonate of soda.
- ♦ Use a fluoride rinse two to three hours before winetasting.

No Alcohol, Please

When you *really* like wine but have to stay away from alcohol, what do you drink? Are alcohol-free wines a good alternative? When it comes to their taste, you're the only one who can decide. No wine drinker has ever been fooled into believing the alcohol-free version was the real thing. But producers have been coming closer to reproducing the tastes.

The wines are fermented normally. Then they're dealcoholized. The exact process of removing the alcohol varies from one producer to another. The wines are reconstituted with grape juice or water and bottled.

One thing you should know is that alcohol-free wines are not necessarily totally free of alcohol. Check the label. You'll usually find the level of alcohol at .5 percent.

Get the Lead Out

Lead crystal is beautiful. And wine looks particularly elegant in crystal glasses and decanters. But, over time, wine can absorb some of the lead. It's not going to be much of a problem drinking a Riesling out of your grandmother's goblets for an evening. But storing a Sherry in a decanter over several weeks is something to avoid.

For new crystal, soak it in vinegar for twenty-four hours and then rinse. And stay away from harsh detergents, which can increase the release of lead.

CHAPTER 19

Visiting a Winery

Nothing beats going to the source to really understand a subject. For wine, that means a visit to a winery for an inspection of the fermentation tanks, a stroll through the vineyards to bask in the same sunshine that ripens the grapes, and—if you happen to be lucky (or plan carefully)—a conversation with the winemaker to witness her passion as she tells you how she blended her cuvée. Oh yes, and sampling wines right where they were made.

Types of Wineries

At last count, the United States had 3,726 registered wineries. With Americans' interest in wine on an upswing, new wineries continue to take form. All fifty states now have wineries. California has almost 1,700. Napa alone has well over 200. And other states have impressive numbers.

- Washington—323
- Oregon—228
- New York—203
- Ohio—100

- Pennsylvania—99
- Virginia—97
- Texas—91
- Michigan—90

In numbers there is diversity. Some wineries are huge enterprises . . . others are mom-and-pop operations. Some wineries are publicly traded, others are owned by families, and still others are owned by celebrities. Most U.S. wineries produce wines from vinifera grapes, but some base their wines on hybrids or fruits. A lot of wineries are located in picturesque settings with spectacular views. Others are housed in industrial warehouses.

Every winery—and every owner—has a story. Sometimes you'll get the story right from the owner himself. Sometimes you'll hear it from a paid employee. It's always a story they want to share with you. And they always have such enthusiasm for their subject. There's just no substitute for a visit to a winery.

Planning Your Trip

With so many options, far and near, the most difficult part of your winery visits will be choosing which ones to go to. Geographical location is the first variable. Do you want to take a day trip close to home—or will you plan a whole vacation around a trip to the wine country of Bordeaux or Napa or Cape Winelands?

Once your location is decided you've got to choose the winery. If you're touring the wineries of Tennessee or Arizona, you'll have fewer alternatives (and an easier decision) than if you're in California or Washington. Faced with a multitude of possibilities, one strategy is to base your selection on the wines you enjoy. You have a penchant for Cabernet? Choose a winery known for their Cabs. If you prefer wines from a particular winery, for goodness sake, go there! It's hard to lose when you choose a winery by personal preference. If you plan to visit more than one, pick out both large and small ones.

Vino Veritas

In Australia most of the wineries are open to the public. But don't look for signs for the "tasting room," because they go by another name. Australians call tasting rooms "cellar doors." Australian producers can make a dizzying number of wines—so there's plenty to sample.

When to Go

When to go is another variable. During the winter months, wineries (particularly those in the more popular wine regions) are much less crowded. You won't have to fight traffic. Of course, the vines are dormant—so you'll see bare trellises in the vineyards.

In the summer the vines are in full vegetation, and the views are spectacular. The downside is that it can be hot and jammed with tourists. Fall is harvest time, and wineries are exciting, bustling places. Each season has it advantages.

Weekdays are less congested than weekends. And mornings are less crowded than afternoons. What . . . you never heard of Zinfandel at 10 A.M.?

Do-Ahead List

The Boy Scout motto is good advice for your winery trip: Be prepared. A little advance planning will make your outing memorable—for all the right reasons.

- **Don't be too ambitious**—Three to five wineries in one day is plenty for the best of wine tourists. Instead of rushing through one winery and scampering to the next, a more relaxed itinerary will give you time to walk through the vineyards and talk to the winemakers. Schedule visits to wineries that are clustered together to eliminate unnecessary driving.
- **Call ahead to the wineries to confirm their tasting room hours**—Not all wineries have tasting rooms. Of those that do, some welcome walk-in visitors and others require that you make an appointment. Some wineries will close during certain months—and, occasionally, they change their hours.
- **Designate a driver**—Wining and driving don't complement each other. If no one in your group is willing to forgo tasting, consider hiring a limo service.
- **Dress sensibly**—That means comfy shoes for vineyard walks and dark colors for potential wine spills. And no perfume. You may not smell it, but the person next to you who's trying to catch the bouquet of her wine will be painfully aware of it.
- **Take a cooler**—If you buy wines on your trip, you'll need a place to store them during the day. Tossing them in a hot trunk might cook them before you get them home. Imagine the disappointment.
- **Take a notebook**—You're certain to taste some wines you like and want to remember. It's guaranteed that, later, you'll forget what they were unless you write down the names.

Tasting Rooms

A tasting room is just what the name says. It's a place—a room or an entire building—that the winery has designated to host visitors, sell their wines, and offer tasting samples. The tasting room may be located at the winery itself, on the winery's property separate from the winery, or offsite in a nearby town. Often a tasting room will offer wine accessories as well as wines for sale. Some wineries provide complimentary tastings of their wines. Others will charge a nominal fee. When reserve wines or otherwise special wines are available for tasting, it usually ups the ante. Occasionally, a winery will apply the tasting fee toward your wine purchases. Call ahead to find out about tasting fees.

Wine drinkers can be nervous about their first winery visit. But their fears usually disappear as soon as they enter the tasting room. When you walk into a tasting room, you'll be greeted by a member of the tasting staff who will enthusiastically tell you about the winery and the wines. She may suggest an order to taste the wines or hand you a "menu" describing the wines: varietal, vintage, appellation, alcohol level, tasting notes. If a tasting order isn't suggested to you, start with whites, advance to reds, and finish with sweet wines.

Message in a Bottle

You don't have to try all the wines. If you're a fan of a particular varietal, say Chardonnay, you may want to sample just those at each winery. This technique can help you learn how different vineyards, different vintages, and different winemakers affect taste. The strategy will give you a greater understanding of that varietal.

Only a small amount of wine—perhaps an ounce—will be poured into your glass. On the one hand, the small portion might seem pretty skimpy. But all those ounces have a way of adding up. On the other hand, you may not want to drink the entire amount—preferring to move on to the next wine. That's what the dump buckets are for. You'll also notice a pitcher of water on the counter. It's for rinsing your glass between wines or between types of wines—like when you go from whites to reds. Just pour a little water into your glass, swirl it around, and dump it out in the bucket.

Alternatively, you can drink the water to refresh your palate before the next wine. If you see a bowl of crackers on the counter, they're for cleansing your palate as well.

Nobody will have his feelings hurt if you dump your wine in the bucket. It's perfectly acceptable—and expected. No one will know whether you hate the wine or are being judicious with your consumption of alcohol. If no dump bucket is in sight, just ask for one.

Tasting Room Etiquette

The temptation is to treat winery visits like big cocktail parties. Yippee! The wine is flowing now! But a more subdued attitude is best. Not reverential—just respectful toward the people who are pouring (who are often the owners), toward winery property, and toward the other visitors.

Yuck, This Wine Is Swill!

You're not going to like every wine you taste. It's fine to express your preferences without offending anyone. Even if you absolutely loathe the wine, keep your remarks from being rude or disparaging.

So, what do you talk about when you're sipping wine across the counter from the winery representative? Remember that you don't have to prove your knowledge about wine to anyone—to the winery employee or to the assembled visitors in the tasting room. You can ask questions. Most winery personnel are trained to provide information and usually jump at the chance to talk about the wines. Their explanations, descriptions, and stories can add to your appreciation of their wines. For starters, ask:

♦ Which grapes they grow in their own vineyards.
♦ Which wines are aged in barrels—and for how long.
♦ What have been the best vintages—and why.
♦ How the winery got started.
♦ What foods would pair well with their wines.
♦ Which wine the winemaker is best known for.

The Ripe Stuff

Will the winemaker be there to answer questions?

It depends on the size of the winery, the time of year, and whether the winemaker is busy making wine. Your chances are better at smaller wineries, where the winemaker produces the wine and also runs the tasting room. If she is there, ask her to sign one of the bottles you purchase.

Spitting Is Allowed

When you visit several wineries in a day, an obvious concern is consuming too much alcohol. You can minimize both the amount and the effects.

- ◆ **You don't have to taste every wine at every winery**—You and your traveling companions can sample different wines. If one of you finds something really special, the rest of the group can try it too.
- ◆ **You don't have to polish off all the wine you're served**—When you've sipped enough to taste, dump it.
- ◆ **You can taste the wine, then spit it out in the dump bucket**—Yes, it's perfectly acceptable. Professional wine judges do it all the time. It may look kind of gross, but it's an option.
- ◆ **Drink lots of water**—It mitigates the dehydrating effects of alcohol. Pack plenty of bottled water for your trip and drink it often.
- ◆ **Eat along the way**—Start with a good breakfast and snack throughout the day. It helps to absorb the alcohol.

If you plan to bring your children along for your winetasting trip in the country, have planned activities for them while you're tasting. They can become easily bored. Be sure to keep them away from breakable objects in the tasting room and from farm machinery outside.

Savvy Sipping

Rules of Two

Under ordinary circumstances, asking for a second taste of one particular wine is inappropriate. However, if you're sincerely interested in buying the wine, let the pourer know your intentions.

When you've paid a tasting fee for one, it's perfectly okay to share your glass with a friend. It's also a way for the two of you to cut your alcohol consumption in half.

To Buy or Not to Buy

You're under no obligation to buy a bottle of wine at the tasting room, but there may be some good reasons to do so. Smaller production wineries have limited distribution and can be difficult—or impossible—to find on retailers' shelves. The only way to buy the wines may be directly from the winery—either at the tasting room or on their Web site.

Some wineries, even high-production ones, restrict the availability of their reserve bottlings or specialty wines to the winery. That's where you can taste them, and that's where you can buy them.

Message in a Bottle

It may seem illogical, but you'll often find wines selling for less at a wine store than at the winery. Because large retailers can get significant volume discounts, they can sell the wine at less than the list price suggested by the winery.

Buy by the bottle or by the case: your choice. Typically, a case discount (and sometimes a half-case discount) applies. It can be a case of one varietal or a mixed case.

Wine Clubs

Most wineries have mailing lists (and, increasingly, e-mail lists) so you can be notified about new releases and order directly from the source. Wineries also have wine clubs. When you sign up, you receive regular shipments of wine during the year—the number of shipments and bottles per shipment varying from club to club. Membership has its benefits—especially when you're partial to their wines:

- You get wines before they're released to the public.
- You receive a discount on wines.
- You get a discount on merchandise purchased from the winery.
- You may be invited to attend members-only special events.

Experiencing Wine Country

Wine country is more than wine. It's food, beautiful vistas, and romance. As you plan your winery visits, keep those other elements in mind.

What could be a greater pleasure than a picnic lunch and a glass of wine overlooking the vineyards? Not all wineries have picnic areas, so call ahead. Your lunch can be as simple or elaborate as you want. But picnic items you should consider taking are plates, eating utensils, table-cloth, napkins, cutting board and knife, wineglasses, and corkscrew. Of course, this *is* wine country . . . so if you don't have glasses and a cork-screw, the winery will usually let you borrow some of their glasses and open the bottle of wine for you.

Savvy Sipping

Remember the most important rule of picnicking at a winery: Always drink that win-ery's wine! They have welcomed you into their "house" and onto their property to enjoy yourself. It's just rude and tacky to take up their picnic space while sipping someone else's wine.

Wine country (any wine country) attracts people who enjoy good food. And it attracts restaurateurs who cater to that crowd. From casual delis to multiple-star eateries, you're likely to find good eating in the area. Some of the larger wineries have their own restaurants.

Getting Around

In wine country there are tour operators who can organize your trip for you. You can join an already scheduled tour. Or with their experience and winery relationships, the tour operators can create an itinerary just for you. Some of your options:

- ◆ **A scheduled tour**—This usually means a preset itinerary. You join others on a bus with a trained tour guide.

- **Limousine service**—You hire a limo with your own itinerary. The limo service may or may not have a driver that can also act as a tour guide.
- **A guided tour**—The tour company provides a van or limo and a tour guide and helps you create an itinerary.

Maybe you want to make your winetasting getaway an entire vacation. There are wine tour operators that can take you to "wine country" anywhere in the world. You can combine winetasting with cooking, biking, boating, or literature. The sky's the limit.

Vino Veritas

Ever thought of having your wedding reception or anniversary party at a winery? It's become big business for some wineries. Couples from around the world have discovered the distinctive opportunity of exchanging (or renewing) their vows in the vineyards—and making it a food and wine (as well as romantic) experience.

Postcards from Winery Visits

Every winery visit is a unique experience. As different as wine personalities are (with thousands of grapes and endless blending options—and effects of terroir), so too are winery profiles. A few generalities may be true for all visits (like you get to taste wine), but each winemaking facility has a character all its own. The following "postcards" from some well-known and some not-so-well-known wineries will give you the flavor of a visit there.

Château Potelle Winery

Have you every discovered a jewel of a restaurant in the middle of a huge city like New York or London that no tourist ever heard of? One that offered exquisite food, breathtaking ambiance, and romance on top of that? If so, you know what a visit to Château Potelle in Napa feels like. The drive is no small undertaking. You'll imagine—more than once—

that you're lost. Once you arrive, though, the view is worth every twist and turn you made. At 2,000 feet, you see all of Napa, its vineyards, its mountains of redwoods.

Pull up the hill past the winery and park at the old cabin-turned-tasting room. You'll be greeted by Tony, the "tasting room guru," who will charm you with his warmth, passion, and sense of fun. And for $5, he'll guide you through five of the winery's outstanding selections of Chardonnay, Sauvignon Blanc, Cabernet Sauvignon, and Zinfandel. Château Potelle produces small quantities of reserve wines and "house" wines (like the late harvest Port-style wine and the southern-French style Rosé) that are only available at the winery. You can taste them for another $5.

Tours need to be arranged in advance. They're conducted by the winemaker herself—Marketta Fourmeaux—who, with her husband Jean-Noël, created Château Potelle. Both are undeniably and captivatingly French. They were originally sent to California in 1980 as "spies" for the French government. Their mission: to learn about winemaking and vineyard management in California. They fell in love with the mountains of Napa and decided to make them their home.

Château Potelle is one of the few wineries in Napa (5 percent, to be exact) with a picnic area for its visitors. So plan to bring lunch.

Another secret: You'll notice the letters "VGS" on Château Potelle wines. They pertain to the quality of the wine—in a very unexpected way. You won't find out here. Just ask when you get there.

Château Potelle Winery
3875 Mt. Veeder Road
Napa, CA 94558
✆707-255-9440
✍*www.chateaupotelle.com*

Open: 7 days
Summer: 11 A.M.–6 P.M.
Winter: 11 A.M.–5 P.M.

Savvy Sipping

For a completely different Napa experience, consider the VIP tour and dinner at the Hess Collection Winery. A group of four will enjoy five courses with five wines, a barrel tasting, a personalized tour of the Art Gallery, and a Hess Collection art book for each guest. Price Tag: $500.

Biltmore Estate Winery

Who would have imagined that the most visited winery in America would be in North Carolina? It's more than a winery really. It's part of the enormous Biltmore Estate, built in 1895 by George Washington Vanderbilt. And the only way you can see the winery is by buying a $39 visitor pass for the estate tour. Every year, 600,000 people do that.

This is no small operation. Think Disney World. As you walk into the winery's visitors' center, you're invited to watch a three-minute video followed by a self-guided tour. You'll pass through barrel rooms and view stainless steel fermentation tanks and read as you go to learn about the winery's history and processes. The tour culminates at the entrance to the tasting room . . . or, make that *rooms*—plural. Once you take your place at one of the many tasting counters, it's time to choose your wines. Of the thirty wines that the winery produces, about a dozen appear on the tasting menu at any given time. Sample one—or sample all. And if the winery's premier wines and sparkling wines seem tempting, you can try those for another $6.

The Biltmore Estate Winery, which celebrated its twentieth anniversary in May 2005, grows about 20 percent of the grapes it uses. The Cabernet Franc, however, is made from grapes that are entirely estate-grown. A good example to sample. The people pouring your wines are well informed and can relate some fascinating facts. A case in point: Canada geese are among the vineyard's biggest pests. Apparently, the geese are really into vinifera grapes and don't like the taste of Concord grapes. So the winery sprays the vines with Concord grape juice. It's proved to be an effective repellent.

The winery has endless shopping opportunities in its store and an on-site restaurant that showcases the products—beef, lamb, fruit—raised or grown on the property. Throughout the year the winery has special events, included in your fee, like wine seminars, behind-the-scenes tours, and cooking demonstrations.

Biltmore Estate Winery
1 North Pack Square (mailing address)
Asheville, NC 28803
☎828-225-6280
✆*www.biltmore.com*

Open: 7 days
Summer: 11 A.M.–7 P.M.
Winter 12 P.M.–6 P.M.

Blue Mountain Vineyards

It may seem an unlikely location to some, but there's wine in the rolling hills of Pennsylvania's Lehigh Valley. From Allentown, it's about a fifteen-minute drive to Blue Mountain Vineyards—and a real escape from civilization. You think you're in the middle of nowhere. As you enter the property, you see a rustic cabinlike building and terraced vineyards up the hills. And way on top of the mountain is the home of Joe and Vickie Greff, owners of Blue Mountain.

Joe is the winemaker, and Vickie hosts the tasting room. She's the one who enthusiastically greets you at the door. The couple is justifiably proud of their wines that they've been producing since 1993. Among other things, their Merlot and Cab were served at a presidential summit.

They started out planting French hybrids in 1986 but soon realized that their microclimate was well-suited to vinifera vines too. They have eighteen different wines for you to try at the winery. And you can taste them for free! They're known for their dry reds, but buy a bottle of whatever is your favorite and take it to their large, outdoor deck. Plan to bring a picnic—or buy some of the winery's cheese and fresh bread to nibble on.

Joe and Vickie will happily give you a tour of the winery and vineyards. Weekends are usually best. If you have a large group, call them in advance. The husband-wife team gears the winery toward special events (like barrel tastings or German night). Every Sunday from 2 to 5 P.M. there's entertainment (and a $5 charge): Sunday afternoon blues, Sangria Sundays . . . the theme changes periodically.

Blue Mountain Vineyards has four dedicated stores in other areas of eastern Pennsylvania where you can also sample their wines.

Blue Mountain Vineyards
7627 Grape Vine Drive
New Tripoli, PA 18066
☏610-298-3068
✍www.bluemountainwine.com

Open: 7 days
11 A.M.–6 P.M.

Whitman Cellars

Not every winery is plunked down in the middle of vineyards. And not all wineries grow their own grapes. Whitman Cellars is a jewel of a winery in a light industrial section of Walla Walla, Washington. They contract with the area's growers to get the best grapes representing the microclimates suited to the wines they make. The grapes come from nineteen different vineyard blocks and are kept in separate barrels until the blending trials are complete.

Owner John Edwards (a successful CPA by day) and his partners Larry and Sally Thomason started the winery in 1998 with their first crush of two barrels of Merlot and one barrel of Cabernet that they blended into a Meritage. Production has expanded since then, but they're still a "boutique" winery, producing about 5,000 cases a year.

When you walk into the winery, straight ahead is a big window to the barrel room, and to your right is the tasting bar. Step right up to the bar for a sample of all their wines. May is the best time to visit—only because you can be assured they'll have all their wines available to taste. You see, they pour samples until they sell out. The Cab, Merlot, and the "Narcissa" blend are always there to taste. But as the year comes to a close, they might be out of the Syrah and Viognier. Whitman Cellars also makes a Port. It's only sold to their wine club members—but if it's available, you get to sample it. There's a $5 charge for tasting, but it's applied toward any purchase you make.

Count on some musical accompaniment to your tasting. The tasting room has a beautiful baby grand player piano, which probably comes in handy for special events too. The winery's barrel room is a popular spot for private parties. It comfortably holds 150 for a sit-down dinner.

Anyone at Whitman Cellars will be happy to give you a tour of the production area and barrel room. Just give them a heads-up. A phone call will help them schedule it.

Whitman Cellars
1015 West Pine Street
Walla Walla, WA 99362
☎509-529-1142
✍*www.whitmancellars.com*

Open: 7 days
11 A.M.–5 P.M.

Warwick Wine Estate

Warwick Estate is about 45 minutes from Cape Town in South Africa's gorgeous wine country. It's situated on the slopes of the Simonsberg Mountain in the Stellenbosch area. When you take the beautiful drive there, be careful not to miss the entrance. It's tucked away on your left-hand side as you're traveling on R44 in the direction of Paarl.

Savvy Sipping

The Warwick estate was originally an eighteenth-century farm belonging to Colonel Alexander Gordon who commanded a regiment in the Boer War. After the war, Gordon decided to stay—so he settled at Warwick (which he named after his Warwickshire regiment) to raise livestock and grow fruit.

Stan Ratcliffe bought the farm in 1964 and started planting Cabernet Sauvignon. Until then, there were no vines on the property. Stan subsequently married, and his wife Norma began to study winemaking. By 1985 they were in full production with Cabernet Sauvignon being one of their first wines. Today the farm is still in the Ratcliffe family and Norma's son Mike has been the managing director for the past few years.

At the end of the "cobbled" road after you've entered the property, you'll find the small tasting room perched on a wooden deck overlooking a dam in the distance. The deck is completely shaded and provides a peaceful atmosphere to taste wines and listen to the birds.

Nerina van Zyl runs the small and cozy tasting room inside. Everyone is so friendly and unhurried and makes you feel like you could spend all day savoring each sip. There's no charge for tasting unless you bring a group of six or more. (And be sure to call ahead if you're bringing a group because there's limited seating.) The wines you can taste range from crispy whites—Sauvignon Blanc and Chardonnay—to full-bodied fruity reds. In addition to their Pinotage and Cabernet Franc, they'll pour you their flagship blends—Three Cape Ladies and Trilogy.

Warwick Wine Estate
P.O. Box 2
Muldersvlei 7807
South Africa
✆+27 21 884 4410
✆www.warwickwine.co.za

Open: 6 days; Sundays, October through April only 11 A.M.–5 P.M.

Louis Guntrum

Talk about history! The Louis Guntrum wine estate, situated on Germany's Rhine River with breathtaking views, was started in 1648 by—you guessed it—Louis Guntrum. It's been in the hands of the family ever since. That's eleven generations.

The location of the winery has changed several times over the centuries because of various wars. This one was chosen in 1923 by the eighth generation. It's the very location where, in 1945, General Patton crossed the Rhine. In fact, Patton and his soldiers made the Guntrum home and winery their temporary headquarters.

Louis Guntrum is only about twenty-five miles from Frankfurt in between the two villages of Nierstein and Oppenheim. The winery doesn't have regular tours, but they always make time to welcome visitors and show them around their winery and vineyards—and to pour samples of their outstanding wines. But be sure to call in advance so they can arrange their schedules. They can accommodate groups from one (although, strictly speaking, that's not a group) to thirty.

There's ample parking when you get there. Depending on everyone's work schedule, you'll be greeted by Angelika Hamm (the head of customer relations), by Rüdiger Steck (the cellarmaster), or by the eleventh generation owner himself—Louis Konstantin Guntrum. One of them will escort you to the vineyards and through the stunning underground cellar system, parts of which date back to 1648. There are about a half a mile of vaulted cellars with wooden barrels of all sizes as well as stainless steel tanks. An awesome sight.

And then, off to the tasting room. The winery doesn't charge for tasting and will enthusiastically pour you samples from their entire range of wines—from dry Riesling, Pinot Gris, and Pinot Blanc all the way up to Riesling and Silvaner Auslese. And possibly even an Eiswein.

Louis Guntrum
Rheinallee 62, 55283   Open: By Appointment
Nierstein, Germany
☎011/49/6133/9717-0
✍www.guntrum.de

CHAPTER 20

Wine Information Resources

There's a big wine world out there! When you go looking for guidance and sound wine information, it's sometimes hard to know where to turn—or in what direction to turn first. Other times you find multiple sources of wine facts, and they're contradictory. Who do you believe? This final chapter provides some reliable sources—to give you a starting point to further your wine education and experimentation.

Who Do You Trust?

Robert Parker isn't the only wine critic around. In fact, there are literally millions of self-proclaimed critics in cyberspace and elsewhere. Everyone who enjoys wine has an opinion. And you don't have to be a Master of Wine to voice your opinion. But some individuals have had years of experience in tasting and judging that gives their opinions context—which is always helpful. When those people also happen to write in compelling, entertaining, and accessible ways, they have much to offer wine drinkers. Here are a few of those wine writers to check out.

♦ Dorothy J. Gaiter and John Brecher, *Wall Street Journal*
♦ Jancis Robinson, JancisRobinson.com (*www.jancisrobinson.com*)
♦ James Halliday, WinePros.com (*www.winepros.com*)
♦ Clive Coates (*www.clive-coates.com*)
♦ Robin Garr, WineLoversPage.com (*www.wineloverspage.com*)
♦ Allen Meadows, Burghound.com (*www.burghound.com*)
♦ Stephen Tanzer, *International Wine Cellar* (*http://wineaccess.com/expert/tanzer*)
♦ Jerry Mead, *WineTrader* (*www.wines.com/winetrader*)
♦ Natalie MacLean (*www.nataliemaclean.com*)
♦ Jennifer Rosen (*www.vinchotzi.com*)
♦ Andrea Immer (*www.andreaimmer.com*)

Wine Magazines, Newsletters, and Web Sites

If you're into sports, you read *Sports Illustrated*. If you're into food, you subscribe to *Gourmet*. When you're into wine, what do you read? The number of choices is staggering. You have national magazines like *Wine Spectator* that you can buy on the newsstand, international publications like *Decanter* that you can subscribe to, regional magazines that focus on wines in your area, and newsletters that spotlight your particular wine interests. There's also *Wine Country International*, a quarterly publication dedicated to increasing the knowledge and enjoyment of wine for wine enthusiasts and experts alike. For wine drinkers who want a fun, straightforward way to pursue wine knowledge, *Swirl Wine News* is a practical bimonthly newsletter that covers topics both general (varietals) and specific (wine-friendly restaurants).

Wine magazines and newsletters aren't limited to the ones you can hold in your hands. Most of the wine writers listed above have online newsletters—daily, weekly, monthly, and bimonthly—that you can subscribe to. Some are free, and some are available by paid subscription.

Message in a Bottle

If you not only enjoy drinking your wine, but also like to experiment in your kitchen or basement with home winemaking, you might appreciate the magazine *Wine-Maker (www.winemakermag.com)*. This publication helps you make world-class wines at home with hands-on articles, expert tips, and great recipes for all levels of home winemakers.

Wine Web sites abound. It would take an entire book to list the ones available today—and another book next week with all the new ones. But here's your starter list for different kinds of wine information.

- **Benson Marketing Group** (*www.bensonmarketing.com*)—Get daily wine news culled from newspapers and news services worldwide.
- **IntoWine.com** (*www.intowine.com*)—Here you'll find an introduction to wine with articles on enjoying wine, wine and health, storing wine, and more.
- **wineanswers.com** (*www.wineanswers.com*)—A fun-filled education site with quizzes, columns, and wine facts of the day.
- **The Wine Skinny** (*www.wineskinny.com*)—You get wine reviews, recipes, party ideas, and more.
- **Free the Grapes!** (*www.freethegrapes.com*)—If you're interested in the issue of direct shipment of wine, this grass-roots organization will keep you up to date.
- **Wine on the Web** (*www.wineontheweb.com*)—WOW is an Internet magazine that offers a *talking* site with consumer advice, wine news, and features.

- ◆ **About.com** (*http://wine.about.com*)—The wine link offers wine basics and articles on wine topics from shopping to parties.
- ◆ **Tasting Wine** (*www.tasting-wine.com*)—This site offers information on the art of tasting wine: etiquette, venues, and terms.

Have Wine, Will Travel

Imagine yourself basking in the Mediterranean sun with a glass of Fiano di Avellino in hand . . . or sailing down the Rhine past thirteenth-century castles while sipping an exquisite Riesling. Wine is about experiencing a place through taste. If terroir is all-important, what could possibly be better than experiencing the wine and its "home" at the same time?

Imagining yourself sipping wine in international locales is one thing. Doing it is quite another. That's why there are travel companies.

Walking and Biking

Seeing wine country on foot or on a bike has a lot of benefits. One, of course, is that you work off all the wine and food calories that you consume along the way. Walking/biking tours let you discover fascinating areas that just aren't possible to see otherwise. You get to experience the people and the culture of the region in a unique way.

Butterfield & Robinson (*www.butterfield.com*) and Backroads (*www. backroads.com*) are two active travel companies that arrange wine country tours as well as other special-interest tours. Between them, they cover Europe and the Mediterranean, North America, Latin America, Asia and the Pacific, Africa, Australia, and New Zealand.

Message in a Bottle

When you're in a foreign country where the wine choices may be unfamiliar to you, go for the best of the local wines. Regional cuisines and wine styles have usually evolved to complement each other. In Italy's Campania region, that could mean a Greco di Tufo. In the Loire Valley of France, your selection could be a Sancerre.

Wine Cruises to . . . Anywhere

Cruise lines offer wine enthusiasts onboard wine programs and wine-focused shore excursions. Silversea Cruises (*www.silversea.com*) has "Wine Series" cruises that incorporate activities both on the ship and onshore. They include lectures, tastings, guided tours to wineries and vineyards—all conducted by experts.

Crystal Cruises (*www.crystalcruises.com*) has "Wine and Food Festival" sailings. In addition to celebrity chefs preparing their signature dishes and demonstrating cooking techniques, wine experts lead tastings.

What should I expect to pay for a bottle of wine in a restaurant in a foreign country?

The Ripe Stuff

It depends on the type of restaurant. If you're in a large city and dining at a four-star restaurant, expect to pay about the same markup as in a U.S. restaurant (double or triple the retail price). However, when dining at local eateries, where the selection may be limited to local wines (and these are your best bets, too!), the markups are miniscule (slightly above retail).

A River Runs Through Wine Country

You don't have to be on the high seas to take advantage of wine vacations. Take a leisurely trip through wine country via the inland waterways. The French countryside is a land of striking contrasts that you can experience on a deluxe barge. French Country Waterways (*www.fcwl.com*) has itineraries to the Loire Valley, Burgundy, Champagne, and Alsace.

If you'd prefer to travel in luxury to destinations closer to home, American Safari Cruises (*www.amsafari.com*) explores California's wine country. You glide along bays and rivers onboard an eleven-stateroom megayacht.

Wine and Golf Are a Vintage Blend

You never have to choose between a golf vacation and a wine getaway. From California to France to South Africa to New Zealand and back to California, golf and wine mix beautifully. Courses around the world are set among scenic vineyards. Some homegrown courses and resorts are:

♦ **The Course at Wente Vineyards in Livermore, California** (*www. wentevineyards.com*)—The Greg Norman–designed course weaves vines and fairways together and flows over 200 feet of elevation change.

♦ **Chardonnay Golf Club in Napa Valley, California** (*www. chardonnaygolfclub.com*)—This semiprivate club has twenty-seven holes and 500 acres that meander through Chardonnay and Merlot vineyards.

♦ **Château Élan Winery & Resort in Braselton, Georgia** (*www. chateauelanatlanta.com*)—The resort includes three championship courses, 200 acres of vineyards, and a French provincial inn and golf villas.

Luxury Wine Country Travel

If ships and yachts aren't quite enough to satisfy your thirst for travel, more luxury options await you. INTRAV (*www.intrav.com*) conducts a nineteen-day tour of Australia's and New Zealand's wine country and transports guests onboard an exclusively chartered Douglas DC-3 aircraft. Needless to say, in between vineyard visits, it's deluxe accommodations all the way.

Abercrombie & Kent (*www.abercrombiekent.com*) is another luxury travel company that will develop customized wine-focused trips. The travel operator started as an African safari company and now arranges both escorted and independent travel in more than 100 countries.

Food and Wine Fun

If dining and feasting on native cuisines while sipping local wines are your requirements for a vacation, there are plenty of tours that offer food and wine pairing adventures. Château Food and Wine Company (*www.chateaufoodandwinetours.com*) is one. They offer the perfect food and wine experience. With packages to Provence or to the heart of Italy, their tours include dining at the top local restaurants with the best wine lists. The real treat is that all lodging accommodations are at local châteaus.

The same type of trip is available in Australia and New Zealand through Wine and Food Tours and Travel (*www.wine-region-tours.com*) with lodgings in historic settings.

For the ultimate foodie who wants to hone her cooking skills, there are private or group cooking lessons and winetasting classes offered in Tuscany. You can learn the art of Tuscan cooking and visit the finest winemakers in the region. Vinarian (*www.vinaio.com*) presents the best of Tuscany's wine and food culture while enjoying fun in their kitchens.

Message in a Bottle

Brown-Wrapper Winery Trips

Sometimes your objectives are more modest. You don't want to plan an entire vacation in some faraway location. In fact, you want to do as little actual traveling as possible. With working wineries in every state of the Union, surely there's one within driving distance of your home. One way to find out is through WeekendWinery.com (*www.weekendwinery.com*). Click on a state, and you'll find a list of wineries with links to the winery sites. Some states have so many wineries that they're subdivided into regions. The site is an especially good tool for planning "rest" stops on lengthy car trips.

The Pleasure of Your Company

Wine is meant to be shared. Experiencing wine in a group—whether it be old friends, new acquaintances, or complete strangers—adds a whole other dimension to enjoying and learning about wine.

Where do you go to find a group? It can be as close as your neighborhood wine store. Enthusiastic retailers organize periodic tastings for customers. Depending on state laws, the tastings might be in the store—or, in states that don't allow in-store consumption—off-site. The tastings might be free or they might have a modest charge attached. But they're a simple, fast, and stress-free way to join a wine group.

Area restaurants are another source. Some restaurants have active wine programs that include getting groups of wine enthusiasts together. The group events can take on a variety of forms:

- ◆ Wine dinners with the winemaker in attendance.
- ◆ Guided winetastings, with a knowledgeable individual (sommelier, wine writer, retail wine manager) presiding.
- ◆ Wine and food pairing presentation.
- ◆ Free-form wine and hors d'oeuvres reception.

Every city has wine events going on—fundraisers, dinners, festivals, auctions, classes, store tastings, winery programs. A good place to find out about them is through LocalWineEvents.com (*www.localwineevents. com*). The Web site lists events in the United States and in foreign countries—so even if you're traveling, you can find the wine calendar for your destination city.

Wine Groups

People with the same interests just naturally seek each other out. Some of them make the relationship official by establishing a formal organization. It applies to wine drinkers the same as everyone else.

A national organization that was founded in 1981 by Julia Child and Robert Mondavi is the American Institute of Wine and Food. Its purpose is to improve the appreciation and understanding of wine and food. It has twenty-nine chapters and 6,000 members. Members attend seminars and social events and get advance information about auctions (*www.aiwf.org*).

Women for Winesense (*www.womenforwinesense.org*) was also started by people involved in the wine industry—in this case, women winemakers who wanted to inject some common sense into the debate about the effects of moderate wine drinking. The organization has ten chapters around the country that have regular winetasting programs.

Vino Veritas

One local winetasting group called Divas Uncorked (*www.divasuncorked.com*) has been hosting wine and food gatherings in Boston since 1999. They're a group of African-American professional women who've helped each other learn about wine while having a bunch of fun. They've expanded their get-togethers to hosting local public wine conferences and special tastings and dining adventures. Their journeys have been featured in the *Wall Street Journal* and *Newsweek*.

In-Home Winetasting

You know the Tupperware concept. You're invited to someone's house for a party, you listen to a Tupperware representative, and then you buy whatever stuff appeals to you. The model has been used successfully for products of all kinds from fine art to sexy lingerie. Count wine among those products.

One company providing this service is the Traveling Vineyard (*www.thetravelingvineyard.com*). You invite your friends over for some wine. A sales consultant conducts a winetasting of their wines. When the tasting is over, you put in your wine order.

The Big Wine Marketplace

Buying wine is a fairly simple proposition for most consumers. If you're over twenty-one and your community allows the sale of alcohol, all you have to do is drive to the nearest wine store—or in some states, grocery store or drug store.

The Internet has made buying wine even more accessible. Retail Web sites, winery Web sites, and auction sites now offer virtual wine selections that are difficult to stock in one physical, standalone store. Some of the major online retailers include:

- Wine.com (*www.wine.com*)
- Wine Library (*www.winelibrary.com*)
- K&L Wine Merchants (*www.klwines.com*)
- Winechâteau.com (*www.winechateau.com*)
- The Wine Buyer (*www.thewinebuyer.com*)
- PrimeWines (*www.primewines.com*)

Know How to Accessorize

In order to enjoy your favorite wine, you need a few accessories. Like a wineglass. And a corkscrew. And if you're going to a BYO restaurant, you'll need a tote. The popularity of wine has spawned new industries. Who ever dreamed up the idea of flattening a wine bottle to make a cheese board? Or hanging little charms around the stems of glasses to keep someone else from inadvertently drinking your wine?

Wine accessories are as ubiquitous as pet products. Nothing wrong with that!

You might not find wine accessories that you might categorize as "essentials" (versus "trends") by taking a trip to the mall. But you will find them from catalog companies. The two most well known are Wine Enthusiast (*www.wineenthusiast.com*) and International Wine Accessories (*www.iwawine.com*). The types of products they offer are:

- Glassware
- Wine cellars
- Wine racks
- Corkscrews
- Cooling units

- Preservation systems
- Decanters
- Carriers
- Home décor

Looking for top-of-the-line wineglasses on a budget? Riedel (who just bought another superior crystal glassware producer, Spiegelau), considered to be one of the finest crystal glassware manufacturers in the world, offers their wineglasses in a lower price "series." Their Vinum collection is reasonably priced and will not break your bank if one of your guests breaks a glass.

Message in a Bottle

Personalizing Your Gift

If you're looking for that consummate gift to give your wine friend—why not a bottle of her favorite vino labeled just for her? There's a multitude of companies that specialize in helping you create the perfect label. You can add your text to a Monet painting, reprint your friend's wedding invitation, copy her family's coat-of-arms, or create your own label in any format you choose. Two online sources are Signature Wines (*www.signaturewines.com*) and 4-Personalized-Wine-Labels (*www.4-personalized-wine-labels.com*). There are also software packages available at your local office supply stores. They require a little extra effort, but worth the savings.

Is a Career in Wine Part of Your Future?

The more you learn about wine, the more you *want* to learn. You probably don't need John Edward to tell you whether your passion for wine will translate into a career. You already know if you want to make wine part of your everyday life (besides drinking it, of course).

The career paths are numerous and varied—depending on what part of the wine growing-making-selling-serving chain interests you. Following are some institutions and their programs and degrees.

College-Based Options

Some college and university programs offer part-time instruction in addition to their full-time degree programs.

- The University of California at Davis and Oregon State University both offer four-year undergraduate programs and postgraduate degrees that range from enology to viticulture to wine marketing.
- The CIA (no, not the one in Langley, Virginia!) is the Culinary Institute of America, home to one of the premier training grounds for chefs. It has lots of classes geared to wine: food and wine dynamics, sensory evaluation of wines, and mastering European wines are among them.
- Boston University's Elizabeth Bishop Wine Resource Center offers courses in all aspects of wine, including wine history, economics, distribution and marketing, and the psychological, physiological, and cultural phenomena of wine consumption.
- Community colleges—particularly in California, Washington, and New York—offer associate degrees on a full-time or part-time basis. The courses are frequently taught by local winemakers or vineyard managers.

Independent Programs

You don't have to be studying for professional reasons to benefit from wine classes. Individuals and institutions offer wine course study programs in many cities around the country—and even self-study courses that you can take at home. *Wine Spectator* offers self-study classes. Topics include regions (Bordeaux, Tuscany, Australia and New Zealand, Burgundy, Rhone), varietals (California Cabs), as well as Understanding Wine, ABCs of Tasting, Advanced Sensory Evaluation, and Wine Collecting.

The Institute for Culinary Education in New York City has a mix of one-session, two-session, and six-session courses devoted to wine. Topics cover regions in addition to Wine Essentials, Wine and Food Workshops, and the ever-popular Really Great Wines for Under $15.

Local Wine Programs

Every major city in the United States offers diverse wine-learning adventures. There's something wine-related for anyone on almost any given day. Maybe it's a Port tasting, a vertical Pinot Noir tasting, or an Australian sparkling sampling. These classes are your opportunity to mix with the wine crowd and learn a little something extra about your favorite wine—or soon to be favorite wine—and maybe give you the edge over your wine crony friend. Some examples are: Executive Wine Seminars, New York (*www.ewswine.com*); the Wine School of Philadelphia (*www.winelust.com*); a no-nonsense wine school in St. Louis (*www.corkdork.com*); Chicago Wine School (wineschool.com); French Culinary Institute in New York (*www.frenchculinary.com*); and Balboa Park Food and Wine School in San Diego (*www.cohnrestaurants.com*).

It's Time to Fly

You've made it! You can wow your friends with your knowledge of wine history, varietals, regions, food matches, and bargains. You can look every bit the expert when you order wine at a restaurant, and you can pronounce *Viogner* like you were born in France. Congratulations. It's the moment you've been working toward—when you can stop reading . . . and start wining!

Pronunciation Guide

Albariño	ahl-bah-REE-nyoh
Alsace	ahl-SASS
Amarone	ah-mah-ROH-neh
Asti	AH-stee
Auslese	OWS-lay-zuh
Banyuls	bah-NYUHLS
Barbaresco	bar-bah-RESS-koh
Barbera d'Alba	bar-BEHR-ah DAHL-bah
Barbera d'Asti	bar-BEHR-ah DAH-stee
Bardolino	bar-doh-LEE-noh
Barolo	bah-ROH-loh
Beaujolais	boh-zhuh-LAY
Beerenauslese	BAY-ruhn-OWS-lay-zuh
Blanc de blanc	BLAHNGK duh BLAHNGK
Blanc de noir	blahngk duh NWAHR
Blauburgunder	BLOW-ber-guhn-der
Blaufränkisch	blow-FREHN-kish
Bollinger	BOHL-in-jer
Bordeaux	bor-DOE
Botrytis cinerea	boh-TRY-tihs sihn-EHR-ee-uh
Bourgogne	boor-GON-yuh
Brouilly	broo-YEE
Brunello di Montalcino	broo-NELL-oh dee mawn-tahl-CHEE-noh
Brut	BROOT
Cabernet Franc	ka-behr-NAY FRAHNGK

Cabernet Sauvignon	ka-behr-NAY SAW-vee-nyohn
Campania	kahm-PAH-nyah
Carmenère	kahr-meh-NEHR
Carneros	kahr-NEH-rohs
Cava	KAH-vah
Chablis	shah-BLEE
Champagne	sham-PAYN
Chardonnay	shar-doh-NAY
Château Cos d'Estournel	sha-TOH kaws dehss-toor-NEHL
Château d'Yquem	sha-TOH dee-KEHM
Château Gruaud-Larose	sha-TOH groo-oh lah-ROHZ
Château Haut-Brion	sha-TOH oh-bree-OHN
Château Haut-Bailly	sha-TOH oh bah-YEE
Château Lafite Rothschild	sha-TOH lah-FEET rawt-SHEELD
Château Lagrange	sha-TOH la-GRAHNZH
Château Latour	sha-TOH lah-TOOR
Château Margaux	sha-TOH mahr-GOH
Château Mouton-Rothschild	sha-TOH moo-TAWN rawt-SHEELD
Château Pétrus	sha-TOH pay-TROOS
Châteauneuf-du-Pape	sha-toh-nuhf-doo-PAHP
Chenin Blanc	shen-in BLAHNGK
Chianti	kee-AHN-tee
Chinon	shee-NOHN
Cinsault	SAN-soh
Clos de Vougeot	kloh duh voo-ZHOH
Cognac	KOHN-yak
Colheita	kuhl-YAY-tah
Condrieu	kawn-DREE-yuh
Copita	koh-PEE-tah
Corton-Charlemagne	kor-TAWN shahr-luh-MAHN-yuh

Côte de Beaune	koht duh BOHN
Côte de Nuit	koht duh NWEE
Côte d'Or	koht DOR
Côte Rôtie	koht roh-TEE
Côtes du Rhone	koht deu ROHN
Crianza	kree-AHN-zah
Cuvée	koo-VAY
Dolcetto	dohl-CHEHT-oh
Dosage	doh-SAHJ
Douro	DOO-roh
Doux	DOO
Eiswein	ICE-vine
Enology	ee-NAHL-uh-jee
Enophile	EE-nuh-file
Frizzante	freet-SAHN-teh
Fumé Blanc	FOO-may BLAHNGK
Gamay	ga-MAY
Gavi	GAH-vee
Gewürztraminer	guh-VURTS-trah-mee-ner
Grand cru classé	grahn kroo klah-SAY
Graves	GRAHV
Grenache	gruh-NAHSH
Grüner Veltliner	GROO-ner FELT-lee-ner
Halbtrocken	HAHLP-troe-ken
Hermitage	her-mee-TAHZH
Heurige	HOY-rih-guh
Kabinett	kah-bih-NEHT
Krug	KROOG
Lambrusco	lam-BROO-skoh
Languedoc-Roussillon	lahng-DAWK roo-see-YAWN

Loire	LWAHR
Mâcon Villages	mah-KAWN vee-LAHZH
Madeira	muh-DEER-uh
Malbec	mahl-BEHK
Médoc	may-DAWK
Meritage	MEHR-ih-tihj
Merlot	mehr-LOH
Méthode champenoise	may-TOHD shahm-peh-NWAHZ
Meunier	muh-NYAY
Meursault	mehr-SOH
Mis en Bouteille	mee zahn boo-TEH-yuh
Moët & Chandon	moh-EHT ay shahn-DAWN
Mosel	MOH-zuhl
Mourvèdre	moor-VEH-druh
Muscadet	meuhs-kah-DAY
Muscadine	MUHS-kuh-dihn
Muscat	MUHS-kat
Nebbiolo	neh-BYOH-loh
Nouveau	noo-VOH
Orvieto	ohr-VYAY-toh
Pauillac	poh-YAK
Penedès	pay-NAY-dahs
Perrier-Jouët	peh-RYAY zhoo-AY
Petit Verdot	puh-TEE vehr-DOH
Petite Sirah	peh-TEET sih-RAH
Picpoul	PEEK-pool
Pinot Blanc	PEE-noh BLAHNGK
Pinot Grigio	PEE-noh GREE-zhoh
Pinot Gris	PEE-noh GREE
Pinot Noir	PEE-noh NWAHR

Pinotage	pee-noh-TAHJ
Piper Heidsieck	PIPE-er HIDE-sehk
Pomerol	paw-muh-RAWL
Pommard	paw-MAHR
Pouilly-Fuissé	poo-yee fwee-SAY
Pouilly-Fumé	poo-yee few-MAY
Premier cru	preh-MYAY KROO
Primitivo	pree-mee-TEE-voh
Prosecco	praw-SEH-koh
Quinta	KEEN-tah
Riesling	REEZ-ling
Rioja	ree-OH-hah
Riserva	ree-ZEHR-vah
Sancerre	sahn-SEHR
Sangiovese	san-joh-VAY-zeh
Sauternes	soh-TEHRN
Sauvignon Blanc	SAW-vee-nyohn BLAHNGK
Sec	SAHK
Sekt	ZEHKT
Sémillon	seh-mee-YAWN
Semillon	SEH-meh-lon
Shiraz	shee-RAHZ
Soave	SWAH-veh
Sommelier	saw-muhl-YAY
Spätlese	SHPAYT-lay-zuh
Spumante	spoo-MAHN-tay
Syrah	see-RAH
Taittinger	that-teen-ZHEHR
Tastevin	taht-VAHN
Tavel	ta-VEHL

Tempranillo	tem-prah-NEE-yoh
Terroir	tehr-WAHR
Tinto	TEEN-toh
Trocken	TROH-kuhn
Valpolicella	vahl-paw-lee-CHEHL-lah
Verdelho	vehr-DEHL-yoh
Verdicchio	vehr-DEEK-yoh
Veuve Clicquot Ponsardin	vurv klee-KOH pawn-sahr-DAN
Vin de pays	van duh pay-YEE
Vinho Verde	VEEN-yoh VEHR-deh
Vino Nobile de Montepulciano	VEE-noh NAW-bee-lay dee mawn-teh-pool-CHAH-noh
Vitis Vinifera	viht-ihs vihn-IF-uh-ruh
Viognier	vee-oh-NYAY
Vouvray	voo-VRAY
Weissburgunder	VISE-ber-guhn-der
Zinfandel	ZIHN-fuhn-dehl

Glossary

acidity
Naturally occurring acids in grapes that are vital components for the life, vitality, and balance of all wines.

aging
Maturing process of a wine to improve its taste.

alcohol
The major component in wine. Also known as *ethyl alcohol.*

appellation
The official geographical location where the grapes used in the wine are grown.

aroma
The smell of a wine.

astringent
The puckering sensation in the mouth attributable to the tannins and acids found in some wines.

austere
A tasting term that is used to describe young wines that have not yet developed a discernable aroma.

balance
A tasting term that describes how well a wine's components complement each other.

barrel
A container used to store or ferment wine.

big
This term used to describe wines that are of full of flavor and with high levels of tannins, alcohol, and grape flavor extracts.

bite
A result of good levels of acidity (especially in young wines).

bitter
Unpleasant taste that registers at the back of the tongue.

blanc de blanc
A white wine—most often sparkling—made exclusively from white grapes.

blanc de noir
A white or slightly tinted wine—and usually sparkling—made exclusively from red grapes.

blend

The technique of mixing wines of different varieties, regions, and barrels from different years.

body

Perception of fullness or texture in the mouth due primarily to the wine's alcohol.

bottle aging

Allowing wine to acquire complexity, depth, and texture in the bottle.

bouquet

The combination of flowery and fruity aromas that come from the alcohols and acids in a wine.

breathe

Allowing air to mix with a wine to develop its flavor.

brut

Dry style of Champagne and sparkling wine.

capsule

The protective cover of tin, lead, aluminum, or plastic that is placed over the top of a bottle of wine to insulate the wine from outside influences.

Cava

The Spanish term for sparkling wines made using the traditional Champagne method.

character

A wine's features and style.

clarity

The appearance of wine that has no cloudiness.

clean

Wines that are straightforward and have no unpleasant odors or flavors.

cloudy

The opposite of clarity; wine that is visually unclear.

complex

Nuances of flavors of a wine often achieved with aging.

cork

The spongy material from the bark of the cork tree used to seal wine bottles.

corked

Wines that have the smell of wood "dry rot" resulting from a defective cork.

crisp

Wines with good acidity and taste without excessive sweetness.

cru

French term meaning "growth."

cuvée

Blend; in the production of Champagne, cuvée is the specific blend of still wines used as a base for Champagne.

decanting

Pouring wine from a bottle into a carafe or decanter.

depth

Wines with full-bodied, intense, and complex flavors.

disgorging

Removing sediment from a bottle of Champagne following secondary fermentation.

dry

Opposite of sweet. All the sugar from the grapes has been converted to alcohol during fermentation.

earthy

Flavors derived from the soil where the grapes have been grown.

enology

The study of wine and winemaking; also *oenology*.

extra dry

Champagne classification where there is a slight perception of sweetness.

fat

A big, soft, and silky wine that fills the mouth.

fermentation

The process that turns grape juice into wine. The enzymes in the yeast convert sugar into alcohol and carbon dioxide.

fining

Clarifying young wine before bottling to remove impurities.

finish

The aftertaste or impression a wine leaves after it's swallowed.

fortified wine

Wine whose alcohol content is increased by adding brandy or neutral spirits.

fruity

The flavor or aroma of fruits in wine.

hard

An abundance of tannin or acidity.

ice wine

Extremely sweet wines made from grapes that have been frozen on the vines prior to harvest; also called *Eiswein*.

late harvest wine

Wine made from ripe grapes left on the vine for periods in excess of their normal picking times, resulting in an extreme concentration of sugar.

lees
The sediment of yeasts and small grape particles that settle in the barrel as wine develops.

maceration
Technique of fermenting uncrushed grapes under pressure to produce fresh, fruity wine.

magnum
A bottle holding 1.5 liters or the equivalent of two standard bottles.

Meritage
Term used for both red and white American wines that are produced by blending traditional Bordeaux grape varietals.

nutty
A fine, crisp flavor often found in sherries and fine white wines.

oak
The flavor imparted to wine by barrel aging. It can be best described as a toasty or woodlike flavor. Sometimes a vanilla flavor will be imparted by fine oak to the wine.

oxidation
Exposure of wine to air, which causes chemical changes and deterioration.

pigeage
A French term for the traditional stomping of grapes by foot.

press
The piece of equipment used to gently separate grape juice from grape skins.

punt
The indentation at the base of a wine or Champagne bottle, which reinforces the bottle's structure.

reserve
A term without a legal definition in the United States but often used to designate a special wine.

richness
Rich wines have well-balanced flavors and intrinsic power.

sec
A term, when applied to Champagne, that describes a relatively sweet wine. Used in the context of still wines, the term means *dry*—without any residual sugar.

secondary fermentation
The process of converting still wine into Champagne that takes place in the bottle. In the production of still wines, the term is

sometimes used in place of malolactic fermentation.

sommelier
French term for "wine waiter."

spumante
The Italian term for fully sparkling wines as opposed to those that are slightly sparkling—*frizzante*.

tannin
Substance found naturally in wine from the skin, pulp, and stalks. Tannins are responsible for the astringent quality found in wine, especially red wines. Tannins form the basis for the long life of wines and, while they can be overpowering in young wines, with bottle aging, they tend to become softer.

terroir
Literally the "soil." A French term referring to the particular character (aromas and flavors) of a given vineyard—or even a small part of that vineyard.

thin
Wines that lack fullness, depth, and complexity.

varietal
A wine named after the grape from which it is produced. In California, for instance, a wine labeled "Pinot Noir" must by law consist of at least 75 percent Pinot Noir grapes.

vineyard
The place where grapes are grown.

vinification
The process of making wine.

vintage
Harvest year of grapes and the resulting wines made from them. Ninety-five percent of the wine in a vintage-designated bottle must be from grapes harvested in that year.

viticulture
The practice (art, science, and philosophy) of growing grapevines.

woody
In most wines this is an undesirable condition indicating that there is a taint of some type from defective wood or an overuse of new oak.

yeast
Naturally occurring, single-celled organisms found on the skins of grapes that are the primary promoters of fermentation. In the fermentation process, yeast turns sugar into alcohol and carbon dioxide.

Index

I

Ice wines, 228–29
Investment wines, 251–52
Italian wines, 86–89, 218

J

Journaling wine preferences, 172–73

K

Kennedy, John F., 13
Kosher wine, 27–30

L

Labels, reading, 46–49, 81, 89, 91
Lambrusco, 104, 218
Late harvest wines, 227–28
Laundering stains, 191
Lead crystal, risks, 268
Lees, 19
Lemberger wine, 120
Lingo, of wine, 127–29
Loire Valley, 85, 217
Longevity (human), wine and, 259
Longevity, of wine, 244–47
Louis Guntrum wine estate, 284–85

M

Mâcon, 83
Madeira, 26, 235–36
Maderized wine, 131
Magazines, 288–89
Magnum, 216
Making wine, 17–33
    aging process, 20–21, 22
    bottling process, 21
    cost of. *See* Cost of wine
    dessert wine, 26–27
    fermentation process, 18, 19–20
    fortified wine, 25–26

harvesting/preparing grapes, 18–19
    kosher wine, 27–30
    organic wine, 30–32
    red wine, 21–22
    Rosé, 23–24
    sparkling wine, 24–25
    vegetarian/vegan wine, 33
    white wine, 22–23
Malbec, 63, 82, 104, 106
Malolactic fermentation (ML, MLF), 20
Manischewitz, 12
Market-driven hot sellers, 157
Marsala, 26
Meritage wines, 45–46, 115
Merlot, 14, 54–55
    aging/longevity of, 244–45
    domestic sources, 112, 117, 119, 120
    food and, 139
    international sources, 80, 82, 98, 104, 107
Méthode champenoise, 208–9, 210
Mold (*Botrytis cinerea*), 27, 227–28
Moscatel, 104
Moscato d'Asti, 218
Müller-Thurgau grape, 41
Muscadet, 85
Muscat, 70–71, 86
Myths, about wine, x

N

Naming wines
    Meritage wines, 45–46
    Old World meets New World, 44
    proprietary wines, 45
    regional names, 42–43, 44
    varietals, 14, 43–44
Napa Valley, 112, 270
Navarra, 93
Nebbiolo, 63, 104, 245
New Mexico wines, 122
New York wines, 115–17
New Zealand wines, 98–100

Sonoma (CA), 113
South African wines, 100–101
Spanish wines, 91–93, 165, 217–18
Sparkling wine, 24–25, 93, 144, 209–10, 217–18, 219. *See also* Champagne
Stains, removing, 191
Steen, 101
Stelvin screw top, 168–69
Storage. *See* Wine cellars
Style preferences, 131
Sulfites, 264–66
Sulfur dioxide, 131
Sultana, 101
Supreme Court decisions, 154
Sweetness of wines, 19
Swirling wine, 126–27
Swishing/slurping wine, 127
Sylvaner, 86
Syrah/Shiraz, 15, 16, 53, 57–58, 97, 104, 120, 139, 144, 245

T

Tannins, 140, 181, 247
Tasting wine, 123–27
   blind tasting, 188
   five senses and, 124–26
   horizontal tasting, 187–88
   in-home parties, 295
   in-store tastings, 162
   physiology of taste, 124–26
   in restaurants, 201–2
   techniques, 126–27
   vertical tasting, 187
   at wineries, 272–75
   winetasting parties, 186–88, 295
TCA, 129–30
Teeth, purple, 267
Temperature, serving, 180
Temperature, storage, 239
Tempranillo, 59, 92, 104, 139
Terms, wine, 127–29

Texas wines, 121–22
Thanksgiving wines, 189–90
Tiers of distribution, 151–54
Time management strategy, 243–44
Tobacco Tax and Trade Bureau (TTB), 47
Tokay (Tokaji) wines, 72, 228
Traminette, 69
Travel resources, 290–93. *See also* Wineries
Trocken, 90
Turkey, 108

U

United States. *See also* Regions, United States
   expansion of wine regions, 14–15
   fads/fashions, 15
   history of wine, 7–16
   Prohibition, 10–12, 106
   sparkling wines, 219
   wine boom, 12–16

V

Varietal wines, 14, 43–44, 103–4, 112, 164–65. *See also specific wine names*
Vegetarian/vegan wine, 33
Vertical tasting, 187
Vine-Glo, 12
Vintages, 49, 133–34
Viognier, 75–76
Vitas rotundifolia, 38
Vitis aestivalis, 38
Vitis labrusca, 37, 41–42
Vitis vinifera, 8, 36, 37
Vouvray, 85

W

Warwick Wine Estate, 283–84
Washington wines, 119–21
Web sites, 289–90
Weight loss, 261–62

The EVERYTHING Series!

BUSINESS & PERSONAL FINANCE

Everything® **Accounting Book**
Everything® Budgeting Book
Everything® Business Planning Book
Everything® Coaching and Mentoring Book
Everything® Fundraising Book
Everything® Get Out of Debt Book
Everything® Grant Writing Book
Everything® Home-Based Business Book, 2nd Ed.
Everything® Homebuying Book, 2nd Ed.
Everything® Homeselling Book, 2nd Ed.
Everything® Investing Book, 2nd Ed.
Everything® Landlording Book
Everything® Leadership Book
Everything® **Managing People Book, 2nd Ed.**
Everything® Negotiating Book
Everything® Online Auctions Book
Everything® Online Business Book
Everything® Personal Finance Book
Everything® Personal Finance in Your 20s and 30s Book
Everything® Project Management Book
Everything® Real Estate Investing Book
Everything® Robert's Rules Book, $7.95
Everything® Selling Book
Everything® **Start Your Own Business Book, 2nd Ed.**
Everything® Wills & Estate Planning Book

COOKING

Everything® Barbecue Cookbook
Everything® Bartender's Book, $9.95
Everything® Chinese Cookbook
Everything® **Classic Recipes Book**
Everything® Cocktail Parties and Drinks Book
Everything® College Cookbook
Everything® **Cooking for Baby and Toddler Book**
Everything® Cooking for Two Cookbook
Everything® Diabetes Cookbook
Everything® Easy Gourmet Cookbook
Everything® Fondue Cookbook
Everything® **Fondue Party Book**
Everything® Gluten-Free Cookbook
Everything® Glycemic Index Cookbook
Everything® Grilling Cookbook

Everything® Healthy Meals in Minutes Cookbook
Everything® Holiday Cookbook
Everything® Indian Cookbook
Everything® Italian Cookbook
Everything® Low-Carb Cookbook
Everything® Low-Fat High-Flavor Cookbook
Everything® Low-Salt Cookbook
Everything® Meals for a Month Cookbook
Everything® Mediterranean Cookbook
Everything® Mexican Cookbook
Everything® One-Pot Cookbook
Everything® **Quick and Easy 30-Minute, 5-Ingredient Cookbook**
Everything® Quick Meals Cookbook
Everything® Slow Cooker Cookbook
Everything® Slow Cooking for a Crowd Cookbook
Everything® Soup Cookbook
Everything® Tex-Mex Cookbook
Everything® Thai Cookbook
Everything® Vegetarian Cookbook
Everything® Wild Game Cookbook
Everything® Wine Book, 2nd Ed.

GAMES

Everything® 15-Minute Sudoku Book, $9.95
Everything® 30-Minute Sudoku Book, $9.95
Everything® Blackjack Strategy Book
Everything® Brain Strain Book, $9.95
Everything® Bridge Book
Everything® Card Games Book
Everything® Card Tricks Book, $9.95
Everything® Casino Gambling Book, 2nd Ed.
Everything® Chess Basics Book
Everything® Craps Strategy Book
Everything® Crossword and Puzzle Book
Everything® Crossword Challenge Book
Everything® Cryptograms Book, $9.95
Everything® Easy Crosswords Book
Everything® Easy Kakuro Book, $9.95
Everything® Games Book, 2nd Ed.
Everything® Giant Sudoku Book, $9.95
Everything® Kakuro Challenge Book, $9.95
Everything® **Large-Print Crossword Challenge Book**
Everything® Large-Print Crosswords Book
Everything® Lateral Thinking Puzzles Book, $9.95
Everything® **Mazes Book**

Everything® Pencil Puzzles Book, $9.95
Everything® Poker Strategy Book
Everything® Pool & Billiards Book
Everything® Test Your IQ Book, $9.95
Everything® Texas Hold 'Em Book, $9.95
Everything® Travel Crosswords Book, $9.95
Everything® Word Games Challenge Book
Everything® Word Search Book

HEALTH

Everything® Alzheimer's Book
Everything® Diabetes Book
Everything® Health Guide to Adult Bipolar Disorder
Everything® Health Guide to Controlling Anxiety
Everything® Health Guide to Fibromyalgia
Everything® **Health Guide to Thyroid Disease**
Everything® Hypnosis Book
Everything® Low Cholesterol Book
Everything® Massage Book
Everything® Menopause Book
Everything® Nutrition Book
Everything® Reflexology Book
Everything® Stress Management Book

HISTORY

Everything® American Government Book
Everything® American History Book
Everything® Civil War Book
Everything® Freemasons Book
Everything® Irish History & Heritage Book
Everything® Middle East Book

HOBBIES

Everything® Candlemaking Book
Everything® Cartooning Book
Everything® **Coin Collecting Book**
Everything® Drawing Book
Everything® Family Tree Book, 2nd Ed.
Everything® Knitting Book
Everything® Knots Book
Everything® Photography Book
Everything® Quilting Book
Everything® Scrapbooking Book
Everything® Sewing Book
Everything® Woodworking Book

Bolded titles are new additions to the series.
All Everything® books are priced at $12.95 or $14.95, unless otherwise stated. Prices subject to change without notice.

HOME IMPROVEMENT

Everything® Feng Shui Book
Everything® Feng Shui Decluttering Book, $9.95
Everything® Fix-It Book
Everything® Home Decorating Book
Everything® Home Storage Solutions Book
Everything® Homebuilding Book
Everything® Lawn Care Book
Everything® Organize Your Home Book

KIDS' BOOKS

All titles are $7.95
Everything® Kids' Animal Puzzle & Activity Book
Everything® Kids' Baseball Book, 4th Ed.
Everything® Kids' Bible Trivia Book
Everything® Kids' Bugs Book
**Everything® Kids' Cars and Trucks Puzzle
 & Activity Book**
Everything® Kids' Christmas Puzzle
 & Activity Book
Everything® Kids' Cookbook
Everything® Kids' Crazy Puzzles Book
Everything® Kids' Dinosaurs Book
**Everything® Kids' First Spanish Puzzle and
 Activity Book**
Everything® Kids' Gross Hidden Pictures Book
Everything® Kids' Gross Jokes Book
Everything® Kids' Gross Mazes Book
Everything® Kids' Gross Puzzle and
 Activity Book
Everything® Kids' Halloween Puzzle
 & Activity Book
Everything® Kids' Hidden Pictures Book
Everything® Kids' Horses Book
Everything® Kids' Joke Book
Everything® Kids' Knock Knock Book
Everything® Kids' Learning Spanish Book
Everything® Kids' Math Puzzles Book
Everything® Kids' Mazes Book
Everything® Kids' Money Book
Everything® Kids' Nature Book
Everything® Kids' Pirates Puzzle and Activity
 Book
**Everything® Kids' Princess Puzzle and
 Activity Book**
Everything® Kids' Puzzle Book
Everything® Kids' Riddles & Brain Teasers Book
Everything® Kids' Science Experiments Book
Everything® Kids' Sharks Book
Everything® Kids' Soccer Book
Everything® Kids' Travel Activity Book

KIDS' STORY BOOKS

Everything® Fairy Tales Book

LANGUAGE

**Everything® Conversational Chinese Book
 with CD, $19.95**
Everything® Conversational Japanese Book
 with CD, $19.95
Everything® French Grammar Book
Everything® French Phrase Book, $9.95
Everything® French Verb Book, $9.95
Everything® German Practice Book with CD,
 $19.95
Everything® Inglés Book
Everything® Learning French Book
Everything® Learning German Book
Everything® Learning Italian Book
Everything® Learning Latin Book
Everything® Learning Spanish Book
**Everything® Russian Practice Book with CD,
 $19.95**
Everything® Sign Language Book
Everything® Spanish Grammar Book
Everything® Spanish Phrase Book, $9.95
Everything® Spanish Practice Book
 with CD, $19.95
Everything® Spanish Verb Book, $9.95

MUSIC

Everything® Drums Book with CD, $19.95
Everything® Guitar Book
Everything® Guitar Chords Book with CD,
 $19.95
Everything® Home Recording Book
**Everything® Music Theory Book with CD,
 $19.95**
Everything® Reading Music Book with CD,
 $19.95
Everything® Rock & Blues Guitar Book
 (with CD), $19.95
Everything® Songwriting Book

NEW AGE

Everything® Astrology Book, 2nd Ed.
Everything® Birthday Personology Book
Everything® Dreams Book, 2nd Ed.
Everything® Love Signs Book, $9.95
Everything® Numerology Book
Everything® Paganism Book
Everything® Palmistry Book
Everything® Psychic Book
Everything® Reiki Book
Everything® Sex Signs Book, $9.95
Everything® Tarot Book, 2nd Ed.
Everything® Wicca and Witchcraft Book

PARENTING

Everything® Baby Names Book, 2nd Ed.
Everything® Baby Shower Book
Everything® Baby's First Food Book
Everything® Baby's First Year Book
Everything® Birthing Book
Everything® Breastfeeding Book
Everything® Father-to-Be Book
Everything® Father's First Year Book
Everything® Get Ready for Baby Book
Everything® Get Your Baby to Sleep Book, $9.95
Everything® Getting Pregnant Book
**Everything® Guide to Raising a
 One-Year-Old**
**Everything® Guide to Raising a
 Two-Year-Old**
Everything® Homeschooling Book
Everything® Mother's First Year Book
Everything® Parent's Guide to Children
 and Divorce
Everything® Parent's Guide to Children
 with ADD/ADHD
Everything® Parent's Guide to Children
 with Asperger's Syndrome
Everything® Parent's Guide to Children
 with Autism
Everything® Parent's Guide to Children with
 Bipolar Disorder
Everything® Parent's Guide to Children
 with Dyslexia
Everything® Parent's Guide to Positive Discipline
Everything® Parent's Guide to Raising a
 Successful Child
Everything® Parent's Guide to Raising Boys
Everything® Parent's Guide to Raising Siblings
**Everything® Parent's Guide to Sensory
 Integration Disorder**
Everything® Parent's Guide to Tantrums
Everything® Parent's Guide to the Overweight
 Child
Everything® Parent's Guide to the Strong-Willed
 Child
Everything® Parenting a Teenager Book
Everything® Potty Training Book, $9.95
Everything® Pregnancy Book, 2nd Ed.
Everything® Pregnancy Fitness Book
Everything® Pregnancy Nutrition Book
**Everything® Pregnancy Organizer, 2nd Ed.,
 $16.95**
Everything® Toddler Activities Book
Everything® Toddler Book
Everything® Tween Book
Everything® Twins, Triplets, and More Book

PETS

Everything® **Aquarium Book**
Everything® Boxer Book
Everything® Cat Book, 2nd Ed.
Everything® Chihuahua Book
Everything® Dachshund Book
Everything® Dog Book
Everything® Dog Health Book
Everything® **Dog Owner's Organizer,** **$16.95**
Everything® Dog Training and Tricks Book
Everything® German Shepherd Book
Everything® Golden Retriever Book
Everything® Horse Book
Everything® Horse Care Book
Everything® Horseback Riding Book
Everything® Labrador Retriever Book
Everything® Poodle Book
Everything® Pug Book
Everything® Puppy Book
Everything® Rottweiler Book
Everything® Small Dogs Book
Everything® Tropical Fish Book
Everything® Yorkshire Terrier Book

REFERENCE

Everything® Blogging Book
Everything® **Build Your Vocabulary Book**
Everything® Car Care Book
Everything® Classical Mythology Book
Everything® Da Vinci Book
Everything® Divorce Book
Everything® Einstein Book
Everything® Etiquette Book, 2nd Ed.
Everything® Inventions and Patents Book
Everything® Mafia Book
Everything® Philosophy Book
Everything® Psychology Book
Everything® Shakespeare Book

RELIGION

Everything® Angels Book
Everything® Bible Book
Everything® Buddhism Book
Everything® Catholicism Book
Everything® Christianity Book
Everything® History of the Bible Book
Everything® **Jesus Book**
Everything® Jewish History & Heritage Book
Everything® Judaism Book
Everything® Kabbalah Book
Everything® Koran Book
Everything® **Mary Book**

Everything® Mary Magdalene Book
Everything® Prayer Book
Everything® Saints Book
Everything® Torah Book
Everything® Understanding Islam Book
Everything® World's Religions Book
Everything® Zen Book

SCHOOL & CAREERS

Everything® Alternative Careers Book
Everything® **Career Tests Book**
Everything® College Major Test Book
Everything® College Survival Book, 2nd Ed.
Everything® Cover Letter Book, 2nd Ed.
Everything® **Filmmaking Book**
Everything® Get-a-Job Book
Everything® Guide to Being a Paralegal
Everything® Guide to Being a Real Estate Agent
Everything® **Guide to Being a Sales Rep**
Everything® **Guide to Careers in Health Care**
Everything® **Guide to Careers in Law Enforcement**
Everything® **Guide to Government Jobs**
Everything® Guide to Starting and Running a Restaurant
Everything® Job Interview Book
Everything® New Nurse Book
Everything® New Teacher Book
Everything® Paying for College Book
Everything® Practice Interview Book
Everything® Resume Book, 2nd Ed.
Everything® Study Book

SELF-HELP

Everything® Dating Book, 2nd Ed.
Everything® Great Sex Book
Everything® Kama Sutra Book
Everything® Self-Esteem Book

SPORTS & FITNESS

Everything® **Easy Fitness Book**
Everything® Fishing Book
Everything® Golf Instruction Book
Everything® Pilates Book
Everything® Running Book
Everything® Weight Training Book
Everything® Yoga Book

TRAVEL

Everything® Family Guide to Cruise Vacations
Everything® Family Guide to Hawaii

Everything® Family Guide to Las Vegas, 2nd Ed.
Everything® **Family Guide to Mexico**
Everything® Family Guide to New York City, 2nd Ed.
Everything® Family Guide to RV Travel & Campgrounds
Everything® Family Guide to the Caribbean
Everything® Family Guide to the Walt Disney World Resort®, Universal Studios®, and Greater Orlando, 4th Ed.
Everything® **Family Guide to Timeshares**
Everything® Family Guide to Washington D.C., 2nd Ed.
Everything® Guide to New England

WEDDINGS

Everything® Bachelorette Party Book, $9.95
Everything® Bridesmaid Book, $9.95
Everything® **Destination Wedding Book**
Everything® Elopement Book, $9.95
Everything® Father of the Bride Book, $9.95
Everything® Groom Book, $9.95
Everything® Mother of the Bride Book, $9.95
Everything® Outdoor Wedding Book
Everything® Wedding Book, 3rd Ed.
Everything® Wedding Checklist, $9.95
Everything® Wedding Etiquette Book, $9.95
Everything® **Wedding Organizer, 2nd Ed.,** **$16.95**
Everything® Wedding Shower Book, $9.95
Everything® Wedding Vows Book, $9.95
Everything® **Wedding Workout Book**
Everything® Weddings on a Budget Book, $9.95

WRITING

Everything® Creative Writing Book
Everything® Get Published Book, 2nd Ed.
Everything® Grammar and Style Book
Everything® Guide to Writing a Book Proposal
Everything® Guide to Writing a Novel
Everything® Guide to Writing Children's Books
Everything® Guide to Writing Research Papers
Everything® Screenwriting Book
Everything® Writing Poetry Book
Everything® Writing Well Book

Available wherever books are sold!
To order, call 800-258-0929, or visit us at *www.everything.com*
Everything® and everything.com® are registered trademarks of F+W Publications, Inc.